AF425828

LANDS OF LOST CONTENT

Also by John Wilson

LANDS OF LOST CONTENT

A Memoir

John Wilson

Library and Archives Canada Cataloguing in Publication

Wilson, John (John Alexander), 1951 -
Lands of Lost Content:/John Wilson

First Published 2020

Cover design by John Wilson
Cover Photo by Susan Scott

For more information on the author and his books, visit:
http://www.johnwilsonauthor.com

*For Jen, who shares this present life,
and Eve and Jim who, unwittingly, gave me so many past
lives.*

Into my heart an air that kills
  From yon far country blows:
What are those blue remembered hills,
  What spires, what farms are those?

That is the land of lost content,
  I see it shining plain,
The happy highways where I went
  And cannot come again.

A. E. Housman

CONTENTS

Prologue

butterfly on a leaf
sips dew above
my father's grave

A Seductive Liar

Nineteen-sixty-one provided a prelude to the decade that has always been the symbol of the baby-boom generation—my generation. It was a year of endings and beginnings, of echoes back to a fading past and faint rumbles of what might yet be. John Kennedy was sworn in as president, the Bay of Pigs invasion failed, the Berlin Wall went up, Adolf Eichmann was put on trial, and Mary and Louis Leakey unearthed Australopithicus in Olduvai Gorge in Tanganyika, a country that was just beginning its three-year-long life as a nation. Yuri Gagarin and Gherman Titov orbited the earth a total of eighteen times between them and Alan Shephard and Gus Grissom poked their heads above the atmosphere for a few minutes each. Joseph Heller's *Catch 22* was published, Bob Dylan performed at Gerde's Folk City and *101 Dalmations* was released. Dashiel Hammett, Gary Cooper, Carl Jung, Ernest Hemingway and Ty Cobb died. Barack Obama, George Clooney, Princess Diana, Eddie Murphy and Wayne Gretzky were born.

In Britain it was also the year that the farthing disappeared and with it the 'four-a-penny' tray of candy at the local store. The soundtrack of that year was provided by The Shadows, Helen Shapiro, Del Shannon, Petula Clark, the Everly Brothers and Elvis. *Hancock's Half Hour*, *Desert Island Discs* and *The Navy Lark* dominated the radio, and *The Lone Ranger*, *The Avengers*, *Danger Man*, *All Our Yesterdays* and *Sunday Night at the London Palladium* filled the small, black and white TV screens. At local cinemas *The Guns of Navarone*, *The Swiss Family Robinson*, *The Time Machine* and *Whistle Down the Wind* were popular.

In a ground floor flat on the corner of a long, sandstone tenement block in Scotland, a young boy sat in the corner of what seemed to him to be a vast room. The ceiling was high and in its centre was a wide circular vegetative moulding from which, the boy imagined, a magnificent sparkling crystal chandelier had once hung. The moulding round the edge of the ceiling was simpler—long straight narrow ridges and wide street-like hollows. The boy often wished that he could defy gravity and crouch on the flat white ceiling, driving his toy cars along those endless roads. Below the ceiling, a wooden picture rail circled the room, separating the plaster above from the faded patterned wallpaper below. Hanging from the picture rail were a couple of abstract oil paintings by an older sister who had gone to art college in London, and several black-and-white photographs of stern people in formal poses.

One wall of the room was lined with low bookcases crammed with dusty hardbacks—history, philosophy and religion—belonging to another sister who had married a vicar in the Anglican church. As a special favour to one of the boy's hobbies, a large plastic model of HMS *Victory* stood atop the bookcase amidst postcards from a third sister in Australia.

The opposite wall was almost entirely taken up with a deep bay window, which looked out over a narrow front garden onto the main road from Paisley down the coast to Greenock where the River Clyde swung south, became the Firth of Clyde and ran past Great Cumbrae, where in 710 CE St Mirin in an echo of St Patrick cast out all the snakes, and Arran where hardy folk went to celebrate Scotland's only official nudist beach.

The boy sat to one side of the hissing gas fireplace, the only source of heat in the room. A large, plain-faced, loudly-ticking clock rested on the mantle bracketed by small framed photographs of the three sisters and one of the boy aged about six. A selection of his most favoured toy cars lay scattered and forgotten around him and, by his shoulder, the television stood grey and silent, turned off because this was "grown-up time".

The grown ups—the boy's parents, an aunt and her partner, and an older cousin—sat in a wide arc facing the fire. The adult conversation lulled and the boy's father stood, expelling a grunt of air as the worn bones of his arthritic hip ground together, and headed over to the table on the far side of the room. A bottle of Famous Grouse whisky, a present from the cousin, stood on a tray beside a photograph of a fourth sister, dead before the boy was born. The man poured a measure of scotch into a crystal tumbler and added a few cubes of ice.

"Can I put the soda in?" the boy asked, jumping to his feet. He loved the astonishing release of the pressurized bubbles from the soda bomb. He loved the very name bomb, for that was what the empty grey cylinders became as they were dropped from one of his model planes onto the ranks of his terrified toy soldiers below.

The man nodded. "Not too much, now," he cautioned.

The boy held the heavy soda syphon shakily and carefully pressed the handle. The bubbling water exploded into the glass, mixing up a chaos of water, gas, whisky and ice cubes.

"Thank you." The man limped back over to his chair. The boy stood and listened to the magical clinking of the ice against the sides of the glass, then he returned to his seat on the floor by the television and listened.

The adult talk over the whisky around the fire did not mean much to the boy. It was mainly about somewhere called the Indian Raj, a place on the other side of the world that he knew little about. Sometimes the conversation intrigued the boy, as when the talk turned to a fish that for some unfathomable reason was called Bombay Duck, and sometimes he laughed along with the others even though he didn't understand the joke, but mostly he was confused.

The boy listened, primarily because at this time of the evening the vast room was the only one in the house being heated and, until his mother went and tucked a hot water bottle into his bed, he didn't want to brave cold sheets. More importantly, though, he listened because the stories of the Raj were told with such a powerful sense of loss that he was utterly convinced that the place they referred to must be so extraordinarily wonderful that it was worth the struggle to understand it.

This feeling was reinforced by the breathtaking stories the boy's father told him: hunting tigers from the backs of elephants, surviving the great

Bihar earthquake, shooting a rabid dog and having his favourite pony killed by a wild boar. The last of these stories was illustrated by the wild boar's tusks mounted on silver stands on the bookcase beside the model ship, and by the man's limp which had been caused by his fall from the dying horse.

The boy finally went to bed, drowning in nostalgia for a lost past. He lay awake imagining the beguiling unreal memory world of the Raj so much more compelling and powerful than the damp grey Scottish reality that trapped him. But, as with all nostalgia, beneath the memories and fantasies there was sadness. The boy was doomed never to recapture his parent's world and yet the seductive liar of nostalgia wove a bewitching silken thread around him, entwining itself around his experiences and perspectives in subtle ways that he was rarely even aware of. Those evening conversations around the fire gave birth to a ghost peering over the boy's shoulder at everything he did, a wisp of history flickering in the corner of his eye yet gone when he turned to look at it.

Even in 1961 as the boy lay in bed making up stories of Imperial adventures in the Khyber Pass, he knew that, except in his imagination, he could never attain this wonderful, perfect place that his parents loved and missed so much. It was the object of such powerful nostalgia precisely because it no longer existed and, although he had no inkling of this, it meant that the boy was destined to spend much of his life trying to go there.

Interlude

Old Pictures

I am surrounded by the dead.
In sepia formality they hang
from the scaffold of the picture rail:
a great uncle killed at Loos
proud in his kilt
before the steamer's sad farewell;
his brother who survived
with a whole body
and forty years of a broken mind;
my grandmother
stern
Victorian
alone
in mourning black forever;
my parents' wedding—
the groom alive with hope,
proud before an empire's collapse—
my mother at eighteen
between giggling sisters,
beautifully shy before the certainty of years.

All are gone,
only the bride's magnificent veil
lies, remembering
in an attic suitcase.

Yet still they live
within the walls of my imperfect memory,
and watch with timeless eyes
my life's amorphous dream unfold.

Who will I look down upon
when I am clay and dust
and stoic, stand and stare
from far behind some dusty pane?

Part 1

Remnants of the Raj

parchment leaf
crumbling beneath
a child's first step

Schoolboys and a Dead Doctor

Thursday, November 29, 1917 was a chilly, misty day in Edinburgh on the east coast of Scotland. This was not unusual. With luck, if the prevailing west wind wasn't blowing, the temperature in the early afternoon might pop up to a balmy 45 degrees Fahrenheit (7 degrees Celsius), before slumping dismally back to somewhere around 38 degrees (3.5 degrees Celsius), when the sun set at 4:30. As they waited, the crowds lining the route from St Giles Cathedral on the High Street to the Dean Cemetery one and a half miles (2.5 kilometres) away, pulled their tweed jackets and shawls tighter, stamped their feet and wrapped their scarves more securely to keep out the chill. Eventually, they heard the tramp of marching feet and the rattle of iron-rimmed wheels on the cobblestones below the castle. A gun-carriage, drawn by six black horses came into view. The coffin on the carriage was draped in the Union Jack and the red, blue and white Serbian flag emblazoned with an elaborate crest of a crowned, double-headed eagle. Around the carriage marched an honour guard of soldiers from the Royal Scots Regiment and men in the green uniform of the Serbian Army. Behind the carriage, dignitaries and a long trailing crowd of citizens followed. At the Dean Cemetery, the mourners watched in silence as the Serbian soldiers lifted the coffin and carried it to the prepared grave near the north wall.

Perhaps, amongst the silent watching crowd were some students from the nearby spired and turreted Fettes College. Fettes was considered "the Eton of the North". Today, it boasts a distinguished list of alumni as diverse as Tony Blair, Tilda Swinton and, according to Ian Fleming in *You*

Only Live Twice, James Bond, but none of the famous were there that day. However, there might have been a twelve-year-old boy beginning his third year as a boarder in Moredun House. The boy had been born in India but had been sent back to Scotland to be educated and subjected to the Fettes regime of constitution-hardening ice-cold baths at 6 a.m.

The funeral ceremony was not to honour some famous military man recently fallen amidst the horrors of Passchendaele, but a short, fifty-three-year-old Scottish woman, Dr. Elsie Maud Inglis. Like the boy, Elsie Inglis had been born in India before moving to Scotland where she studied medicine and, in 1892, obtained her license from the Royal College of Physicians and Surgeons. Shocked by the low standards of medical care for women, Dr. Inglis became a political activist and opened a maternity hospital for the poor. She also joined the suffrage movement where she became secretary of the National Union of Women's Suffrage Societies.

In the formal photographs of the time, Elsie Inglis seems to be always trying to suppress the smile that threatens to overwhelm her face. Yet she was not someone to be trifled with. On the outbreak of the First World War, she established the Scottish Women's Hospitals for Foreign Service Committee with the aim of providing female-staffed medical units. She proposed the idea to the War Office in London and was condescendingly told, "My good lady, go home and sit still." Instead, Dr. Inglis offered her idea to the French, who jumped at it and organized for a group of doctors and nurses to go to Serbia.

Austro-Hungarian troops had invaded Serbia in 1914 to enforce the ultimatum that had followed the assassination of Archduke Franz Ferdinand in Sarajevo in June but, by Christmas and despite heavy casualties, the battle-hardened Serbian army—they had fought two brutal wars against various neighbours in the two years prior to the latest invasion—had driven them back across the border.

The situation was quiet when Dr. Inglis arrived to take over the unit in May and she even had time to propose a scheme to introduce fresh water fountains into rural communities. However, in the fall, the Austro-

Hungarian and Bulgarian armies attacked crushing the exhausted Serbian army and forcing the survivors to flee to Albania and Russia. In February 1916 the Scottish nurses and doctors were captured and forcibly repatriated to Britain.

Despite the horrors they had witnessed, Dr. Inglis and her colleagues immediately began raising money and organizing a new venture. In late August 1916, they set sail for Archangel to provide medical aid for a Serbian division fighting with the Russian army. For a year the unit worked in Russia and Romania, retreating and establishing mobile hospitals as the situation allowed or demanded.

Dr. Inglis wrote extensively describing conditions. In a station waiting room: "A crowd of people was collected at one end with boxes and bundles and children. One little boy was lying on a doorstep asleep, and against the wall farther on lay a row of soldiers. On the bench to the right, under the light, was a doctor in his white overall, stretched out sound asleep between the two rushes of work at the station dressing-room; and a Roumanian officer talked to me of Glasgow, where he had once been invited out to dinner..." and later during the retreat, "The night was inky black; the only lights were our own head-lights and those of the ambulance behind us, but they revealed a sad and never-to-be-forgotten picture...it was like a dream or a play; it certainly was a tragedy. No one spoke; we just waited and watched it all; to us it was a spectacle, to these poor homeless people it was a terrible reality...We arrived at Braila to find 11,000 wounded and seven doctors, only one of them a surgeon."

In March 1917, revolution broke out adding more unrest and chaos to the difficulties of war, but none of this daunted Dr. Inglis. A group of "Russian Citizen Soldiers" strained their command of English to write to her: "The wounded and sick soldiers from all parts of the army and fleet of great free Russia, who are now for healing in the hospital which you command, penetrated with a feeling of sincere respect, feel it their much-desired duty, to-day, on the day of the feast of Holy Easter, to express to you our deep reverence to you, the doctor warmly loved by all, and also to your honoured personnel of women. We wish also to express our sincere gratitude for all the care and attention bestowed on us, and we bow low before the tireless and wonderful work of yourself and your personnel."

Despite fighting an agonizing personal battle with bowel cancer, Dr. Inglis struggled on, refusing to leave Russia before her unit was repatriated. On November 7, 1917, she and her companions took ship from Archangel to face the ordeal of a winter voyage through the Arctic and across the North Sea. She arrived in Newcastle-Upon-Tyne on November 25 and died the following day in a room in the Station Hotel on Neville Street.

In honour of Elsie Inglis the British Residence in Belgrade is named after her, her picture graces the back of Scottish banknotes and there is a plaque where her funeral service was held in St Giles Cathedral, but her greatest memorial was constructed at the opposite end of the Edinburgh High Street from the cathedral. The Elsie Inglis Memorial Maternity Hospital opened in 1925 and before its closure in 1988 many thousands of babies were safely brought into the world there. Dr. Inglis would have been pleased.

Whether the boy from Fettes watched the funeral or not, he would certainly have known about it and been aware of Elsie Inglis and her achievements. What he could not possibly have known was that, at 10:10 a.m. thirty-three years eight months and four days later, his son, John, would be born in the maternity hospital named for the extraordinary woman buried that chilly day.

~~~~~

In 1951, James Annan Wilson or Jim as he was always known, after fathering four girls the oldest of whom was about to turn twenty years old, wasn't prepared to entertain the possibility that number five would be a son. When my sister phoned to tell him of my arrival, at first he didn't believe her. However, proof was forthcoming and, unaware of the confusion I had caused, I squalled my way back to my new home at 10 Duddingston Crescent in Portobello, equally unaware that a few minutes walk away on Duddingston Ave was the house where, almost exactly three
~~~~~

years later, the infant who was to become my wife would also come home. Had I stayed, grown up and met and married the girl around the corner, this would not be remarkable, however my stay in the neighbourhood was brief and our meeting was in a very different time and place. Even if unintentional, the tangled webs we weave begin early.

Prior to my arrival, Jim had lived much of his life in India. He had even been born there, in Lucknow, on January 20, 1905, but returned to Scotland around 1909 to live with his uncle, James, in Helensburgh. In 1915 he crossed the country to Edinburgh to attend boarding school at Fettes before, in 1921, beginning a five-year apprenticeship in engineering at North British Locomotive's Hyde Park Works in Glasgow. North British mainly built steam engines and Jim would have worked on several Ab class 4-6-2 Pacific tender steam locomotives for New Zealand railways. One that he probably knew, Ab 745, crashed fifty feet down an embankment between Wanganui and New Plymouth in 1956 and lay buried until 2001 when it was purchased for a dollar. It now sits in a Rimutaka Incline Railway Heritage Trust shed in Maymorn, awaiting restoration.

In 1927 Jim returned to India to take up a post with the Bombay and North Western Railway where he rose to be a Chief Mechanical Engineer and acted occasionally as 'Government Surveyor of inland steam vessels' for the Government of Bihar. A few weeks leave in each of 1935, 1939 and 1945/46 were the only times he went back to Britain before his final return not long before my arrival.

My father's contribution to the jewel of the British imperial crown came to an end with partition and independence on August 15, 1947. On May 20, 1950—he stayed on to help with the transition to independence—he walked down the gangplank of the S.S. *Stratheden* in London. Jim's wife, Eve, had travelled down from Edinburgh to meet him off the boat. It must have been a strange homecoming. They had not seen each other for four years and only for less than six months since September, 1939. In that time three of Jim and Eve's daughters had grown up and the fourth had been born and died. Jim was forty-five years old, overweight and, although entering his profession as Government Official in the ship's passenger list, he was unemployed and had precious little experience of living in the changing world of mid-twentieth century Britain. The train journey back up north must have been bleak.

For my parents, after such long separation, the adjustment of recreating a life together in a dreary post-war Scotland, a land that they barely knew and that life had hardly prepared them for, must have been incredibly harsh and stressful. Into the middle of all of this and blissfully unaware, I arrived.

As I grew, I only had a vague sense of how difficult life was for my parents. I was aware that we had very few Indian possessions. All my relatives who had lived in India had houses filled with faded memorabilia: intricately inlaid tables, hammered brass bowls and trays, moth-eaten tiger skins, and, in one case, an elephant's foot worked into a stool. It was only years later that I discovered the reason for this gap in the family history.

Like many refugees from the Raj, when they returned to Britain, my parents brought with them trunks and tea chests filled with their most treasured possessions: silverware, crockery, cutlery, pictures, small favourite items of furniture, ornaments, pieces of Indian work that would always remind them of their lost past. After Jim came home, my parents' Indian life was put into storage until the family became settled. The settling didn't happen and there was never enough money to recover the possessions from storage. Eventually, everything was sold off to pay for the storage costs.

I suspect that this cruel wrench from the life that she loved broke my mother's heart and contributed to her dislike of the world I grew up in, but I was oblivious. All I remember from India were easily transportable things that had never gone into storage or had survived our many moves. There was old-fashioned bone-handled cutlery and increasingly chipped willow pattern cups, plates and bowls, but the things that fascinated me were the remnants of Jim's life: the tusks of the wild boar that gored his horse, a *kukri* (a Gurkha knife), a selection of books riddled with silverfish holes, and a 1915 vintage, .455 calibre Webley Scott Mark 1 Self-Loading Pistol. All that remain are the *kukri*, the tusks and a 1924 edition of Lord Roberts' *Letters Written During the Indian Mutiny*, but it was the pistol that occupied my young imagination the most.

Interlude

My Father's Gun

My father's pistol lived in a metal box,
in the bottom of the wardrobe,
hidden from the children
beside the Christmas presents
in my favourite hiding place.

I loved that dark cave of musty smells and mothballs
on the borders of Narnia,
but mostly I loved the gun:
its weight that I could barely lift,
the blue-steel of its barrel,
the smell of its oil,
the roll of its name on my tongue
Webley Scott.

With that gun I shot countless burglars,
lions,
bad guys,
good guys,
and once, in an ecstasy of expectation,
we took it into a field and killed
a rotting tree stump.
For days afterwards my ears rang
and the bad guys exploded like dead wood.

Then one day the wardrobe contained
only lifeless clothes.
For an age I wondered if my father was a spy
who had to kill an enemy agent,
or if someone had stolen the gun
to return and murder us all.
How would I protect everyone?

Eventually, I asked my mother,
"That old thing, your father sold it
I never liked having it around."
So I went back to plastic guns,
but I knew I would never again
stand a chance
against the bad guys.

How to Skin a Crocodile

The death of a parent can throw what we don't know about them into painfully sharp relief. Jim died in March 1985 and, like many sons, I could fill a book with detailed, never-asked and probably unanswerable queries. Fortunately, he loved to tell stories of his life in India. Unfortunately, for much of my childhood there was only one question I wanted to ask.

I was that eager kid in the First World War poster, steeped in stories from a later war and certain that my dad must have done brave and extraordinary things.

"What did you do in the war, Dad?" I eventually asked.

"Nothing much."

"But you were a captain."

"Acting captain," he said, setting his book aside. "I was really only a lieutenant. Everybody on the railways had to join." He smiled at me. "The Bengal and North Western Railway Battalion."

"And you've got a gun," I persisted, referring to the heavy oiled pistol in its metal box in the bottom of the wardrobe in my parent's bedroom.

"You mustn't touch it."

"I just look," I lied. I loved how I could barely lift the gun and how cold its steel felt even on the hottest summer day.

"One day, when you're older, I'll show you how it works."

The thought of that wonderful day-to-come distracted me for a while. Then I remembered something else I could use. "You won a medal."

"It was just an MBE. Everybody got one."

I have the medal in its velvet-lined case, and a scroll dated 12 June, 1947 and signed by the king. It begins: "George the Sixth by the Grace of God of Great Britain, Ireland and the British Dominions beyond the Seas, King, Defender of the Faith, Emperor of India and Sovereign of the Most Excellent Order of the British Empire to Our trusty and well-beloved James Annan Wilson Esquire Greeting....We have thought fit to nominate and appoint you to be a Member of the Civil Division of Our said Most Excellent Order of the British Empire..." etc. etc.

Years later, looking at the medal and the scroll, I thought, "No, Dad. Not everybody got one." But if they were uncommon, what did James Annan Wilson Esquire do to become "trusty and well-beloved"?

I have some clues. I do know that the railway workshops Jim was in charge of were turned over to the production of munitions and the building of three ambulance trains. My sister told me that, in the spring of 1944, one of the trains needed to be driven as close as possible to Kohima and Imphal where desperate fighting was going on to halt the Japanese invasion of India. No one wanted to undertake the hazardous trip so Jim volunteered and took the train.

Perhaps that journey was enough for the Most Excellent Order, but I have one other intriguing, isolated piece of information relating to that time. It is from the archives at Fettes College. Fettes keeps track of the activities and achievements of its old pupils after they have left and were very helpful in confirming several details that I already knew about Jim. However, their records added something startlingly new: "1939-45 War; Capt. Punjabis; POW". Since I can find no confirmation from military records or family of his being either in the Punjabis or a prisoner of war, it is almost certainly an error, but...

As Jim told me, European engineers and administrators working on the railways of the Raj automatically became officers in the Auxiliary Forces of India. In another fancy document from the time of George VI's dad, Jim, already "trusty and well-beloved", is made a 2nd Lieutenant in the Bengal and North Western Railway Battalion. He became a full Lieutenant two years later on 1st June, 1934 and was a Captain by the time the battalion was disbanded in 1947.

The job of the railway battalions was simple, keep the peace. The Bengal and North Western Railway Battalion, with a strength in 1939 of 110 Europeans and 180 Anglo-Indians (as the children of mixed Indian and British parentage were designated in those days), was tasked with "providing armoury guards during periods of civil unrest", although as "civil unrest" increased in India during the 1930s and 40s, I suspect that many of the Auxiliary Forces were used for other purposes. What those other purposes might have been is suggested by one of the stories Jim told me about his military career in India.

One evening, we were watching an old movie on television. I don't remember the details but there was a scene where a small group of brave British lads were faced by an angry mob of locals in some far corner of the British Empire. The soldiers fired over the heads of the advancing crowd and were then overwhelmed by it.

"Nonsense," my dad said. "That's not how you handle a riot."

"But how can you?" I asked. "There are a lot more rioters than soldiers."

"Yes, but your squad is disciplined and armed. The idea is to use the least amount of force necessary to quell the riot. If you fire over the heads of the crowd the leaders will simply say 'See, their bullets cannot harm us' and you're no better off. First you blow the bugle to get the crowd's attention and then read the riot act."

"Does that stop them?"

"Sometimes."

"If it doesn't stop them?" I asked, trying to tease out more of the story.

"Every crowd has leaders: the man with the megaphone, the man leading the chanting and urging the others on. While the riot act is being read, you get the two or three best shots in the platoon and point out the major ringleaders in the crowd. If the crowd keeps coming, you order those men to fire at the targets you've given them. That beheads the crowd and without leaders to give it focus a crowd is much more easily dispersed."

As I pondered this, Jim went on. "The problem was that permission to fire on a crowd had to be given in writing by the local magistrate. Local magistrates were Indian and could hardly ever be found when trouble was brewing."

I loved the story of facing down an enraged mob but it was only years later and too late, that I wondered how my dad knew in so much detail what to do with a squad of soldiers amid the chaos of a riot, and regretted missing the opportunity to ask him.

I was told other stories to the soundtrack of clinking ice in a crystal glass.

"I remember once in the rebellion of 1942, Jock MacIntosh was alone when he was faced in the railway yards by a hostile crowd. A young Indian in the crowd harangued him with, 'Bloody Englishman. We don't want you here.' Jock shouted back, 'I'm no an Englishman. I'm a Scotchman.' While the mob wondered at this, Jock jumped onto a nearby train and escaped."

Clink.

"Troopers from the Bihar Light Horse were once paraded before a visiting senior officer. They were a scruffy bunch and the officer wasn't impressed by the lack of spit and polish. He gestured at the lined up men and pointedly asked the Sergeant Major, 'What is that?' Without missing a beat, the Sergeant Major replied, 'They're a corps of gentleman, sir. They owns their own horses, don't clean nothing and salutes nobody.'"

Clink.

"I felt bloody helpless during the Bengal famine of 43/44. It was dreadful, bodies in the streets, no more than skeletons. And it was all made worse by the merchants stocking full granaries to drive up prices."

Clink.

"Explosions are strange things. One time in 1944 a munitions ship, the SS *Fort Stikine*, blew up in Bombay harbour. A railway man I knew, Bob Scott, was walking along a street near the docks with a friend. The explosion knocked him out. When he came to he was unharmed but his friend was down the street, naked and without a mark on him, but stone dead."

Not all Jim's stories were about the war. One day he returned to the bungalow to learn that the family dog, Mac, had been behaving oddly and had been locked in the shed. My dad peered through the window and saw Mac, tearing wildly around, snarling, foaming at the mouth and obviously rabid. He got his shotgun, opened the door a crack and pushed the gun through. In a frenzy, Mac seized the barrel and my dad pulled the trigger. When he withdrew the gun he noticed that Mac had left teeth marks on the tempered steel.

Much as I loved Jim's stories, I never made any attempt to fit them into a reconstruction of his pre-me life. It's impossible now but I have other clues from other sources.

My sister Susan remembers our father being very drunk one night shortly after he came back from India for good. He was wildly waving a gun around and shouting, "They're coming to get me." Who?

Once, in the bookcase in Paisley, amidst the tomes on religion and philosophy, I unearthed a well-worn book in a stained brown paper cover. It dealt with living with alcoholism.

On another occasion, shortly before I married, my fiancee and I went to visit my parents. My mom took my fiancee aside and advised her that I would have affairs and that she should ignore them. Do these three events suggest horrific war experiences, alcohol problems and affairs? Certainly, wartime India was not calm, heavy drinking was a part of the colonial culture and Jim must have been excruciatingly lonely for long periods.

It's tempting to build a story out of all this but that would be mere speculation and this is not a novel. All I can do is accept the stories for what they were, isolated anecdotes that were powerful enough to punch through my self-involved childhood. And that they certainly did. I loved all of Jim's tales, but my absolute favourite was the one about the time he went crocodile hunting on the Ganges River.

~~~~~

On June 23, 1757 the world's first global conflict was raging across Europe, North and South America, and West Africa. At dawn that day,
~~~~~

Robert Clive, a factor for the East India Company and a lieutenant-colonel in the British Army, stood thoughtfully on the banks of the Bhagirathi River some 150 kilometres north of Calcutta. On the face of it, Clive was doomed. His 3,000 British and Indian troops, 8 cannons and 2 howitzers were ranged against 50,000 infantry and cavalry and 300 pieces of artillery belonging to Siraj ud-Daulah, the Nawab of Bengal. The Nawab was confident that morning, but what he didn't know was that Clive had bribed the leader of a large portion of his forces to stand idle and not take part in the coming battle in exchange for becoming the new Nawab. The Battle of Plassey was a confused affair that lasted all day. It resulted in a victory for Clive and the British and marked the end of French colonial and commercial interest in India and the beginning of almost 200 years of British rule.

One hundred years to the day after Plassey and almost 1,000 kilometres to the northwest, another battle took place. This was part of a much smaller war, the Indian Rebellion or as it's known in India the First War for Independence, but it was the turning point in the history of British rule in India.

Prior to the mid-nineteenth century India was administered as a commercial enterprise by the East India Company who maintained order and put down revolts using their own private army consisting of Indian soldiers under British officers. In the Bengal Army, disaffection over several political and religious issues erupted into open rebellion in the spring of 1857. All across northern India, soldiers killed their officers and any British civilians they could find. They captured Delhi and proclaimed the aged Bahadur Shah Zafar, the last descendant of the Mughal dynasty, emperor. Many other smaller towns were overrun and the British residents fled, were killed or took refuge and were besieged.

In Cawnpore (now Kanpur), the British officer in charge, General Sir Hugh Massy Wheeler, relied on his cordial relations with the local Indian leader, Nana Sahib, to protect the Europeans in the city. After all, Wheeler had lived in India for fifty years, was married to the daughter of a Hindu woman, spoke the local language fluently and was popular with his troops. Unfortunately he miscalculated and, with around 1,000 Europeans and loyal Indians, was forced to take refuge in a couple of hastily fortified buildings outside the city.

Despite the unsuitability of the defensive position, shortages of food, water and ammunition, continuous shelling, and little chance of rescue, the dwindling number of defenders held out for three weeks. On June 23, encouraged by a prophecy that said British rule in India would end exactly 100 years after Plassey, Nana Sahib attempted to storm the entrenchment. The attacks were repelled, but it was obvious that the end was near. Two days later, Nana Sahib sent a note to General Wheeler offering safe passage for the survivors downriver to Allahabad.

With no sign of the relief column and little chance of repelling another onslaught, General Wheeler accepted Nana Sahib's proposal. On the morning of June 27, the 700 or so pitiful survivors of the siege, including many women and children, headed down to the Ganges River. On the way the wounded who fell behind and the Indian soldiers who had remained loyal were killed.

The pathetic survivors reached the river at Sati Chaura Ghat where, inauspiciously, Indian widows had as recently as thirty years before been expected to immolate themselves on their husbands' funeral pyres. As promised, the boats to take them downriver had been provided but they were stranded on the wide sandbanks exposed by the low water. As the survivors of the entrenchment struggled to clamber aboard, firing broke out from soldiers along the banks and several of the boats burst into flames. In the ensuing massacre all the men from the entrenchment, with the exception of four who managed to escape down the river, were killed.

After the massacre at Sati Chaura Ghat, about 120 women and children were taken into Cawnpore where they were joined by captives from nearby Fatehgarh. Around 200 women and children were imprisoned in a house called the Bibighar. Two and a half weeks later, on July 15, as the British relief force eventually fought its way to Cawnpore, butchers armed with cleavers and swords were ordered into the Bibighar where they slaughtered all the prisoners. The following day the bodies were dumped down a nearby well.

The atrocities at Cawnpore shocked British public opinion and triggered brutal reprisals that cost many thousands of Indian lives. It also meant the end of East India Company power and in 1858 jurisdiction was transferred to the British crown and the Raj (a Hindi word meaning rule), was created. It also gave me my favourite story.

"The Ganges crocodiles can live to be 100 years old," Jim told me, "and they're scavengers. They can drag a buffalo into the river, drown it and store it in their den until it rots a bit and is easy to eat, but they'll take anything that floats along.

"They're also very difficult to shoot. Most bullets will bounce off their armoured skin and if you only wound one, it goes back into the water and you lose it. You have to hit the brain. Do you know how big a crocodile's brain is?"

This was not something I was being taught at a Scottish grammar school, so I shook my head and raised a speculative clenched fist.

"No," my dad said and held up his thumb. "It's about the size of a walnut, and you can't shoot it from the front, skull's too thick. You have shoot from the side or behind, so you need a very powerful gun and good aim.

"First thing you do when you shoot a crocodile is skin it. You do that by making a cut all around behind the head and then peeling the skin back towards the tail. It's like removing a glove."

I loved the way my dad told me things as if there was the remotest chance that this information would ever be of use in my late 20th century life. But I was riveted nonetheless.

"Crocodile skin's tough. It can be made into bags and shoes, so it's worth money. Do you know what you do next?"

Wide-eyed, I shook my head.

"You cut open the stomach."

"But the stomach's not worth anything," I pointed out, struggling and failing to imagine what the inside of crocodile's stomach was like.

"No," my dad agreed, "but what's inside might be. If a crocodile eats someone with a few *rupees* in their pocket, after a while there won't be much left of the person but the coins will stay in the stomach."

"Did you find much money?"

"No but I'll tell you what I did find one day. It was not long after I went to India. A friend took me crocodile hunting on the Ganges. We didn't have much luck until we found a big old crocodile—it must have been nearly 20 feet long—laying on a sand bar. My friend shot it, we skinned it and cut open the stomach."

He paused. "What did you find?" I asked, totally absorbed.

"A watch," he said with a smile. "Not a wrist watch, like the one that you have, but an old-fashioned pocket watch."

"Did it still work?"

"No. It had been there a long time and the workings were very corroded, but the cover of the watch was gold and gold doesn't rust. We cleaned it off."

"and..."

"There was an engraving on the inside of the cover. 'To subaltern Thomas Atkins on his departure for India. January, 1857.'"

"That's old," I said, slightly disappointed that there was no secret code or treasure map. Then my dad said that he had been hunting downriver from Cawnpore and he told me the story of the massacre at the boats.

"His parents probably gave Thomas the watch as a parting gift as he boarded his ship for India. Most likely, he was stationed in Cawnpore, survived the siege and was killed at Sati Chaura Ghat that day. His body floated downstream and a young crocodile found it. It ate him and the watch in his pocket and the watch stayed there until we shot the crocodile all those years later."

"Do you have the watch?" I asked hopefully.

My dad shook his head. "My friend took it. It was probably lost many years ago."

I can't begin to count the number of hours I spent, daydreaming at my school desk or in bed at night, making up stories about what might have happened to Thomas Atkins and how his watch ended up in the crocodile. I never wrote anything down, but I was already an author.

Were my Dad's stories true? I doubt if they were in a strict sense and details were added to keep the flow going. For example, Thomas Atkins is generic slang name for a British soldier, so I very much doubt if that was the name on the watch. But all the tales were probably based on some real event that Jim had experienced or heard about. In any case, I don't think the literal truth or lack of it is important. What is important to me is how my father's life in India, or at least his retelling of it, encouraged a love of stories in his son. In fact, four decades later, the watch-in-the-crocodile story and the historical events around the massacre at Cawnpore became the basis for a novel, *Where Soldiers Lie.*

So Jim's tales contributed greatly to the creation of my storytelling life. But what of my mother? She too was born and lived much of her early life in India. She was also alone for many years in wartime and postwar Britain. What contribution did her experiences make to moulding her late-arriving son?

Interlude

Last Call

"Last call for Flight 16."
To where?
My future,
hopeful, solid, imaginable,
a chaos of children,
journeys unforetold.
Your past?
Unfamiliar, ethereal, strange,
a different world
that I can never know.

"Will passengers proceed through Gate 3A."
I must go
while you recede through memories of
magic ships in deserts—port out starboard home,
bridge,
chota pegs beneath the waving punkah,
Mac, rabid enough to leave his teeth
imbedded in your gun,
great quakes of snaking rails, broken earth,
rescued infants in the Ayah's arms,
hailstones large as tennis balls,
tiger hunts and ponies gored by pigs unstuck,
and freedom, dohti-wrapped, that sent you home.
To what?
Sad memories of childhood loneliness
half spent in icy Fettes baths
before apprenticeships to rule,
hotels unvisited so long they must be but a dream,
shipyards dying of old-age,
used cars and ironmonger's shops,
and this and that,
until again the loneliness returns.

"Complete a customs form."
Declare my memories
of one who loomed so large he could do anything,

although that "damned bad hip" precluded any games.
Not true,
you taught me chess, whist,
to never blink at a royal flush,
to see the world as something magical,
how to fix a car,
to hold a silence which could sometimes scare me more than any fist,
and how to live within myself,
you, who only really came alive
when conversations turned to thoughts of yesterday
across the world.

"I wish to hell I could come with you."
No.
There's just this one embrace,
the only one in forty years,
awkward, forgiving
a tear
no
look away
security is beckoning.

My father stands
a heavy shape
stick-propped
with only that damned cancer
for a friend.

Two Worlds

Six weeks before and fifty miles to the south of where the dying Elsie Inglis landed at Newcastle-Upon-Tyne, No. 107 Squadron of the Royal Flying Corps (RFC) was formed at Catterick airfield. Although not supplied with aircraft until May of 1918, by which time the RFC had become the Royal Air Force (RAF), the Airco DH.9s of the squadron were busy as day bombers attacking enemy airfields, railways and, spectacularly in July, a large ammunition dump west of Reims. In 1919, the squadron was disbanded, but it reformed in 1936 as a light bomber squadron.

When the Second World War broke out, 107 Squadron was immediately involved, undertaking the RAF's first raid of the hostilities when four *Blenheim* bombers of the unit attacked German shipping in Wilhelmshaven on September 4. The raid was not a success, with three of the planes shot down and one returning without being able to drop its bombs. The squadron also provided the first British prisoner of war when Sergeant George Booth's plane was shot down on the same day.

In 1942, the faster, sturdier *Bostons* replaced the *Blenheim* bombers and the squadron went on several daring missions over occupied Europe, including bombing shore batteries in support of the failed Dieppe Raid in August. On December 6, twelve *Bostons* of 107 Squadron took part in Operation Oyster.

The huge Philips Radio Works in the occupied Netherlands was supplying sophisticated radio parts for much of the German army. Putting it out of commission would be a major blow to the Germans, but it would be a difficult task. The Philips works were a large target, but the two factories were in the middle of the city of Eindhoven. To ensure accuracy and minimize civilian casualties, the plan was to launch a low-level daylight raid using 93 aircraft of various types (36 *Bostons*, 47 *Lockheed Venturas* and 10 of the new *Mosquitos*).

RAF cameramen on the raid produced stunning footage of the aircraft flashing over the north sea and the Dutch countryside at less than 50 feet, being fired at and firing on the anti-aircraft guns on top of the Philips complex, and of bombs exploding in the factories.

The first hazards of the raid were from panicked birds which rose in flocks at the sound of the low-flying planes and several aircraft returned with the remains of gulls, ducks and in one case a heron smeared over them. Despite heavy anti-aircraft fire, the planes precision-bombed their target at 12:30 p.m. leaving many of the factory buildings in ruins under the thick cloud of smoke from the many fires.

Turning for home the bombers had to run the gauntlet of the *Focke-Wulf FW190* fighters that had been scrambled from nearby Schipol airfield. Pilot Officer Jack Peppiatt dramatically described what it was like: "...we were all down hugging the ground for comfort...as *FW190s* appeared...10 or 20 aircraft were screaming along, full throttle in a loose mass; no one wanted to be at the back where the *Focke-Wulfs* were coming in to attack and wheeling away for another go... I distinctly saw cannon shells hitting plowed fields in front of me...at one point a fighter slid past us and just sat to my right as he slowed—so close I could stare at the pilot...I was sliding and diving constantly. The astonishing thing was that we didn't collide, as aircraft constantly criss-crossed in front of each other."

The raid was a success and the Philips factory did not resume full production until six months later. Because of the low level of the attack (between 1,000 and 1,500 feet), the bombing was for the most part very accurate; however, several bombs fell short, killing over a hundred civilians. Of the 93 aircraft involved, 13 failed to return. No. 107 Squadron lost three *Bostons* to the *Focke-Wulfs* on the return trip. The last to be shot down was aircraft AH740, which crashed at 12:59 three miles off the Dutch coast killing all four crew. Their bodies were never found.

AH740 was piloted by the Squadron Commander, Peter Hiley Dutton. He was twenty-nine years old and left a young wife, Marjorie, and two infant daughters, Jane and Felicity. Marjorie and her girls spent the rest of the war in rural Scotland with her older sister, Eveleen Victoria Marguerite Wilson, my mother.

~~~~~

Eveleen Victoria Marguerite Dyer, always known simply as Eve, led a parallel but different life from my father. Jim's father, John, had been the first generation of his family to go to India. Taking his young bride Emily, he went out to Calcutta in 1902 where my aunt, Helen, was born later that year. My father followed in 1905. Unfortunately John's life in India was short and he died in Calcutta in 1920. Eve's family had deeper roots.

In 1876, the British Prime Minister, Benjamin Disraeli, in an attempt to bind India more firmly to Britain, had Queen Victoria proclaimed Empress of India. On November 20 of that year my great grandfather, Dr. James Alexander Dyer, a Free Church of Scotland missionary and accomplished eye surgeon who had arrived in India only the year before, married Elizabeth Margaret Hay Scott in Calcutta.

For forty-five years Dr. Dyer worked tirelessly with the Santal people of West Bengal. I have a photograph from the late 1800s of him dressed in tweeds on the verandah of a bungalow, operating on a patient's eye, while others line up behind him.

I also have an account he wrote to the Geological Survey of India about his experiences in Giridih during the Great Assam Earthquake of 1897: "On turning to look at the house I found extraordinary movement taking place...I could see most distinctly the heaving motion, and compared it in my mind to what might have been produced by an elephant under such a roof, if he had his back against it from north to south...We stood so long in the sunshine that I dreaded sunstroke, and ran for shelter and shade to a small house."
~~~~~

Dr. Dyer's oldest son Alfred was home in Britain when the Assam earthquake occurred, but he would have his own experience. At 2:28 on the afternoon of January 15, 1934 the Bihar Earthquake struck causing immense devastation and loss of life in Nepal and northern India. Perhaps Alfred's father had told him stories of the earlier quake to pique his interest, but he filled two photograph albums with pictures of collapsed buildings, fissures in the earth, fallen bridges and rails snaking across the ground like twitched lengths of string.

Jim also experienced the Bihar Earthquake, although it affected him differently. When he was back in Scotland on leave in 1935, he went to see a movie in the huge Odeon movie theatre on Renfield Street in Glasgow. As he was settling down, he heard the deep swelling reverberations of a major earthquake. Without thinking, he leaped from his seat and fled up the aisle, only to realize that the building wasn't shaking and that everyone else was sitting, staring open-mouthed at him. Sheepishly, he returned to his seat as the underground train out of Central Station rumbled beneath the cinema.

Only my mother, Alfred's daughter Eve told me a story of her experience of the actual quake. As the chandeliers swayed and furniture crashed about her, my mother grabbed my two-and-a-half-year-old sister and fled to sit in the relative safety of the front lawn as the earth heaved and shook around her. The family *Ayah* (a servant hired to look after the children), was horrified to see the infant sitting in the afternoon sun without her hat, which had been forgotten in the panic. Despite my mother's entreaties to never mind, she rushed back into the collapsing building to retrieve it.

Like my father, my mother was born in India, on September 11, 1912 in Samastipur. On October 18, 1922, the ten-year-old Eve with her father Alfred, mother Victoria, and younger sisters, Dot and Marjorie, boarded the *City of Marseilles* in Liverpool after a summer of being shown off to the family back home. Eve was returning to begin her preparation for her role as a memsahib. The role didn't require an extensive formal education, it was mainly picked up by watching the world around and with lessons in the more formal elements of protocol from older female members of the family. It was tricky to run a household of many servants whose duties were rigidly defined by each individual's place within the immensely complex Hindu caste system. No less subtlety was required in organizing dinner parties so that none of the European guests' noses were put out of joint by being placed out of *their* narrowly defined role in the ruling hierarchy's caste system. It was a lot to learn and it didn't suit the student for life in a world wider than the restricted confines of Imperial India, but that wasn't an issue in the confident days of 1929 when Eve was considered ready to come out into society.

Coming out for a girl was code for finding a husband and the season of dances, parties and balls was when and where she would find one. If she failed in this task in the first two seasons or so, she became a spinster, doomed to settle for an unsuitable match far below her on the social scale or, if she was strong-willed enough and lucky, to find a measure of freedom doing something she loved on the fringes of society.

In 1929, Eve was strikingly good-looking with her hair waved in the latest style and wearing fashionable dresses from Britain. She once told me that she loved the social whirl of that season of balls and parties—and why not—she was beautiful, privileged and doing what she had spent much of her young life being trained for. The glittering world of the Raj was eternal and the idea that Gandhi and the Indian National Congress would ever force the British to leave must have seemed ridiculous. In photographs from that time, Eve looks happy and secure, looking out at the future with a slight, wistful smile. She never had any difficulty filling her dance card.

At the balls and parties that season, she met two handsome young men. One could dance beautifully and the other couldn't. Dancing well was an important skill in British India society and the seventeen-year-old Eve was impressed. However, after much teenage agonizing, the less accomplished dancer's sense of humour won out and, in Christ Church at the top of the Mall in Simla, on September 27, 1930, sixteen days after her eighteenth birthday, Eve married my father.

It was a spectacular occasion with the service performed by the local Bishop. In the photograph afterwards, Eve stands in white holding a bouquet of lilies, and with the train of her veil flowing out onto the ground in front of her. Her head is tilted slightly and that smile is threatening to break through. Jim stands staring straight at the camera dressed in his formal Scottish regalia. The couple are surrounded by family dressed in their best and all look out through the camera, with the rather odd exception of Alfred who is staring off to one side.

A year less two weeks after that splendid day, their first daughter, Helen known as Eelin, arrived. Three years on, the second, Dorothy, appeared on the scene to be followed in 1937 by the third, Susan. Life in the Raj was broken up by trips back to Scotland, in 1933 and 1934. Traditionally, these trips involved a four- to five-week sail from Bombay or Calcutta to either Tilbury or Liverpool in April, with a return in October. Jim stayed working in the heat of an Indian summer while Eve travelled alone with the children. The 1934 visit was different. Eve was pregnant and gave birth to my sister Dorothy in Edinburgh that September. Consequently, she stayed over the winter. My father returned on leave for the summer of 1935 and although they both travelled back to India that fall it was on separate ships. James sailed on September 13 on the S.S. *Rawalpindi*, a ship which was later converted into an armed merchant raider and was famously, as Jim told it, sunk in a hopeless battle against the German battle cruisers *Scharnhorst* and *Gneisenau* on November 23, 1939. The captain's last message was: "We'll fight them both, they'll sink us, and that will be that. Good-bye." Eve, accompanied by a nurse, sailed on October 26 on the much more mundane S.S. *Strathmore*.

The next trip home, following Susan's birth, was on April 29, 1938, once more aboard the *Strathmore*. Eve, aged 25, and the three girls arrived at Tilbury downriver from London. The voyage had been good. Eve later said that a young woman travelling alone with small children was pampered on the P&O Liners.

After the arrival formalities were completed. The four travelled by train up to Edinburgh where, as in 1933 and 1934/35, they stayed in a large, sandstone semi-detached house at 7 Lygon Road with Jim's sister, also Helen known as Eelin. The visit was planned to be similar to the two previous trips, a five-or six-month opportunity to show off the children to relatives, and in this case to arrange an eye operation for three-year-old Dorothy—but this visit was different. Like many other passengers on the *Strathmore*, Eve put down her country of permanent residence as India, but she was wrong. Neither my mother nor my sisters would ever return to India.

~~~~~

Tensions in Europe steadily rose over the summer of 1938 as Hitler incorporated Austria into the Third Reich and gradually increased his demands to absorb the ethnic German population of Czechoslovakia. Politicians shuttled back and forth attempting to find a solution to an insoluble problem—as early as May 30, Hitler had ordered his army to prepare for an invasion of Czechoslovakia on October 1.

Many people were convinced that war was going to break out that summer. It didn't because the governments of Britain and France caved to Hitler's pressure and, at 1:30 in the morning of September 30 in Hitler's office in Munich, signed an agreement that dismembered Czechoslovakia and presented Germany with the Sudetenland and 25% of the armaments that were, within two years, used in the invasions of Poland, Denmark, Norway, Belgium, Netherlands, Luxembourg and France. The British Prime Minister, Neville Chamberlain claimed that the agreement would bring "peace for our time" but few believed him. Churchill called the agreement a "total and unmitigated defeat" that would only be "the first foretaste of a bitter cup".

Amidst the uncertainty and rumours of war that summer, it was decided that Eve and the girls should stay in Britain for the time being. This decision was confirmed the following year when Jim returned in March for a brief leave. In September, as the German tanks rolled through Poland, my father returned to India and the responsibilities of protecting the Raj. He left Eve in Aberfeldy, north of Stirling with three young
~~~~~

children and, although he couldn't have known it at the time, pregnant with their fourth daughter.

As the war progressed, the family moved a few miles east to Strathtay. Life in Strathtay for Eve and her four young children (Fiona had arrived in the spring of 1940), wasn't easy. I remember my mum saying how much she had hated the wartime bread and powdered eggs. Even with extra rations for the children, life was hard and making do was not something that someone trained to live in Imperial India with all its servants was used to. And yet I recall my mother saying that those years in the Scottish countryside were among the most enjoyable of her life. It was a community of women and children and the war made everyone come together and help each other. The idyll came to an end as the war did.

Eve and my sisters moved back to Edinburgh shortly before Jim returned home on leave on August 29, 1945 after six years away. This wasn't a leisurely four week boat trip but a hurried plane journey with only a brief stop in Egypt and my dad brought bad news. Throughout the war my mother's cherished assumption was that something close to the life of privilege she had known in India would be continued after Germany and Japan were defeated. It was not to be. By 1945, the world had changed. It was obvious to everyone that India would be given independence in a very short time. Jim had work to do on the railways and helping with the handover to the new countries of India and Pakistan, but there was little point in bringing the family out. On February 15, 1946, James boarded a plane flying east for what turned out to be a four-year separation.

I know little about those postwar years other than one shattering event.

~~~~~

An Egyptian stele from around 3,400 years ago is thought to be the first representation of a victim of the Poliomyelitis Enterovirus. The disease is transmitted through contact with human faeces. Ironically, in the days of poor sanitation, prolonged infant exposure to the virus accorded an immunity and the disease was rare. It was only after improved sewage
~~~~~

disposal and the provision of clean water greatly reduced contact with the virus that polio epidemics became a factor in developed countries. Even in the days before vaccination the majority of people exposed to the polio virus never even knew it. Of those who were diagnosed, the majority suffered fever, headaches and an upset stomach and recovered. In a few cases, the virus attacked the central nervous system and some form of paralysis resulted, and in some of these cases the paralysis was permanent. In a fraction of one percent, polio killed.

In Britain, polio was at its worst in the 1940s and early 1950s, when it killed up to 750 people a year. Compared to diphtheria (which annually killed an average of 3,500 children in Britain before vaccination), tuberculosis (which accounted for between twenty and thirty thousand deaths each year during the 1930s and early 40s, many of whom were children), or, in earlier years scarlet fever and influenza, polio was a relatively minor killer of children, but it was one of the most feared. Philip Roth strikingly captured that fear in his novel *Nemesis*: "Finally the cataclysm began – the monstrous headache, the enfeebling exhaustion, the severe nausea, the raging fever, the unbearable muscle ache, followed in another forty-eight hours by the paralysis."

Before the polio vaccine became widely available in Britain, I remember seeing and hearing about kids in iron lungs and wearing heavy leg braces that today would not look out of place in some weird steampunk science fiction movie. That was the image that horrified adults, a tiny fragile child trapped in a cold, unyielding mechanical contraption.

When Salk's and Sabin's vaccines became available in the late fifties and early sixties, parents rushed their children in to doctors and clinics. Of all the vaccines I received as a child the only one I remember was going down with Eve to the Russell Institute on Causeyside Street in Paisley to get my polio shots. It wasn't because it hurt more or was more unpleasant than any others, it was because of my mother's tension around each visit.

One morning in October 1948, my eight-year-old sister, Fiona, complained of a headache and stiffness. My mother checked and discovered a fever. Aspirin didn't do the trick and by late afternoon things were bad enough for my mother to call an ambulance. The ambulance arrived and took Fiona to hospital just as her older sister was arriving home from school. Forty-eight hours later Fiona was dead.

The suddenness and horror were devastating, but it was not a devastation that I experienced. For me, my lost sister was a ghostly black and white photograph that sat in the living room of every house we lived in while I was growing up—and the urgency with which my mother took me to get my polio vaccine shots.

~~~~~

For the first eight years of their married life, my parents were apart a lot. That was the way it was in the Raj. In the days before air-conditioning, between May and October each year, women and children escaped the brutal heat of the Indian plains by taking refuge in a hill station such as Darjeeling, Mussoorie or Simla. Except for brief visits to the hills whenever they could, the men remained in the lowlands. The wives and children saw little enough of their husbands and fathers for those months, but they saw nothing at all if they went back to Britain between April and October, which Eve did in 1933 and 1934.

By 1938 my parents were used to being apart, but after that things were much worse. In the twelve years from the end of April 1938 to late March 1950, Eve and Jim were together for no more than ten months— five in 1939 and five in 1945/46.

Renewing a marriage after a twelve-year separation is hard on any relationship. How much more difficult is it if you throw in a world war, the birth and death of a child, and the collapse of the only world you know? My father took refuge in whatever work he could find and may have augmented that out of a bottle, but what was it like for my mother?

Eve was part of a largely unrecognized lost generation—one of the 45,000 or so European women living in India and Burma around 1947. Most returned to Britain either before the war or in the years after Independence. The vast majority came from middle-class families and were not independently wealthy. A list of the occupations of my ancestors
~~~~~

in the generation or two prior to the move to India included a tailor, a baker, two blacksmiths, a stone mason, and a cork cutter. In India, the women of my mother's generation had been trained for little other than running a household full of servants within the rigid social structure of the imperial rulers. Back in Britain they were bereft of servants in a world they either didn't understand or detested. They found themselves in a grey, wet country struggling for money in an economically depressed climate, and surrounded by people who didn't care about them, didn't help them, and whom they didn't much like. The Raj and the rest of the British Empire was gone or rapidly going. Imperialism, in all its complexity, was dismissed as a dirty word and those who had participated in it as grumpy, inflexible old fossils out of synch with the bright new world of hope that blossomed in the 1960s.

My mother wasn't a storyteller like my father, although she did tell me about the earthquake and the time a rabid dog ran through the house and my infant sister had to endure a series of extremely painful injections into her stomach. Her filtering of the India experience through to me was more subtle.

I sometimes confounded my school friends by getting the *doodh* (the Hindi word for milk) from the fridge. Of course, whether they realized it or not, they themselves used many words that the British had derived from Hindi: bangle, bungalow, cot, dungarees, jungle, khaki, loot, monsoon, pyjamas, shampoo, thug, typhoon, veranda. But there were many that were in common usage in our house that they didn't know: *begum* (a high born lady, usually used by my mother for someone with ideas above her station), *choky* (a chair), *palavar* (an unnecessarily long discussion), *ghee* (clarified butter), *chota peg* (a small drink), *burra peg* (a large drink).

I grew up firmly closing my mouth when passing a bad smell in the street, looking with fascination at women who smoked in public or wore bright lipstick because both were signs of low morals, and being far too conscious of class distinctions that only existed in my mother's mind.

I once got into terrible trouble from my mother for suggesting out loud that we were working class, which from a financial point of view of course we were.

I learned to talk on the Isle of Skye and picked up a soft, highland lilt which was derided when I went to school in lowland Paisley. I had to learn to talk differently at school and I had to remember to change the way I spoke when I went home because, to my mother, a west coast lowland accent was lower class.

All my school friend's parents were much younger than mine and seemed to understand at least something of the world that their children were growing up in. Not only were Eve and Jim older, but their lives in the fossilized society of the Raj added an extra generation to the gap.

I often felt that I was growing up in two worlds, my home life and everything else. I wished for a life identical to my peers and didn't appreciate until much later what I had been given. Growing up in two worlds teaches you to always see the other side, to never take things at face value, to always distrust the person who has a simple answer and is convinced that he or she is right, in short to be skeptical. It is probably no coincidence that two of my favourite authors since I was a teenager are George Orwell and Albert Camus, both independent thinkers who grew up in two worlds: Orwell in England and Imperial Burma, Camus in Algeria—then a colony of France.

My mother hated Britain, and that gave me her other great gift. Scotland in the 1950s and 60s was the anti-Raj. Where India was bright and colourful, Scotland was dull and grey. Where India was sunny and dry, Scotland was continually overcast and rainy. Where India glittered and was vibrant, at least for the rulers, Scotland was drab and listless.

It didn't help that my parents were always struggling to make ends meet. Jim's pension from India was never paid and his first venture in Scotland, running a hotel on the Isle of Skye, failed. He worked in shipbuilding on Clydeside until technology made engineers of his training and background redundant. He ran a driving school, managed gas stations and operated a hardware store. Eve worked shifts as an Auxiliary Nurse in the children's ward at the Royal Alexandra Infirmary in Paisley. It was always tough and my mother's constant theme was what a dreadful place Scotland was. My sisters all left the country: for Australia, Africa and Canada, and I was repeatedly told that, after I had an education, I had to leave and make my future elsewhere. Of course, the unstated subtext was, "Go out into the Empire, young man," but when I opened the door to leave and asked which way the Empire was, there was nothing left. It didn't stop me moving and that is the other thing I have to thank my mother's Indian imperial experience for, a love of being in different places.

I doubt if my parents intended to raise a skeptical storytelling traveller, but that's the way it turned out. Of course, growing up I didn't know the directions I was going in or the influences that were steering me, but my parent's lives in India had, in ways that I am still discovering, an immense formative influence on the person I was to become.

At the beginning of April 1982, Eve had a stroke. According to Jim she had had several before that had changed her personality and made her a bit difficult to live with, but this one was massive and sent her into a deep coma. I flew home from Canada to be with my dad in the small cottage my parents owned in Letham. Early in the morning of Good Friday, April 9, the hospital in nearby Forfar called to say that Eve had died.

Three years later Jim was dead and my last direct link to his and Eve's world was gone. All that remained was that boy sitting shyly in the corner of the room listening to incomprehensible tales of a magical lost world and all that was left for me to do in order to try to make sense of it all was the obvious. I would do what my parents, sisters and aunts and uncles never did, I would go to India and see what remnants were left of their world.

Interlude

Dancing

My mother loved to dance.
Through the glittering ballrooms of empire
she danced;
through the sirens and the doodlebugs
she danced;
through my unforgiving childhood
she danced.

Now the damp grey air
has sucked the colour from the world.
Around a bottomless hole
we silently remember
the happy bright woman
who loved picnics in the woods
and the smell of babies
and try to ignore
the hopeless embarrassing sobs
of a weeping aunt.

Am I the only one
who wants to dance?

Beggars and Gentlemen

My sister, Eelin, and I once discussed how much fun it would be to go together to India and explore all the places from our family past, but it never happened. At my prompting as to whether they would like to go back my parents gave differing reactions. Jim expressed a vague interest in seeing how things had changed but accepted that it would never be financially possible. Eve was dead against any thought of a return, even for a nostalgic visit.

"I would hate it," she said. "It would be too sad. Everything would be different."

Actually, it wouldn't have been that different, only the veneer, the world Eve had lived in, was gone, the rest of India was remarkably unchanged. There is an immense inertia in India against change for its own sake. We tear down city buildings and put up new ones every generation or two. In India, there is an abandoned city that hasn't changed since the sixteenth century. In the 1980s I showed photographs of Simla to an aunt who had lived there half a century before. She could identify every building and claimed that it hadn't changed one bit. Of course under the surface Simla had changed, the buildings were not used for their old imperial purposes and the statue of Queen Victoria at the top of The Mall had been replaced by one of Gandhi, but the physical presence of the town was identical. What my mother meant by change was not physical and not even large scale. She didn't want to return because she thought her culture—which in any case was an artificial, transplanted one and even at the height of the Raj made up only a tiny piece of India as a whole—had vanished. Even that was not entirely true and, as I was to discover, there were tiny remnants of the Raj, sometimes in the most unexpected places.

Despite the best efforts of my missionary great grandfather, Christianity never really took hold in India; there are only about 28 million Christians distributed among India's 1.324 billion population. Still, it has left the most obvious remnants of European rule. Churches in India range from the soaring neo-gothic edifice of the Anglican All Saints Cathedral in Allahabad to the modest, sensible, red brick, presbyterian St Andrew's in Simla. Some are still used for their original purpose, others have been repurposed (St Andrew's was used for evening classes at the University of Himachal Pradash when I visited), and some have fallen into ruin, like the Rosary Church in Shetihalli which is flooded when the water rises in the nearby dam every monsoon season.

The dour Scottish Presbyterian monotheism of my ancestor's Church never had a hope of supplanting the rich, vigorous Hindu culture that, some say, offers 330 million gods. Today there are a mere 8 million Protestants in India spread amongst a surprising array of 31 denominations. The Catholic church, both Roman and Eastern Orthodox, with its mystery and ceremony was always more attractive and has garnered two-and-a-half times as many converts. Christianity is, perhaps unsurprisingly, most in evidence in one of the oldest enclaves of imperialism. But it is a tiny piece of the subcontinent that was never a part of the British Raj.

In December 1961, a two-day war in India resulted in 52 deaths and the end of 451 years of European occupation. In 1510, the Portuguese defeated the local sultan and established a colony at Velha Goa, or Old Goa, on India's southwest coast. It rapidly became a centre for missionary activity led by Francis Xavier who voyaged as far as Japan and established the Goa Inquisition, which was mainly notable for the enthusiasm with which it tortured and burned Hindus, Buddhists, Jews and lapsed Catholics. All of this religious fervour has left a World Heritage site of impressive churches, some ruined, some still in use.

My visit to Goa in 1987 coincided with that of a Soviet Naval Commander who strode hurriedly around the Archaeological Museum amidst a collection of large security guards in ill-fitting suits. Afterwards as I was sitting in the cool of the vast Se Cathedral, the church deacon introduced himself with, "Excuse me, sir, I'd like to ask your advice." To my certain knowledge, it is the only time a member of any church has asked my advice.

Apparently Se Cathedral had been on the whirlwind agenda of the Soviet naval officer. He had come in with his retinue and asked if they could go up to the altar. While the deacon went to check with the priest, the visitors had gone over the low railing designed to keep people away from the altar and posed for a group photograph. This was what was upsetting the anxious deacon. "Had they blasphemed, sir?" "Am I at fault for failing to prevent them?" "Will my job be in jeopardy?" I had not the slightest idea how to answer his questions, but tried to reassure him as well as I could. It seemed to work as I met him later in the garden where he cheerfully offered to share his lunch with me.

The Portuguese stubbornly regarded their colony at Goa as a detached but integral part of their country, which was why a war was necessary to make it a part of India. Even at the height of the Raj's power, the British never felt that. For the sahibs and memsahibs, India was always the other —an exotic alien culture that offered wonderful opportunities for those adventurous enough to brave its harsh climate and terrifying diseases. However, Britain (specifically it seemed Eastbourne or somewhere else on the south coast), was always 'home'. While I loved Goa with its almost Mediterranean feel, ruins and spectacular beaches, it was the British experience that I sought.

<div align="center">~~~~~</div>

My first visit to India lasted only 24 hours, yet it encapsulated many of the divergent annoyances and joys of a much longer sojourn, and introduced me to one of the two things that, it is said, India inherited from the British —the bureaucracy.

It was December 23, 1986 and, with my wife Jen, I was just over six weeks into a year-long backpacking adventure around the world. Already, I had been tear-gassed in Seoul, propositioned in an unrecognized Thai brothel, and had wept at ground zero in Hiroshima. Now, I was heading for some trekking in Nepal. The plan was for a short, two-and-a-half hour flight from Bangkok to Calcutta (now Kolkata), and an even shorter ongoing connection to Kathmandu.

My farewell to Bangkok was harsh after a sleepless night, missed taxis and excruciating airport delays. Long after dark, exhausted and hours after my connecting flight would have left Calcutta, I was ushered out towards the waiting Air India plane. Harsh floodlights snapped on and Thai police in full riot gear watched us all file slowly across the wet tarmac. I guess a grubby backpacker with a beard and long hair was fair game. I was pulled aside and frisked. Standing in the glare with legs apart, arms out wide and head slumped despondently on my chest as I was searched, the image of Brad Davis in the airport scene in *Midnight Express* flashed uncomfortably into my mind.

Eventually I was let on the plane and it was then that India came to my rescue. I was presented with a single rose and a cool cloth to wipe my brow then, in a scene that my father would have appreciated, the immaculately dressed First Cabin Officer approached me and said, "Would you like a whisky after take-off, sir?" It was a moment in which I could have forgiven imperialism almost anything. Then we arrived in Calcutta.

The bureaucracy kicked in at immigration in Calcutta airport. Because I was supposed to be in transit I had no visa, yet the next flight to Kathmandu was not until the following evening. After much back and forth, discussion and paper stamping, I was allowed through to collect my backpack. Because I was technically in transit, I was allowed to stay in the nearby Airport Rest House.

The Airport Rest House was a large bungalow that had once been a part of the Dum Dum Barracks where the British had invented the Hague Convention-banned expanding bullet of the same name. My excitement at being in a piece of British imperial history was somewhat diminished by the fact that the place looked as if it hadn't been painted, the bathrooms cleaned or anything repaired since my father might have stayed there. The only bright spots were that I had had the foresight to purchase a bottle of duty-free Glenfiddich during the interminable wait in Bangkok and the bungalow was stocked with glasses and ice, so I sat in a cane chair on the generous, screened verandah and, to the clink of ice in a glass of whisky, toasted Eve and Jim's vanished world.

The next day was Christmas Eve and I felt refreshed enough to consider searching out some other Raj remnants in the old imperial capital city. A cheerful official gave me my first sighting of the Indian head nod that could mean yes or no, or anything between, and confirmed that it was a wonderful idea to go into the city even if the bus to downtown would leave, "Maybe ten. Maybe later", and he had no idea when the bus back might be. He also attempted to encourage me by telling me that a "holy man" was going to be in the city and that there would be, "...millions of people downtown. So many crowds that, if you fall over, you will not fall down. You land on people." Enticing though this inner ring of Dante's Hell sounded, I decided to confine myself to the Dum Dum Barracks and spend the day reading.

That evening, after more waiting and bureaucracy, I caught my flight to Kathmandu where, in a surreal change of scene, I checked into the Sheraton (at the trekker's rate), discovered the Gurkha Bar and drank and ate peanuts in lieu of supper.

After a month's trekking and rafting in Nepal, I returned to India on a luxury overnight bus with reclining seats. I soon discovered that reclining wasn't a guarantee but more of an either/or—my seat didn't recline, the one in front did. As a consequence I spent the night uncomfortably bolt upright a few inches from the over-greased hair of the blissfully snoring passenger in front.

Varanasi, or Benares as my parents' knew it, is the site where Shiva dropped the severed head of Brahma after he tore it off in battle. It is also the site of a minor massacre in 1799 (five Europeans were killed) and a much larger one at the beginning of the rebellion in 1857. Colonel James Neill of the 1st Madras Fusiliers, in a fit of Old Testament passion, declared that "the Word of God gives no authority to the modern tenderness for human life." He then promptly ordered his artillery to open fire on a confused mass of soldiers and Sikhs and proceeded to hang anyone suspected of rebellious intent. It was not an auspicious place to begin my exploration of India's imperial past.

Unfortunately, I remained unaware of one of the strangest remnants of the Raj. Somewhere in Varanasi's bustle there is a banquet hall with a large dining table kept exactly as it was laid out in 1906 for a visit by the Prince of Wales (later one of the Georges who thought my father "trusty and well-beloved").

What I did discover was that Varanasi was a popular place for weddings, all of which seemed to involve brass bands playing all night, and that the holier a shrine, the dirtier and the more overrun it was with beggars. It was also very crowded and the options of getting around were: risking twelve passengers to a *tuk tuk* (a motorized rickshaw designed to carry four), braving insane and often crooked traditional rickshaw haulers or walking, which involved avoiding strolling cows, being pummelled by crowds and having betel juice spat down one's legs.

The other thing I learned about India in Varanasi was that, however bad a day has been, it is often followed by a stunningly beautiful sunset that can persuade the tired traveller to forgive the country anything. In Varanasi's case, it is best seen from a boat on the Ganges River as the buildings above the burning ghats turn ethereal shades of orange and red.

The second thing that India inherited from the British was something my father spent his years there working on. India possesses the fourth largest railway network in the world (after America, Russia and China). It carries over 22 million passengers per day between 8,500 stations on 120,000 kilometres of track of five different gauges at speeds that range from impressive to snail-like. In honour of Jim's memory, I was looking forward to travelling on the trains. Consequently, I had purchased a first-class railway pass in advance and had it activated, bureaucratically, in Varanasi.

Travelling by train, at least back in the 1980s, was probably as close to recapturing my parents' world of privilege as possible. Many trains were still steam in those days and first-class compartments were often quiet idylls of gleaming wood panels, the smell of leather, mirrors ornate with gilt foliage, and heavy windows that, at the pull of strap, disappeared with a loud thump into a gap in the carriage wall. Beneath the seats of one carriage, there were even metal-lined boxes with a separate door opening to the outside through which, in the days before air-conditioning, large blocks of ice were introduced.

The people one met in these compartments were Indians, but in some cases more British than the long-vanished rulers. One businessman who was old enough to remember the Raj even spent an hour lecturing me on how he wished the British would return because life had been so much better when they had ruled. What he selfishly meant was how much better life had been for him.

He reminded me of an Indian I had worked beside in Canada. He was a keen photographer and had the remarkable talent of taking pictures of his crowded homeland with no people in them. When I asked him why there were no people in his pictures he told me that he was not interested in photographing people and described hundreds of millions of his fellow countrymen as "insects". Even the most strident class and race-conscious memsahib would have been hard pressed to compete with that level of superiority.

~~~~~

Occasionally when the two legacies of British imperialism intersected the results were startling. In Delhi I went to the main station to book the next leg of my journey.

"How long will you be in India?" the clerk behind the desk asked.

"About another five weeks," I said.
~~~~~

"Very well," the enigmatic head nod, "then tell me where you wish to go and I shall book it."

"But I don't know exactly."

"No matter. It can be changed."

The clerk unfolded a large map of India and over the following half hour we worked out an itinerary that took me to all the major places I wanted to visit.

"Very good," the clerk congratulated me. "You will see much of India. Come back tomorrow."

Without much faith, I returned the next day. My clerk stood and waved a greeting at me above the heads of the other less-fortunate travellers. "Everything is done," he said, handing over a printed itinerary. "Please enjoy your stay in my country."

If this had happened in Japan, where people get upset if a train is a minute late, I would have believed our clerk, but after ten days in India I was getting used to travel uncertainty. Miraculously it worked perfectly, the trains were where they should be, mostly when they should be, even at the places where there was only a half hour connection.

Of course, the trains didn't always run on time. One train, already scheduled to take nearly fifteen hours to cover 250 kilometres, was two-and-a-half hours late arriving, and some routes were better than others. High speed trains ran between some major centres, but on rural lines it was still sometimes necessary to change trains because the gauge of the rails changed. The highlight was when, four weeks after my visit with the clerk in Delhi, I arrived at two in the morning at Madras (now Chennai) station to find my name handwritten in careful gothic script on a board on the platform, a reserved sleeping car complete with bedding, and a smiling attendant who, unasked, brought breakfast in the morning. Perhaps Jim's ghost was looking after me.

India is, and I suspect has always been, a land of staggering divergence —cleanliness and filth, peace and violence, gentlemen and beggars. I suspect this is why so many people find it so difficult to adjust to travelling in India. From one moment to the next you can never be totally certain on which side of the contrasts you are about to land. Most of these disparities can be encountered on the railways.

My favourite railway companion was a gentlemanly Parsee, Mr. Pavri, on a journey down to Bombay (now Mumbai). He was an education specialist and we conversed pleasantly on the relative strengths and flaws of education in India, Canada and Scotland and he told me about his religion and his sorrow that his three sons were in America and would not be able to care for him in his old age.

Every so often, he would break off the conversation with a, "Please excuse me for a moment." He would then produce a tiny transistor radio from his pocket and press it to his ear for a moment or two before returning it to his pocket. Noticing my puzzled expression, he explained, "Cricket. The test match with Pakistan is on just now. It is the third day and we are not doing so well." I suppose that is the advantage of a five-day-long cricket match—one doesn't need to pay attention all the time.

As the train reached Bombay's sprawling suburbs, Mr. Pavri invited Jen and I to get off a stop before our destination. He took us in a taxi to a restaurant and bought us dinner, although he didn't eat, "My wife will have prepared something for me," and took us back to the station to complete our journey.

On the other side of train travel in India, I was targeted by a beggar girl on a platform in Jhansi. She was 10 or 12 years old and had the most incredibly annoying whine imaginable. By then I had been travelling for a while and was used to beggars and took precautions around keeping my packs at my feet, if possible with a foot through a strap. The fact that this girl had followed me through the station and stood about four feet away whining incessantly and unbearably should have given me a warning, but it didn't. Eventually, I could take no more. I stood up, took a couple of steps forward and yelled at her to shut up and go away. She vanished into the crowd, and so did the daypack that had been at my feet.

I looked around, but it was futile, the theft was professional and the pack long gone. I went to report the loss to the railway police and bureaucracy kicked in. I was asked politely but repeatedly what colour the pack was, how big it was and what was in it. My only consolation was that opening the pack must have been a disappointment for the thief since most of the contents were either personal—prescription glasses, address book, etc.—or of low value—small camera or bottle of perfume. The most frustrating loss was the trip diary from Nepal.

After two hours of alternately being asked the same questions and sitting waiting for a report to be drawn up, I had an idea. There was no hope of getting the pack back but I needed something official for the insurance company back home. I got a piece of paper from a policeman, wrote out what had happened and what had been stolen and signed it. I then took it up to the desk and pushed it over. The policeman didn't speak English so I pointed to the impressive array of rubber stamps on his desk and mimicked stamping the letter. He got the idea and entered into the spirit of things, smilingly stamping the letter with an impressive collection of Hindi stamps. I don't know what the insurance company made of them all but I was eventually reimbursed.

Of course not everyone one meets on an Indian train is as gentlemanly as Mr. Pavri. On a commuter train in Bombay, Jen and I were separated in a crowd so dense that neither of us could move. Jen was shamelessly groped by the men around her. When we pulled into a station and the doors opened, I had to physically haul people out of the way to get Jen off the train. The passengers thought it was a great joke and only later did we learn that there were separate carriages for women.

Taxing though the railways could be, there were worse modes of transport. I feared for my life on numerous occasions as taxi drivers played chicken at high speeds with approaching buses, and I almost lost an arm as I careened through traffic clinging onto the side of a *tuk tuk*. Once, an insane rickshaw driver hurtled round a corner into the middle of a funeral procession. Amidst much angry shouting and gesticulating, the linen-wrapped corpse was thrust under my nose to point out how inappropriate the rickshaw driver's actions had been. At least on the trains, there were times when I was close to being alone and the railways were always a connection with my parents. I travelled by train to see sights all across India from the Taj Mahal to the beaches of Goa, but there were two places where I could be certain that I was walking in Eve and Jim's footsteps.

~~~~~

The governor at Lucknow, Sir Henry Lawrence, prepared the city for the Indian Rebellion of 1857 much more effectively than did General Wheeler at Cawnpore. When the rebellion broke out, over 2,000 British and loyal Indian troops and civilians, including many women and children, took refuge in the fortified Residency buildings in the centre of the city. They held out from May 30 to November 27 when they were finally relieved. Oddly, they had been relieved once already. On September 25, Colonel (now Brigadier-general) James Neill, who had been slowly slaughtering his way from Varanasi, led his 1st Madras Fusiliers as part of a relief attack on the city. It succeeded, but there were not enough soldiers left to force a way out, so they became part of the defence in a second siege. Neill, in a touch of poetic justice, was killed in the attack.

After Lucknow was relieved, the Residency was kept in its ruined state as a memorial and it remains so today. Jim was born in Lucknow in 1905 and visited the ruins several times as a child and as an adult, so was able to tell me many exciting tales of the Residency's defence. When I went to visit the ruins, they looked as they had eighty years before, so I could half-close my eyes and imagine a small boy in short pants or a young man in *jodhpurs* and *solar topi* walking ahead of me.

After visiting the Residency, I spent a pleasant afternoon wandering around the quiet tree-lined streets of the cantonment area of Lucknow. This was where the British had lived during the Raj and their bungalows were still there although, according to the name plates by the gates, now mostly occupied by high-ranking Indian army officers.

While I was peering at one bungalow, an aged Indian gardener poked his head above the rose bushes and asked who I was and what I was doing. I explained that I was from Canada and that my father had been born in Lucknow many years before.
~~~~~

"What was his name?" the old man asked. I told him and he nodded his head. "This is the house he was born in."

Of course it wasn't, at least no more likely than any of the other identical bungalows, but it was a delightful idea. It was told in a genuine attempt to be helpful and friendly and not in the insincere way of so many attempts to scrounge baksheesh. To the gardener there was no difference between working for an imperial engineer on the Bengal and North Western Railway and a general in the Indian Army.

If you know anything of the British Raj, walking through Simla (now Shimla), is like entering a time warp. The Viceregal Lodge, now the Indian Institute of Advanced Studies; Christ Church, where the minister showed me the entry in the church annals recording Eve and Jim's wedding; the toy train from Kalka, which is still hauled by steam locomotives over 864 bridges and through 102 tunnels; the immaculately uniformed waiters in the high-ceilinged tea rooms on the Mall; the countless slowly decaying imperial bungalows; and the sad overgrown cemeteries filled with sahibs, memsahibs and their children, are all incredibly evocative of the nostalgia I recognized around the fire in Paisley. With the exception of the wedding in Christ Church, I had no specific locales in Simla to evoke my parents, but the whole town was like a museum to Eve and Jim's lost past.

Churches, crumbling bungalows, overgrown cemeteries, cricket, an incredible railway network and a ponderous bureaucracy are the legacy of two centuries of British rule in India. Personally, the Raj of my parents, their remembrances of it, and what it made them, have all played their part in creating who I am. However fascinating it is to explore the past, one's own or one's culture, it is a not particularly profitable or healthy activity. After Simla, I still had several weeks in India, travelling on my father's trains but experiencing an India that he and my mother were never a part of. For a westerner, India is not an easy country to know and there were times on my travels when I sincerely wished for the closeted, protected, privileged existence that Eve and Jim had enjoyed. However, the Indian culture, which had existed for thousands of years before the Raj, which had absorbed from the Raj what it wanted, and which continues to evolve and change in its own ways, is where I was and where I wanted to be.

I went to India seeking remnants of a very specific, personal past, but I ended up appreciating a much larger history that gifted me extraordinary days wandering around and appreciating Fatehpur Sikri, Hampi, Ellora and Ajanta, Arunja's Penance, and a host of other magical places. I suffered dirt, noise, suspect food, crooked rickshaw drivers, interminable waits, and numberless beggars and thieves, but I also met some of the kindest, gentlest people on earth who made my travelling exceptional in countless tiny way: Mr. Pavri who bought Jen and I supper; the taxi driver who refused to charge us for the trip because the temple at our destination was closed; the aged, turbaned, impressively moustachioed Sikh guide who showed us round the palace where he had once been a retainer for the long-vanished Maharaja.

The perspectives that I inherited directly and indirectly from my parents—skepticism and a love of story, history and travel—are much more important than the eroding specifics of the world that I searched for in India. I loved standing in the doorway of Christ Church in Simla where Eve and Jim's wedding photograph was taken and was enchanted by the myriad tiny remnants of the Raj that I encountered. However, if I am honest, I can never capture the nostalgia of my parents, but then I suppose that is the nature of nostalgia. Even in Simla the nostalgia is simply a bonus that spices and enlivens the history that, at the root of it, stirs my emotions.

I am an atheist but I can stand in absolute awe for an age in the nave of Chartres Cathedral; I have never been a soldier and I can come close to tears standing in no-man's-land where the Newfoundland Regiment were slaughtered in half an hour on July 1, 1916; I am a slightly cynical skeptic and yet I can feel the excitement of being a twelve-year-old boy standing by Hadrian's Wall watching seventy or so middle-aged Italian re-enactors marching back and forth and play-fighting as Roman legionaries. The Raj, through my parents' expression of their nostalgia for it, gave me those gifts, but they would be nothing had they not been crafted and polished by countless other experiences, an early one of which was an odd congruence of castles.

Interlude

Indian Images

Goa

> Awake to a room
> by the beach at Goa,
> a high white cave
> of slumbering heat,
> the lazy fan
> painting the walls
> with brush-strokes
> of wave sound.
>
> Outside the endless sands
> preserve the naked footprints
> of a thousand gods,
> sandwiched deep between
> the layers of crashing waves.
>
> And ghosts of fevered Jesuits,
> gaunt as Greco Christs,
> haunt the tombs
> of mouldering laterite Notre Dames
> to whisper in the souls of travellers
> vying still for puny man's eternity.
>
> Miracles still keep
> the flesh and bone of Xavier
> as young as yesterday
> before the wondering eyes
> of faithful devotees.
> Once, long years ago
> a woman overcome with ecstasy,
> perhaps the one true convert,
> bit a toe from off that sacred foot.
>
> Upon the wall above, bejeweled Ganesa,
> huge amidst his happy fragile acolytes,
> a garish ponderous rolling bulk

of comfort, peace and succour
celebrating as he smiles enormously
the rotund joviality of our too brief lives.

If he were mine
I would not give him up
to drink the blood
and eat the flesh
of promises uncertain
and days of pain and thorns and suffering.

Kajuraho

High upon the dusty Deccan plateau
I sit amongst the dancing ancient stones
while prancing priapetic princes
copulate with energetic friends
and happy jewelled concubines
in mock disapprobation
avert their eyes and preen themselves
for pleasures ever to be locked in stone.

Did Kajuraho's princes fight and kill and die
as ever princes have been wont to do?
Were pleasures taken as reward for valour
or with captive fair or bestial?
If so they did not think it true enough
to be immortalized in stone
for here no one can die, except perhaps from ecstasy,
and days in endless leisure spent
pile one atop the next to reach
the sacred mountain peak.

This culture of unbridled joy
eight centuries before I came
could celebrate with such abandon
as to make the silent rocks alive
and tell this tale so unalike
the grubby world of now
where loveless gods look down
and sneer at our sad procreation.

Part 2

Castles and Cannibals

drifted blossoms
fill carved letters
R.I.P.

My First Castle

The sparse ruins of Duntulm Castle sit on a promontory of volcanic rock that juts out from the west coast of the Trotternish Peninsula at the most northerly tip of the Isle of Skye. Looking northwest from the castle it is possible to see Lord Macdonald's Table and the romantically-named *Fladaigh Chùain* (Flat Island in the Ocean), where the nuclear submarine, HMS Trafalgar, ran aground and suffered five million pounds worth of damage in 2002 because important navigational features had been obscured by tracing paper laid over the chart. In the distance, on clear days, the Outer Hebridean islands of Harris and Lewis and North Uist rise out of the cold water.

Around 170 million years ago in what is now the bay to the southwest of the castle, vast long-necked sauropod dinosaurs left trails of footprints as they ponderously went about their business. Much more recently, around 1662, the flat fields above Tulm Bay to the northeast of the castle were occupied by Duntulm Farm and the settlements of Duntulm and Erisco. All that remains of the settlements are a few stone walls but the farm was converted to a hotel, Duntulm Lodge, in the 1930s. In the winter of 1951/2, the Wilson family, Jim, Eve, youngest daughter Susan and infant son John, moved from Edinburgh to take over the running of the hotel. To entice visitors they stressed the scenery, the romantic adventures of Bonnie Prince Charlie and Flora Macdonald, and hot and cold water in all bedrooms. I suspect that an echo of Jim's life in India snuck in with the offered, "Salmon, sea trout and trout fishing on lochs and rivers. Shooting over 21,000 acres." All of this was available for a mere twenty-five shillings per day or seven to eight guineas per week.

The first memory I have that I am certain is genuine, is of sitting on a bench beside my mother on a ferry. Across the way is a young woman with an infant who will not stop crying. The noise is bothering my mother and she says, "Why can't she keep that baby quiet?" This was out of character for Eve and I suspect that is the reason it has stuck in my memory. I was turning four years old and after the failed attempt to make a go of the Duntulm Lodge Hotel we were retreating south to Milngavie (pronounced Mulguy) where Jim was to begin work as a Planning Engineer at Mechan's Ltd. Mechan's, an engineering firm on Clydeside in Glasgow, dated back to 1862 and was noted for building steel lifeboats, engine room telegraphs and watertight doors for the British fleet in the years prior to the First World War. However, they were a general firm and also made steel structures for gold mining operations and machinery for water, cyanide and sugar plants. Jim was to become one of the 1,000 employees at their 20 acre factory.

The reality of my past becomes slowly solid and defined after Skye, like a figure walking forward out of a thick fog. Skye itself is a blank so, if all I can remember of Skye is leaving, why say anything at all about it? Because I have been told stories of it by others.

I "remember" Jim having to climb out a window to dig snow away from the front door, which opened outwards, and him taking me fishing or checking lobster pots in the rowing boat that was kept in Tulm Bay. I was told about a neighbour who was a die-hard Free Presbyterian, "Wee Frees" we called them. He was dead against the ferries to Skye running on Sunday—there was no bridge in those days so I suspect the Devil has unlimited access now. He also frowned upon children playing on a Sunday and spent the hours between the several Kirk services sitting at home reading *Pilgrim's Progress* out loud. Apparently because all our neighbours and those who worked in the hotel spoke Scots Gaelic amongst themselves, I could speak a few words at four years old. All I remember now is *Slàinte mhath*, which means good health when raising a glass of *Uisge Beatha* (whisky), although even that might come from reading Robert Burns.

I had my first pets at Duntulm: a very friendly spaniel called Sally, a less friendly cat called Black Devil, and a duck, inevitably named Jemima, which had been hatched and raised in a cardboard box on top of the huge AGA cooker. Apparently I spent hours peering into the straw-lined box waiting for the egg to hatch and, consequently, I was the first thing Jemima saw at birth and so she was imprinted and followed me around in the belief that I was her mother. Amidst copious tears, all pets had to be relocated and left behind when we went south.

I also have photographs, small grey grainy images of me in Skye: on my mother's shoulder, in my pram, in a snowsuit, in my dad's rowboat and, rather apprehensively, meeting a cow. In many, beneath my pudding-basin haircut, I seem dubious about what I am involved in and often positively worried about something. I am happiest playing in the snow, on the beach, or in the boat. Apart from one shot where he proudly holds up a large lobster, Jim is invisible, busy with the hotel. As soon as I could get about on my own, Eve mostly disappears into the role of photographer. The person most commonly with me is Susan, my sister closest to me in age. My two older sisters, Eelin and Dorothy, were old enough to stay in Edinburgh and go to University or finish school but Susan was only fourteen and so accompanied us to Skye to go to school in Portree, so it was often her task to look after me.

For a toddler it was a fairly solitary, adult-centred existence. The only children in evidence in four years of photographic history are cousins who appeared for a brief summer visit. I think Skye gave me a sense of comfort being on my own or around adults but not children my own age. It also contributed a love of open, barren countryside and gave me the soft, highland accent that was to be a handicap going through my troubled teenage years in the lowlands. Over everything in those years, literally and figuratively, loomed the ruin of Duntulm Castle.

Duntulm Castle was on a good defensive site protected on three sides by sheer cliffs that disappeared into the grey treacherous waters of the

Minch. It was additionally protected by the Blue Men of the Minch, mythological creatures who sought to overturn ships and drown shipwrecked sailors. They would gather around a ship and their leader would rise up and recite two lines of poetry. The only way a ship's captain could save his vessel was by competing poetically with the Blue Man. One tale gives the following exchange where the captain outsmarts the attacking poet:

> Blue Chief: Man of the black cap what do you say
> As your proud ship cleaves the brine?
> Skipper: My speedy ship takes the shortest way
> And I'll follow you line by line.
> Blue Chief: My men are eager, my men are ready
> To drag you below the waves.
> Skipper: My ship is speedy, my ship is steady
> If it sank it would wreck your caves.

After the Norse left in 1266, the castle changed hands numerous times as the local clans struggled for power. Eventually, in 1618, the Macdonalds of Sleat won out and ruled relatively peacefully until the castle was finally abandoned in 1732. From then on it provided a handy stone quarry for the local crofters until it became, when Susan was in charge of me, her favourite place to keep me occupied when the busy hotel required my absence. While we walked up the grassy slope, she would tell me a story.

"Once upon a time, hundreds of years ago, Donald, the chief of the clan Macdonald lived here. One day his cousin Hugh came to visit. In those days there was a law of hospitality, anyone who showed up on your doorstep had to be invited in and given food and a bed for the night. The trouble was that Hugh had plans to murder Donald and become clan chief himself. Fortunately, one of Hugh's servants told Donald of the plot and Hugh had to flee the castle in the middle of the night. He went over to Uist and hid there but Donald never forgave him for violating the laws of hospitality, so he hunted him down and captured him. He brought him back to Duntulm and imprisoned him in the deepest dungeon in the castle where the tide came in every day. He gave Hugh salt meat to eat but no water. After a while, poor old Hugh went completely mad. He beat the stone walls with his fists and screamed and shouted, but Donald just laughed. Eventually, Hugh died a horrible lonely death in his dungeon. It is said that on nights when a storm comes in, Hugh's ghost can be seen walking the castle ruins and that all the screams of the storm aren't just from the wind."

Of course by this time I was totally entranced. We would reach the castle and my sister would lead me over to a deep, damp hole in the ground and tell me with great glee, "And this is the dungeon where Hugh went insane." It didn't matter that the hole was far above the high tide mark and could only fill with water during a truly massive tsunami, I was fascinated by that hole in the ground and its appalling history. I don't remember having any nightmares around my sister's tales but perhaps it wasn't just from Jim that I got my love of storytelling.

Interlude

Skye

Where I grew up some folk believed
the calm intelligence of seals
in human guise could walk the land,
except on Sunday
when a God so stern
he would not let the ferries run
held sway.
With *usquabae* the people talked
the ancient tongue of seers and poets;
so soft it made the wandering Danes remain
an age before the sound was turned to screams
beneath the redcoats' guns.

I remember fishing with my father
amongst the rocky barren isles,
wondering where the oily swell was from
while he read the waves
and told me of a dream he knew
where viceroys and beggars strode
across a scape of alien, shimmering beauty,
and sacred rivers washed the living and the dead.
A vanished world not happily exchanged
for this Atlantic cold.

In searching for that dream,
I ransacked Africa for gold and memories
and found dry hills and hatred;
I rummaged through the dusty wheaten prairie
where silent oceans lap the bones of dinosaurs
and found a rolling sky drowning in a
distant waterless horizon.

I travelled just to leave,
and found in frantic quest a circle of escape
ending nowhere.

It was all so long ago and near forgot,
but now I live again upon an island
perched upon the ocean's shuddering rim
and listen in the quiet lonely nights
for the seals to call me home.

Dead Rabbits and Conkers

After Skye we lived for two years in Milngavie on the north side of Glasgow. I remember nothing about the house other than there being an alcove bed in the kitchen and frames upon which laundry was hung to dry before being hauled up out of the way near the high ceiling.

Eve was in hospital for a spell when we lived in Milngavie and Jim and I went to visit her. We travelled through the countryside on the bottom floor of a double-decker bus. At one point a woman was coming down the twisting stairs at the back of the bus when she slipped and fell onto the platform at the bottom. Everyone turned to look and I asked Jim in a loud voice, "Is she dead?" She wasn't and everybody laughed. I couldn't understand why. It seemed like a perfectly reasonable question.

In my memory the most significant event from that time is my first day of school. It was 1956, I had just turned five and my sister was given the unenviable task of taking me along the road to Milngavie Primary. Having very little experience of interacting with groups of other children, the idea of school horrified me. On top of that, the school was an imposing red sandstone building and, probably because of stories of Duntulm Castle, I was convinced it was some kind of prison where I was to be locked away forever, perhaps in a dungeon like the unfortunate Hugh Macdonald. I had to be dragged screaming and in floods of tears along the road. The teacher, I suspect without total confidence, told my sister that this sobbing mess in front of her would be fine and it would be easier (for whom?) if my sister left.

She did and when when she returned with a certain trepidation that afternoon I was happy and cheerfully skipped along the road beside her.

"So we won't have any nonsense like that again tomorrow morning," she said.

I stopped dead in my tracks. Tomorrow morning? It wasn't just one day. I hadn't survived this hideous experience. It was to go on another day, another year, forever? The first of life's disillusionments.

Or perhaps it didn't happen that way at all. My memory is that it was my oldest sister, Eelin, who dragged me there that morning and much of my memory is based on what she told me later. However, Eelin lived in Newcastle when I lived in Milngavie, so it was unlikely that she would have been available to escort me to school. My sister Dorothy was away at art college in London and so it couldn't have been her. This leaves my youngest sister, Susan, she of the Duntulm Castle stories. Susan was attending Jordan Hill Teachers' Training College in Glasgow and used to come home to Milngavie on weekends (when, incidentally, I was removed from my bed to give her a place to sleep). She also came to look after Jim and I when Eve was in hospital for a spell. During that time, she took me to museums and on my first tram ride and, because my sister Fiona had made such a fuss on her first day of school, Susan was given the task of taking me. As she remembers it, I went happily with no fuss at all and the the only stress was her worry at the looks she, still a teenager, got from the other children's mothers.

So my memory of my first day of school is false. In fact, the opposite happened. The false memory grew up through misconceptions, misinterpretations, confusions with later bad days at school, a conflation in family lore of my and Fiona's first days at school, and just plain exaggeration by Eelin to improve a story. And yet I believed for most of my life that it had happened exactly that way. As such, it influenced and helped shape my perspectives as I grew up. In a small way, the fiction became a part of who I am. The story is not verifiable, definitive truth, but it is my truth.

I have a photograph of me taken on July 23, 1956. I am scrubbed and resplendent in short-sleeved white shirt, sandals and pressed shorts, standing with my sisters at Eelin's wedding in Edinburgh. Eelin's husband, Frank, was my first brother-in-law and, since my sister was twenty years older than me and Frank was seventeen years older than her, he seemed incredibly old to the almost-five-year-old me.

After Eelin married Frank they moved down to Newcastle, but when she came home or I went to visit her she told me stories that broadened my horizons beyond the dark deeds of the Macdonald clan. Before I was allowed to go to the movies, I knew the exciting tales of *Shane* and *3:10 to Yuma*. Before I could read the originals, I knew the terrifying narratives of *Dracula* and *Frankenstein*. My internal life was getting richer.

Also in Milngavie, I began to make friends. Ten days after Eelin and Frank's wedding, there are four other small boys with me in a snapshot of my fifth birthday party. We all have cups of juice in front of us and a large chocolate cake that is obviously the focus of attention. But the Milngavie experience was brief, by age six we had moved once more.

~~~~~

Castle Semple had none of the dark character or storytelling possibilities of Duntulm. When Eve, Jim and I moved into a house along a dirt track from the castle in 1957, all that remained was the shell of a church built by Lord Semple and a 'temple folly' on a nearby hill. The original castle was probably more interesting when it was built around 1492 when castles served a purpose, but it had been rebuilt many times and, in 1735 when castles were no longer of use, was torn down and replaced by a gothic-revival style mansion, which in its turn, when mansions were going out of style, conveniently burned down in 1924.

Like Milngavie, our stay near Castle Semple was a mere two years, but it is etched much more clearly in my memory. The house was small but that didn't matter as my sisters had all left home by this time, and it seemed to me large, mainly because of the wonderful views across an open field that sloped down to the Glasgow to Ayr railway before the land rose to the hill
~~~~~

where the folly stood. Across a yard large enough for me to exhaust myself on my red tricycle, stood a prodigious barn that provided a wonderful play area, especially after the farmer had filled it with hay bales to climb.

Jim believed in a good hearty breakfast and so woke early to cook up the oatmeal that had been soaking overnight so that he could eat before leaving for work at Mechan's. He kept a single shot .22 rifle in the cupboard in the kitchen and occasionally I would be woken to the sound of gunfire out the kitchen window and go through later to find a cleaned rabbit lying on the kitchen table. The skins of several of these unfortunate yet tasty creatures were nailed to dry on the barn door and made me a rather smelly but much loved Davey Crockett hat after I had been taken to the cinema in nearby Johnstone to see my first movie—Fess Parker and Buddy Ebsen getting the better of the bad guys in *Davey Crockett and the River Pirates.*

It was at Castle Semple that I was given pet replacements for the small zoo I had access to on Skye. First was a hamster called Henry who was given free run of the living room in the evening. Apparently convinced that hard times were looming, Henry worked hard collecting food and storing it inside the furniture.

Much more memorable was the arrival of a grey tabby kitten called Tibby. I was thrilled but the association did not begin well. Tibby was asleep one evening on my bed, obviously convinced that any human who doted on her as blatantly as I did must be a good bet for a lasting relationship. Sadly, I didn't look before jumping onto my bed and sat on Tibby. The poor beast screeched, leapt off the bed and shot through to the safety under the sideboard in the front room. I too leapt off the bed and burst into floods of tears, convinced that I had killed my new pet. Both Tibby and I were eventually calmed down and Jim told me later that it had actually been very funny when he turned at the noise to see a distinctly flat-looking cat shoot into the room and slide under the sideboard. Tibby and my relationship never recovered and it was always to someone else in the family that the assorted dead or dying small animals that she had stalked and caught in the field were proudly presented. Henry succumbed to old age but, somewhat oddly, I have no recollection of what became of Tibby.

Castle Semple appears idyllic in my memory, possibly because it recreated the open spaces of Skye. I had free run of the field behind the house, all the way down to the railway line that Eve and I used to walk along eating wild strawberries and collecting lumps of coal that had fallen from the passing trains. My friends included the girl who lived at the bottom of the road and a couple of boys with whom I would sneak over the wall of a nearby estate to steal apples and chestnuts. To give our activity some added spice, we built up the owner of the house behind the wall as an angry old man who would chase kids with a stick. However, since we were not the most subtle of thieves and were never chased, I suspect that he was perfectly aware of our activities and was probably laughing behind a window somewhere.

The apples we collected for obvious reasons but the chestnuts, or conkers, were special. The best of them, selected by each child's private arcane ranking system, were placed in a very low oven to harden, had a hole drilled in them and were suspended on a length of knotted string, often a shoelace. The point of this was to play a game also called 'conkers'. One player held his conker suspended while the other took a shot at hitting it. The positions were then reversed and repeated until one conker broke. Victorious conkers gained a point for the victory and also collected any points that the defeated conker had. Scores were kept religiously and high-scoring conkers were treasured. In case you think this childish and abstruse, the World Conker Championships were established in 1965 and take place annually on the second Sunday in October. Despite threats from failed conker harvests, the Horse-chestnut leaf miner moth and Covid, the event commonly draws around 400 fanatical competitors from around the world and some 5,000 spectators.

In my conker-playing years, I attended primary school in the nearby village of Howwood. It was about a two kilometre walk along a rural road, which in the early days my mother accompanied me on and later I was allowed to go on my own or with other kids. I had overcome my screaming horror of school, but was still not convinced it was a good idea.

I learned about social hierarchies at Howwood. After every break, we had to line up at the door when the bell went, boys in one line, girls in another. It was a status thing to stand at the front of the line and there was always a rush to get there. The largest boy in the school usually won. One day he was delayed with some activity and I found myself proudly at the head of the line. Unfortunately, the dominant male didn't meekly go to the back of the line. He rushed forward and lunged to the head of the queue, knocking me aside into the school wall. I hit the back of my head and was taken bleeding and in tears to the school nurse who patched up what turned out to be a minor scrape. I remember walking home in front of my mother in hopes that she would notice my 'war wound', but I had too much hair in those days.

On another occasion I recall getting into a fight with the same boy, although the reason for the altercation is lost. From my point of view it didn't end well but, since it was obvious that I wasn't a very good fighter, I learned the benefit of conflict avoidance and gradually developed the skills necessary to remain as invisible as possible.

As a child, despite the government issue cod liver oil and orange juice, I was sick a lot. At Castle Semple, at least some of this was eventually diagnosed as tonsillitis. Back then that involved the complete removal of the offending organs and a couple of days in hospital. I was sold on the idea by being told that, since my throat would hurt, all I would be given to eat would be ice cream. There were long conversations on which flavour and I think strawberry was finally decided upon.

Very nervous, I went into hospital and had the operation. Upon recovery I could barely wait for my first bowl of ice cream. The nurse eventually arrived with two pieces of dry toast. "Where's my ice cream?" I asked plaintively.

"We always give toast," she said unhelpfully. "Eat up, now."

Disconsolately and painfully, I worked my way through the toast, not yet old enough to appreciate that much of life is being offered strawberry ice cream and being given dry toast.

Having been sensitized by the sudden death of my sister, Fiona, from polio, my mother was protective whenever I got sick and I soon discovered that if I played up the symptoms I could squeeze and extra day or two away from school. I did suffer from real illnesses, brutal colds and flu every winter, but it was the vaguer afflictions like a sore tummy or a headache that produced the best results.

One day while walking with my mother into Howwood, I complained of a sore tummy. When asked where it hurt, I pointed to the lower right hand side of my stomach. It produced a surprising reaction and I was whisked into the doctor who poked and prodded and recommended keeping an eye on me as that was right where the appendix was. Without the faintest idea how much stress I must have been causing Eve, every sore tummy was located by me on the lower right of my tummy, so I was diagnosed with a "grumbling" appendix. Eventually, it was decided to remove what was then thought to be a completely useless vestigial organ. I had my second week-long visit to hospital and came home in pain but proudly sporting a four inch long scar. I didn't have my appendix which Eelin had persuaded me to ask for in a bottle of spirits—the doctor had declined to grant my wish.

As the 1950s turned to the 1960s, there were major reshuffles in the dying heavy steel shipyards of Clydeside and Jim was laid off, not an enticing prospect for a fifty-four-year-old engineer with a background in steam engines and heavy steel. Certainly there was nothing anywhere close to Howwood or Castle Semple, so we moved into the city.

Interlude

Nonsenses

The Beglup and the Scribbling

There's a sunrise every morning,
A sunset every night,
Between then both it's either dark
Or very, very light.

The Beglup shuns the light of day,
The Scribbling fears the dark,
Thus they will never ever meet
At dusk down by the park.

It cannot be both light and dark,
Tis either one or t'other.
So the Beglup and the Scribbling
Knew nothing of the other.

Until one eve the bright daylight
Was slow in going to bed
And darkness fell a bit too fast,
Or so it has been said.

In any case, for one bright blink
In darkness thick as leather,
The Scribbling fierce and Beglup bold
Were face-to-face together.

They stopped and stared, then screamed and fled,
Their meeting could not be
For each was far too frightful for
The other one to see.

So be mindful of that fated dusk
When next you're deep in play,
And want to stay up far too late,
Or lie in bed all day

Beware the Aardvark's Supper

So darkly, darkly shines the moon
At night on Christmas Day
When down below in silver hue
The three-legged fishes play.

They leap and jump o'er hill and dale
So happy to be free
From that sticky pea-green ocean
Which hides them all from me.

They sing a sort of fishy song
In scales of their own choice
Without a single thought or care
For danger's lovely voice.

From out the east the Aardvark comes
With jaws as wide as stairs
To feed upon the happy fish
Who frolic unawares.

"Oh comely, comely little fish,"
The earth-pig sings out loud,
"Pray jump upon my glittering spoon
And we shall dine most proud."

The fishes wander to-and-fro
Enraptured by the tune
And one by one they step upon
The Aardvark's dining spoon.

When sudden one small voice is raised
Amidst the wails and tears,
"I cannot hear enticing tunes
There's darkness in my ears."

Then quickly quickly little fish
Pluck darkness from the night
And stuff it in your tiny ears
To quell the sound and fright.

The Aardvark blusters "Come back here!"
As fishes skip away
Back to the hilly sea they run
To swim another day.

The Aardvark glumly then goes home
With rumbling, empty tummy
To dine on porridge and brown toast
And cups of dark red honey.

Witches and Weaving

In the Zoroastrian mythology, Zarathustra planted a cedar tree in paradise. The tree bent under the weight of the Muslim invasion of Persia and became a curved symbol, the *boteh*, which was a sign of strength as well as modesty. The symbol spread through the Middle East and, with the expansion of the Mughal Empire, into India where it became popular as a design pattern on intricate Kashmir shawls. The East India Company introduced the shawls into Europe in the 17th century and the pattern on them became so popular that they could not import enough to meet demand. Local manufacturing began in France and elsewhere and by the 19th century so much was being woven in the Scottish town where I grew up that the pattern became forever known as Paisley.

In keeping with the theme of castles associated with the places where I lived, the first district we moved to in Paisley was called Castlehead. There was even less evidence of a castle here than at Castle Semple, the story being that it was the site of a long-vanished Roman settlement that had been established by Agricola and called Vanduara by Ptolomy in the second century.

After the Romans left, few paid much attention to Castlehead until, in the mid-19th century, it became a trendy place for rich Paisley merchants to live. For a couple of thousand pounds one of them had a two story sandstone mansion called St Cuthbert's built on Main Road. In the spring of 1959, Jim and Eve rented the ground floor of St Cuthbert's.

I wasn't even eight-years-old and it was the fourth place I'd lived—not that I had time to settle in here either. After Mechan's Jim was looking for a job but he had no luck despite a glowing reference letter from his time in India, his MBE, his recent work on Clydeside and, perhaps less usefully, an ability to speak French and Urdu. Undeterred and with few other options, Jim took over an ironmongers (hardware) store. I had little interest until I was given the job of clearing some dusty, junk-laden shelves in the back of the shop. It was boring work until I moved some scrap and found a treasure—the casing and nose of an 18 pounder shrapnel artillery shell from the First World War. I rushed through to the front shop to show Jim. He must have had a moment of utter horror seeing his young son rushing happily at him clutching an artillery shell, but he determined that it was safe and I was allowed to keep it. For many years it stood in my bedroom and contained my meagre collection of foreign coins. I still have it and it's a great hit when I present on the First World War in schools, although I only use it as a prop at places I don't have to fly to.

Sometimes I got to work behind the counter in the shop. There was a construction company working nearby renovating some old apartments and the workers occasionally popped in to pick up small items that they needed. They were a cheerful bunch and often joked with the kid behind the counter. On one memorable occasion, an apprentice who had just started with the firm and was hardly more than a handful of years older than me came in.

"Hello," he said, scanning the shelves behind me. "The boss sent me down to pick up something."

"What is it?" I asked when it became obvious he wasn't seeing what he was looking for.

"Bubble for a spirit level."

"What?" I had no idea what he was talking about. I knew what a spirit level was but as far as I knew the bubble was just air floating in liquid.

"He needs a new bubble for a spirit level," the apprentice repeated.

I was beginning to feel flustered and totally out of my depth. Then I glanced out the window and spotted two workers from the site grinning broadly. I realized that the joke wasn't on me. In retrospect, I wish I had gone along with the joke and asked the apprentice what size of bubble and whether he wanted a round one or an oval one, but I was young. I merely said, "Sorry. We're completely out of them," and he left to inform his boss.

My grandfather, John Wilson, died in 1920 at the age of 44 and my grandmother on the other side of the family, Victoria Dyer, died shortly before I was born. Grandmother Emily died in 1953, so the only grandparent I ever knew was Alfred Dyer. He was a traveller who went around the world a couple times while I was growing up. There being no cruise ships in those days, he travelled on the mail boats with only a tiny suitcase to carry a change of clothes. On visits home, he brought me back postcards and once, a small, crudely-carved wooden mask from some obscure stop on his peregrinations.

Alfred was a keen photographer and carried a miniature camera everywhere to record the people and places he saw. In addition to the two albums recording the effects of the Great Bihar Earthquake of 1934, he filled several others with images of the people he met and places he visited. After his second world tour he came to stay with us at Castlehead and, of course, photographed my mother and I in the back garden.

One morning instead of breakfasting in the kitchen as was normal before I went to school my sister suggested that, since it was such nice weather, we could breakfast in the garden. We did and to entertain me Eelin told me a story. I enjoyed the change of routine and went happily off to school. Only when I came home that afternoon was I told that grandfather Dyer had died in his sleep the night before.

I don't remember my emotional reaction to my first encounter with death on a personal scale but I do remember becoming aware over subsequent days that old people die. With the calm rationality of a nine-year-old, I observed the obvious fact that my parents were considerably older than my school friends' parents and took from it that one day they too would die. I suppose the thought must have scared me at the time but it became absorbed into my childish world view as simply the way things were.

A happier event in the fall of 1960 was the birth of my first niece, Fiona, to my sister Dorothy. Dorothy had gone to art college in London where she met an architect, Alan, whom she married in 1959. Babies didn't interest me that much, but becoming an uncle at nine years old was cool and helped me acquire a certain minor status at the unimaginatively-named South Primary School and in my local Cub Scout pack.

Our part of the mansion on Main Road came furnished and included a grand piano in the living room. My sister Susan decided that, in addition to my burgeoning storytelling talents, some skill in music would be a good idea and proceeded to teach me how to play the piano. We progressed reasonably well and I could soon play a stuttering version of *When the Saints go Marching In*. Unfortunately, what negligible musical potential I possessed was to remain unfulfilled. One day I was messing around instead of learning to play and dropped the keyboard lid on Susan's fingers, effectively ending the piano lessons. I'm sure the piano lid incident wasn't the reason, but soon afterwards Susan became a *Ten Pound Pom*. In those days Australia was desperate to increase her population and offered passage out for a mere ten pounds. Of course implicit in the offer was 'white' population and a young, newly-qualified teacher from Scotland perfectly fitted the bill.

Eve and Jim never hit me, even though a spank on the bottom was perfectly acceptable in those days. I got into trouble the usual number of times and was undoubtedly disciplined, however, there was only one time I remember being actually scared.

A friend from up the road had come round and we were playing darts in the garden. Essentially, this involved trying to hit the tree in the middle of the lawn. Egging each other on, we added spice by one of us climbing the tree while the other threw the dart. Inevitably it went wrong and a dart stuck in my arm. I pulled it out and as it bled my friend panicked. "What'll we tell your parents. We have to make up a story."

I agreed and, exercising my nascent storytelling skills, suggested saying that I had fallen out of the tree. Falling out of a tree onto a dart was an unconvincing tale at best but in the confusion and upset of the moment it was all I could think of. My friend abandoned me and I took my injured arm into the kitchen for attention.

Of course the pitiful story wasn't believed and I had to admit the truth. Eve was upset at the possibility of tetanus from the wound, but more so by the fact that I had lied. She couldn't think of a suitable discipline so she said, "Wait until your father comes home."

I spent a totally miserable afternoon feeling angry at my friend for deserting me, guilty about lying and imagining all the possible horrors that Jim might unleash upon me when he returned. In the event, he simply looked at me sternly, said it was a stupid thing to do and was silent. I've done other stupid things since then but I learned never to climb a tree and allow a friend to throw darts at me.

One interesting yet irrelevant fact that I was unaware of at the time was that, in the graveyard around Castlehead Church at the bottom of Main Road, lay the remains of US President Ronald Wilson Reagan's maternal grandparents, John and Jane Wilson. Both Wilson and John are and were very common names in the west of Scotland, so these kinds of coincidences crop up quite often and sometimes can erroneously be absorbed into family folklore.

One story of my father's was that we were descended from the last man to be publicly hanged at the Gallowgate in Glasgow. As Jim told it our namesake had been accused of "resisting the English invaders marching up the High Street." Apparently, back in the 18th century, there had been a riot, a not uncommon occurrence in Glasgow at that time, and English troops had been called in to restore order. The troops were led by an officer on a white horse and, as they marched up the High Street to confront the mob, a shot was fired and the officer knocked off his horse. The troops charged the crowd and arrested several rioters, one of whom was my ancestor. He and two others were subsequently hanged.

It was a great story and I told it whenever the opportunity presented itself, usually embellishing it with my ancestor being caught because he was too drunk to run away with the rest of the mob. Unfortunately, neither my embellishment nor any other part of the story was true.

Despite its name, Gallowgate was not the place of public execution in Glasgow. That was Jocelyn Square beside Glasgow Green, and the last man publicly hanged there was not a Wilson. In 1865, Dr. Edward William Pritchard poisoned his wife and mother-in-law with antimony. He had previously been suspected of foul deeds in 1863 when a servant girl in his house had died in a suspicious fire, but no charges were brought. This time an anonymous letter accused Dr Pritchard. The bodies were exhumed, antimony found and Pritchard was convicted. The case was a *cause célèbre* and many thousands filled Glasgow Green in the early morning of July 28 to witness Pritchard's end and grab a last chance to witness a hanging.

There *was* a James Wilson publicly hanged in Glasgow on Wednesday, August 30, 1820 for treason. He was a sixty-year-old radical weaver from nearby Strathaven (pronounced Strayven), who had been involved in the Radical War of that year. Having been told by *agent provocateurs* that the revolt was supported by the French and much more widespread and advanced than it was, Wilson led a small group of his colleagues toward Glasgow under an eccentrically-spelled banner reading "Scotland Free or a Dessert." It soon became clear to Wilson that he had been misled in more than the spelling and he returned home, but it was too late. He was arrested, tried and, despite pleas for clemency, sentenced to be hanged and beheaded.

The Glasgow Herald newspaper reported that amidst cries from the crowd of "Murder" and "He's a murdered man", Wilson was led up the scaffold and hanged. The Herald report gives a glimpse of what was considered an easy death in 1820.

"About five minutes after the body was suspended, convulsive motions agitated the whole frame, and some blood appeared through the cap, opposite the ears, but on the whole he appeared to die very easily.

"At half past three, after hanging half an hour, his body was lowered upon three short spokes laid across the mouth of the coffin. His head was laid on the block with his face downwards, and the cap taken off, when there was again a repetition of disapprobation of the crowd."

The executioner then, "...advanced to the body, which was placed at the front of the scaffold amidst the execrations of the people and, after calmly feeling the neck for a moment, he lifted the axe and at one blow severed the head from the body, which he held up, and proclaimed, 'This is the head of a traitor'.

"Vehement cries of 'It is false, he has bled for his country!' were heard from different quarters."

Wilson was buried in an unmarked paupers grave but his daughter and niece dug up his remains and removed them to Strathevan where they were secretly buried and where a monument stands today. Two other leaders were also executed and those three were the last beheadings in Britain.

So the story of James Wilson's sad end could have inspired Jim's tale although I can find no evidence that he was an ancestor. As for the riot, there were plenty to choose from in Glasgow in the late 18th and early 19th centuries, but none fit exactly and I can find no mention of an officer on a white horse being shot, although there is a pub called the White Horse on the Gallowgate. One of the things about researching an autobiography is finding out the truth or lack of it in fondly-believed family tales.

~~~~~

St Mirin, after having dispatched the snakes from Great Cumbrae on his way over from Ireland, founded a religious community in Paisley during the 7th century and an abbey was established on the site 600 years later. William Wallace may have been born nearby and was possibly educated at the Abbey, which might explain why Edward I had it burned down in 1307, two years after had watched Wallace be hanged and torn apart in London.

St Mirin's legacy lives on in Paisley in the beautiful rebuilt abbey and in several local names, including that of my local football team, but Paisley's fame rests on other supports.
~~~~~

John Wilson

Christian Shaw was a "respectful and sensible child" who lived a relatively comfortable life, at least for the end of the seventeenth century. Her father, John, was the Laird of Bargarran in the west end of Paisley and in 1696 eleven-year-old Christian had a large bedroom to herself on the ground floor of the Bargarran home. One day in August, Christian spotted one of the servants, Katherine Campbell, stealing milk and, being a good child, reported the theft to her mother. Campbell was admonished and unwisely lost her temper and cursed Christian. Four days later in an unrelated incident an old local woman, Agnes Naismith, who lived nearby and existed by begging around for alms and food, dropped by and finding Christian in the courtyard inquired after her health and age.

It was all very innocuous until Christian fell ill with pains, paralysis and convulsions. She was temporarily struck dumb and when she recovered her voice, she accused Campbell and Naismith of bewitching her. Over succeeding months, Christian accused more and more people with wilder and wilder stories, began pulling coal, gravel, straw, chicken feathers and balls of hair out of her mouth, and according to some witnesses occasionally travelled around her room at high speed without her feet touching the floor.

Hysteria spread just as it had a few years before at the Salem witch trials in America. This was helped by the death of John Hardie a local minister. Hardie was old and although he died in pain, this was not unusual at the time. Also not unusual in the day was the sudden death of an infant, but several infant deaths were attributed to the witches. For good measure the witches were also accused of inciting the devil to sink the Erskine ferry over the River Clyde, causing the deaths of two men and several horses. In all more than thirty people were accused of witchcraft but this was whittled down to seven, four men and three women, including Katherine Campbell and Agnes Naismith. The seven were found guilty and sentenced to be hanged and burned. One of the men, a local blacksmith called John Reid, hanged himself with a his scarf but the other six were led out on June 10, 1697 for what was to be the last mass execution of witches in Europe. They were hanged individually and their bodies thrown on a huge bonfire. A rather gruesome story has it that a couple of the victims were still alive when thrown on the bonfire and the executioner borrowed someone's walking stick to poke the twitching limbs back into the flames. Apparently the owner refused to take the walking stick back because it had touched a witch, although I suspect there may have been a more rational explanation for his refusal.

As she was led to her execution, Agnes Naismith laid a "dying woman's curse" on those present and all their descendants. For generations afterwards, everything that went wrong in Paisley, and there was much, was blamed on the "witches' curse." An iron horseshoe was buried in the ground above where the witches' charred remains were interred, just to be on the safe side.

These grisly events give us a slight shudder of disgust and a comforting, although perhaps misplaced, feeling that we have progressed since those appallingly unenlightened days. But what happened to poor little Christian Shaw? Surely after all of the vomiting of unpleasant objects, flying round the room and meeting the devil she ended up a traumatized wreck? Actually, no. Christian grew up to be a ruthless and very efficient businesswoman, no mean feat in the early 1700s. She married the Reverend John Miller, who unfortunately died in unsuspicious circumstances three years later. After that, she went to Holland and stole the secrets of thread production and some pieces of machinery, improved them and established the Bargarran Thread Company. Bargarran thread was stronger and whiter than Dutch thread and became highly prized. With her profits, Christian established a spinning school in Edinburgh and collected donations which she distributed to the young trainee girls. Still unlucky matrimonially, she married a glove manufacturer in 1737 but she died in the September of that same year.

Christian Shaw is credited with founding the Renfrewshire thread industry. Bargarran Thread Company no longer exists but the techniques that Christian pioneered became industrialized in the eighteenth century and eventually expanded into a truly global business.

If you buy a spool of Coats thread today, it might have been made in India, Mexico, Poland, Egypt, or a host of other places around the world. If, however, you had bought some Coats thread one hundred and fifty years ago, it would have been made in the first Coats mill in Ferguslie in the west end of Paisley, a mere stone's throw away from where the Bargarran witches met their ghastly end.

Weaving and the Paisley Shawl were what the town became famous for, but it would not have been possible without thread, and the industrialization of its manufacture in Paisley made the Coats family very rich. The Ferguslie Mill sprawled over several acres on either side of the Cart River and employed hundreds of workers. The owners lived in a mansion on landscaped grounds to the north of the mill. The mill manager lived in a respectable two-storey sandstone villa behind a walled garden a bit closer to the north gate of the mill. Behind the manager were terraced houses for the overseers and senior staff and at the end of the terrace was a whitewashed house that dated from 1820 and was where the Coats family had lived before their thread empire took off and they could afford to build a mansion. The workers lived in much less salubrious and overcrowded accommodation in Paisley itself.

The Ferguslie Mill was a complex of nine mills and was largely torn down in the 1990s. The Coats mansion, which in an echo of Castle Semple had been built on the site of a medieval castle, was demolished in 1920 but its gardens and ornamental pond are now a pleasant park. Curiously, the oldest building, the white house, still stands as do the terrace and the manager's house in its walled garden. It was to the ground floor of the manager's house, now called Ferguslie Villa, that the Wilson family moved in early 1961.

As I turned ten, Eve and Jim were respectively approaching fifty and sixty and concerned with getting by in a difficult, post-India world. Of my siblings, Eelin was married and living in Newcastle, Dorothy was beginning a family in London and Susan was making a life in Australia. I was alone again, but this wasn't the pleasant rural solitude of Duntulm or Castle Semple. I was facing a complex adaptation to city life at a time when my generation were struggling with changes of their own. Sometimes, it didn't go well.

On the bright side, it snowed a lot in the winters at Ferguslie, which presented opportunities for snowball fights and sledding. The best sledding spot was the park where the garden of the Coats mansion had been. A gentle slope led down from some trees before giving way to a precipitous drop onto the path beside an ornamental oval pond. If you had the skill and the courage to stay on the sled as it rocketed down the slope, your momentum was enough to carry you over the path onto the frozen surface of the pond and, if conditions were just right, as far as the small island in the centre. The first person down after a snowfall was the bravest since they tested the thickness of the ice and the consequences of getting it wrong were an abrupt stop and a dunking in two feet of icy water.

The big walled garden of Ferguslie Villa was shared with the inhabitant of the top floor but since she was an old lady with only a budgie called Joey for company we had it to ourselves. My only interactions with the old lady were the occasional times she would invite me up for juice and biscuits and to show off how well Joey could say, "Who's a pretty boy then?"

I got my first two-wheeler bike in Ferguslie and learned to ride it around the garden. Because my Mom thought that my fervently desired ten-speed bike with dropped handlebars was dangerous, all I got was three speeds and straight handlebars. However, considering my early skills, that was probably a good thing. I wasn't a very adventurous cyclist and confined myself to the streets round about and the local school playground on weekends.

For my tenth birthday, the year I mastered my bike, I was given a puppy. She was a pedigree Scotch Terrier named Ferguslie Meg, although she was always just Meg. A subplot in the story of Meg was that we would breed from her and sell the puppies. We did this twice with the grandly-named Toryglen Tambingo and Toryglen Tallboy. Both times Meg produced six puppies and both occasions are etched vividly in my memory.

The first event was a minor tragedy. With mounting excitement, I watched Meg grow and then deliver the puppies over several hours one evening. The last to arrive was a sickly runt that my dad said was going to die. I railed against this idea and sat up long and alone into the night with the runt on my lap. It was a very tearful few hours and I bargained my life away to God if only the puppy survived. It did not and I think, through the childhood sorrow, helplessness and anger at the unfairness of it all, the first seeds of atheism took root.

Several months later, Toryglen Tallboy showed up for an afternoon and despite some hesitation or lack of experience on his part the process was repeated. Again I watched as six puppies arrived and shuddered when the last one was a runt. Once more, I sat up, but there were no bargains offered this time. Remarkably the runt survived and I persuaded my parents that we should keep him. My idea probably wasn't that hard a sell as no one wants to buy the runt of a litter, and so at the end of September 1963, Fergus Faraway, always known as Mac, joined the family.

Meg was a calm, intelligent, easily trained dog. Mac, on the other hand, although he grew into a fine physical specimen of Scotch Terrier, was a trifle lacking in the intellectual sphere. He tended to get excited and run into solid objects or chase rabbits by running in completely the wrong direction. He wasn't an aggressive dog, although he wouldn't back down from a confrontation. On one occasion I was letting Mac run in the park when we were charged by a vicious-looking Alsation (German Shepherd). Mac immediately went for the other dog and I was terrified that he would be badly hurt. Fortunately Mac had a plan. He ducked under the Alsation's head and grabbed the loose skin hanging from its neck. Surprised and unable to bite Mac, the other dog began trying to shake him off. Mac swung wildly from side to side but retained his hold. Eventually, the Alsation tired, Mac released his grip and the vicious attacker of moments before slunk off. Perhaps Mac wasn't as dumb as we all thought.

We lived in Ferguslie Villa for three years, only slightly above average for the first twelve years of my life, but they were important years. I moved from South School to West School and, in September 1963, nervous in a new jacket, tie, shirt, socks and shoes, I boarded the local bus to be taken across town and deposited outside the imposing red sandstone building that was to be a huge part of my life for the following six years.

Interlude

Paisley Nights

Dark drunken Paisley nights,
the sociability of bus stops
amidst the gobs of spit
and wet discarded piles of
wasted beer and chips.
An old unshaven man prevents
the stop from falling,
arms wrapped round the cold steel pole
with much more love
than he has ever shown at home.
A pocket, loose,
raggedly protects a brown-bagged bottle.
Fortified, the label says,
as if its strength will stop
the stomach heaves
and keep the drinker from the cold.

A boy goes past
nervously arrogant without his gang,
caught halfway between being lord of the street
and just another one of father's punching bags.

A woman passes hurriedly,
eyes down,
late shift at the hospital,
already seen enough
to fill one night's imaginings.

Taxis rumble by
distributing their loads
to other lives.

The old man coughs and swigs his wine
the bus is late—so what?
The stop is friendly.
What's at home anyway?
Kids are gone,

silent wife'll never understand.
Life's been shite since the factory closed.

He takes another drink, and slips.
The bus stop, treacherous, has moved
betraying a friend.
The bottle falls, shatters.
"Fuck," the man slurs.
He weeps to watch his hope run down the gutter.
Around his feet a blowing paper wraps,
plastering his skinny legs.
An ineffectual kick opens up the sheet.
"Man Lands on Moon"
the headline reads.

From Sawney to Spain

Alexander "Sawney" Bean was a caring paterfamilias. Born near Edinburgh sometime in the early fifteenth century, Sawney apparently married a witch, Black Agnes Douglas. This offended the locals who drove the couple away. Eventually the wandering Sawney and Agnes arrived at Bannane Head near Ballantrae in Ayrshire on Scotland's west coast. There they discovered a large cave in the cliffs above the beach and decided to set up house. For twenty-five years, despite the cave mouth being cut off at high tide, the Beans struggled to raise a family.

Disinclined by nature to undertake honest work, Sawney and Agnes took to a life of crime. Venturing out of their rather dank home at night they waylaid solitary travellers, murdered them and stole their money. As time went on the family grew and ultimately, eight sons, six daughters, eighteen grandsons and fourteen granddaughters shared the cave in a web of relationships that I try not to think too hard about. The growing family presented certain practical problems, not least of which was how to purchase enough food with their ill-gotten gains without attracting too much unwelcome attention. Caring father that he was, Sawney overcame this difficulty in an ingenious way: the Beans would eat their victims, pickling what they couldn't manage at one sitting. This, as it were, killed two birds with one stone, solving the food crisis while conveniently disposing of the evidence.

Of course, the people in the surrounding area became suspicious as the numbers of disappearing travellers mounted and partly dismembered body parts washed up all along the coast. Searches were mounted but the cave remained hidden. In frustration, the locals lynched various innocent strangers without much effect. However, sooner or later things were bound to go wrong for the Bean's unorthodox lifestyle.

One night the family surrounded a couple returning from a local fair. They murdered the woman but the husband put up an unexpectedly vigorous resistance, holding the family off with his sword until help arrived. Four hundred men and bloodhounds soon discovered the Bean's happy home and led the forty-eight family members away in chains while they tried to prevent their shocked minds dwelling on the sights they had seen in the cave.

Sawney and the male members of his clan were killed by having their hands and feet cut off and being allowed to bleed to death in front of the womenfolk. The women were then burned alive.

Serious historians have cast doubt on the Sawney Bean story, not least because there are no written records and it does stretch credulity to imagine a family of forty-eight cannibals living undetected in a cave for a quarter century while they happily murdered and ate hundreds of people. Of course, that didn't bother my fourteen-year-old mind on a family holiday to Ballantrae in 1965 and I shuddered deliciously as I peered into what legend identified as Sawney's cave. It apparently also didn't bother movie director Wes Craven, who used the tale as the basis for his 1977 horror film, *The Hills Have Eyes*. Craven revelled in the cannibalism, incest, and violence, but balked at the Scottish weather and set his version in the desert of the America southwest. Wes Craven was smart to avoid the bracing elements of the Sawney Bean story.

One of the many meanings of "brace" in the *Concise Oxford Dictionary*, is "invigorate." This is what my mother meant by her favourite word on family holidays in Scotland. It was usually brought out when I was dressed in every stitch of clothing I possessed, bent double against a force eight North Atlantic gale as the foaming rollers crashed on the shingle at my feet. I would beg to go back to our cozy bed-and-breakfast, and be told, "Don't be silly, it's bracing." I never understood what she meant because it was the opposite of what I was told at home, "Put a jacket on, you'll catch your death of cold out there." Why freezing half to death should be a bad thing at home and a good thing on holiday always escaped me but, despite being braced to excess, I enjoyed these holidays.

I don't remember our family car before we moved to Paisley, but at Ferguslie Villa we owned a large, black, square four-door Morris Ten Four, one of the 49,000 or so built between 1933 and 1935. This was back in the days when cars were still such a novelty and roads so quiet that people used to go for a relaxing drive on a Sunday afternoon. On many Sundays we piled into the old Morris and drove aimlessly around the Renfrewshire countryside. Sometimes we would pack a blanket and recreate an Indian Raj picnic. We didn't have servants or hot weather but Eve would enthusiastically pack tuna sandwiches, hard-boiled eggs, some recent baking and flasks of tea and we would stop at a likely spot, walk into a field or convenient small wood, spread out the blanket and sit and eat while Mac and Meg explored the countryside round about in search of rabbits. It was all delightfully pointless.

More purposefully, the car was also used to take us on holidays. Sometimes this was simply a day trip to Largs on the coast, but some years, like 1965 in Ballantrae and 1963 in Troon, it was a proper summer holiday. In 1961 we went to a bed-and-breakfast on the tiny island of Lismore in Loch Linnhe off Oban. The island is only 9 miles long and 1 wide, but there are several good lochs where Jim taught me fly fishing. I had my photograph taken with two small trout, which the landlady of the B&B kindly cooked up for me as an addition to her already vast breakfasts.

For most of the two weeks on Lismore it rained and I sat in a window alcove betting against myself on raindrops racing each other down the glass. There was a bookcase in the house and, when raindrop races bored me, I read Robert Falcon Scott's diary of his tragic dash to the South pole. I was fascinated by Edgar Evans going mad, Lawrence "Titus" Oates saying, "I am just going outside and may be some time," before walking nobly out into the snow, and Scott's descriptions of himself, Henry Bowers and

Edward Wilson dying in their tent. Even through Scott's imperial self-aggrandizement and his widow's careful editing, I sensed that mistakes had been made and things could have been better done. Later reading has convinced me of this, but I still hope that Oates said his iconic sentence.

I was also impacted by two local stories about Lismore. One was of a piper who, with his dog, planned to walk underground between two caves. He played his pipes and they could be heard all over the island, then the sound ceased. The piper's dog emerged, blind and hairless, but the piper was never seen again. I shivered at the description of the piper's end in his lament, "I was drowning and howling amongst the horrid pools."

Oddly, there is an almost identical story from St Andrews on the other side of the country. There a piper went into a tunnel near the castle to trace old coal workings. People on the ground above followed the sound of his pipes until they stopped. The piper was never seen again and a pattern in the cobbles of the main street is said to be where his pipes fell silent.

The other Lismore tale was about the time two early Christian worthies, St Molaug and St Mulhac, argued about who should build a monastery on the island. They decided to settle it by having a boat race. The first to Lismore got monastery rights. As they neared shore it became obvious to Molaug that he was going to lose. Resourcefully, if somewhat extremely, he cut off a finger and hurled it onto land thereby claiming that a part of him had won the race. Founding a monastery was a very big deal in those days.

Car journeys in the old Morris were always an adventure, not least because Mac had a weak stomach and would throw up after the first two or three miles. This was a problem until my mother worked out what fraction of a sleeping pill would safely put Mac out for the requisite number of hours.

Mac wasn't the only problem. Occasionally I was. One time, deciding that it would be a good father/son bonding experience, Jim suggested that he and I go camping for a weekend. Eve prepared some food, Jim checked the car and I collected the sleeping bags, stove, tent, etc. With me feeling thrilled and very adult, we set off. In those days there were few campsites and it was common to simply camp wherever looked suitable beside the road. As dusk thickened, we pulled into a field and began unpacking.

"Where's the tent?" Jim asked.

"It's..." I said before the slow hideous realization dawned that it was lying on the couch in our living room back in Paisley. I had forgotten the tent and all my misplaced pride in being an adult vanished. Fortunately it wasn't raining and the old Morris had a high clearance. Jim slept under the car and I scrunched miserably into the back seat. We went home the next day.

On another occasion we were driving at night down to the south of Scotland to visit my aunt. With a surprisingly loud thump we hit a pheasant, which shot up in the air and landed stunned on the road behind us. Jim stopped, ran back, wrung the bird's neck and with a "Pity to waste it," threw the limp body onto the back seat beside me.

Several miles farther on, Jim was broadening my education. "It's a shame we didn't hit two," he said.

"Why?" I asked loyally.

"Game meat has to be aged to taste its best," he said. "To do that properly with pheasant you need two, a brace. You hang the birds in a cool shed and leave them. When one rots enough to fall off, you eat the other one."

While Eve said, "Jim, don't tell him things like that," I silently gave thanks that we only had one pheasant. The pheasant itself, which had apparently only been feigning death, decided that now was the time to begin trying wildly to avoid this unpleasant fate. Now, you may not think that a pheasant is a particularly large or threatening bird but, if you are a small boy and one is hysterically flapping around in the back seat of a Morris Ten Four with you, it appears immense and deadly. While my mom attempted to calm me down, my dad stopped and dispatched the pheasant again, this time efficiently.

I used to love the visits to my father's sister Helen's place down near Newton Stewart. It was a small cottage called Banks of Dee but it was set on a large estate around which I had free run. Jim taught me to shoot his .22 rifle there and I would hunt pigeon whenever I had the chance. I used to dream of coming upon a deer but, given that I only had a .22 and no idea how to clean a deer, it was probably just as well I didn't encounter one. My cousin Ken did, however, and presented my dad and I with a complete haunch. This coincided with Eve spending a week visiting Dorothy, Alan and their growing family in London, and Jim and I roasted the haunch and, in fine medieval fashion, cut off hunks of venison whenever we felt hungry.

Eventually, as it approached its fourth decade of life, the Morris faltered. It wasn't worth much, but Jim decided that he might get a little more for it if it was repainted. He hired me and a school friend to do the job. Unfortunately he gave us too much leeway with the colour. We could see no reason why cars should be black and so decided on a pleasing powder blue. When Jim came back from work, I took him into the garden and proudly showed off the careful job we had done. To his credit he took it very well, commenting only that the car looked like an ice cream van. I was undoubtedly ahead of my time for the early 1960s but I doubt if my colour choice added much to the car's value.

~~~~~

As I got older, the holidays began to change. By the mid-sixties, Dorothy, Alan and their four kids had moved to Armagh in Northern Ireland. For a couple of summers I was put on a boat in Greenock and met in Belfast by my brother-in-law for a two-week holiday. I loved these holidays with new countryside to explore, my nieces and nephews to entertain and the wonderful chip shop around the corner. I drank Guinness with Alan and visited his family at their echoing mansion in Omagh. I went down to stalk the second-hand bookstores on the banks of the Liffey in Dublin and gaze at the ruined stump of Nelson's Pillar, which had recently been blown up by the IRA. The only downside was a sleepless night if I was there on July
~~~~~

12 when, outside the pub on the corner, Orange Order celebrants hammered tunelessly and repetitiously on huge Lambeg drums throughout the night.

One thing that Armagh offered was encouragement for my nascent interest in the distant past. Just outside town was Navan Fort which in the 60s was being extensively excavated. It was not actually a fort but a huge, circular Neolithic ceremonial site. The archaeologists took weekends off so I would wander around the deserted site peering down post-holes and under tarpaulins. I dreamed of stumbling over a horde of gold coins but soon realized that was not going to happen. What I did find was almost as exciting.

The last major structure on the site had been a vast, circular timber structure around 130 feet (40 meters), in diameter. For some ritual reason that neither I nor the archaeologists understood, around 100 BCE the building was partly filled with rock, burned down and buried under an earth mound. As the scientists worked, they moved the rocks into piles outside. The rocks were limestone which had formed on a seabed around 340 million years ago. To my delight they were loaded with a suite of impressive fossils. I brought my rock hammer and chisel and spent many hours happily banging away at the waste pile and in a nearby quarry. Out of the hard rock, I patiently chipped three-hundred-million-year-old corals, crinoids and *productid* brachiopod shells, the largest of the latter being four or five inches across. My background reading told me that there were fossil fish in the quarry, but I never came across one. It was always a challenge heading back home on the ferry with my treasures. People sometimes offered to assist this obviously struggling boy, but I soon learned that few were as interested in heavy bags of rocks as I was.

Any possibility of holidays to Armagh ended in 1969. Dorothy and the kids were in the front garden when a man ran around the corner. He shouted, "Better get the kids inside, Missus. There's been a man been shot on Cathedral Road." The shot man was a Catholic civilian, John Gallagher and he had been killed by Ulster Special Constabulary officers. Gallagher's death, along with the other seven who were killed in the rioting that

August in Northern Ireland, marked the beginning of the modern Irish Troubles. Within a year, Dorothy and her family had moved to Canada.

Despite speaking a few Gaelic words when I was very small, I do not have a facility for languages. Because it was the early sixties and Paisley Grammar School had certain educational pretensions, I had to do a couple of years of Latin. They were taught by an old teacher who was close to retirement and, I am certain, knew deep down just as certainly as we did that what he was doing was utterly pointless. He had the same perspective on Religious Instruction, although he gave me an appreciation for the English of the *King James Bible* and a love of I Corinthians Chapter 13. He drank like a fish and smoked like a chimney and when he retired in my third year of high school the class clubbed together and bought him a half bottle of decent Scotch and a pack of good cigarettes, a gesture that reduced the poor man to tears.

Latin not being compulsory past third year, I was left battling with only French, a struggle that was never going to be anything other than a complete rout. For the O level (Ordinary Level), national exams in fourth year I was in the lost cause class. We were given into the care of new teaching graduate and we reduced her to tears as well, but not for the same reasons as our Latin master. Remarkably that year was one of the worst in O level history and, since the national results were bell curved, against all the odds every single one of us lost-hopers passed.

The point of this story is that having passed O level we were then expected to progress into an A level (Higher Level) class, albeit the lowest one. I never thought this was a good idea and after the teacher (not the same one) burst out laughing in the middle of my French oral presentation I gave up, skipped class regularly and became quite proficient in billiards at the local workingmen's club. The bright spark in the class was that at the end of the year the teacher and one of his buddies led a class trip to Austria. As far as I know, no one questioned why they were taking a French class to Austria, but it said something about what they thought of our linguistic abilities.

Anyway, we travelled by train to Salzburg and by bus up to Fuschl am See, which our teacher gleefully explained had been a favourite holiday haunt of Joseph Goebbels. We didn't see any Nazis but we had a great week wandering around the town, swimming in the lake, climbing the hill behind the town, playing cards for money and underage drinking at the local disco. We were, at least in theory, supervised but it was the first non-family holiday for all of us. At the end we were all given awards by the teachers: best card player, heaviest drinker and so on. I won the award for dancing with the best looking girl at the disco, a stunningly beautiful, almost cliche gorgeous, blond blue-eyed German called Trixie. Of course, a dance was all it was and brief totally unrealistic fantasies of skinny-dipping in the lake at midnight came to naught.

My first real on-my-own holiday came in the summer of 1969. I had a job that paid the princely sum of eight pounds a week—more if I did a few split shifts—in the kitchens of the fancy restaurant at the new Glasgow Airport. I almost didn't last the first few weeks. My initial job was to clean three years' grease off the kitchen walls. This involved a lot of violent scrubbing with some vicious chemicals and each night I went home exhausted, red-skinned and coughing. The plus was that I could imagine myself as George Orwell in Down and Out in Paris and London. Fortunately the staff turnover was high and after I had stuck it out for few weeks I had risen to the lofty heights of pot-scrubber and salad-maker.

The head chef was Italian and quite possibly certifiably insane. He treated the trainee chefs, of which we had three, as if they were medieval serfs and used to throw knives in their general direction and laugh uproariously as they leaped out of the way. My torture was different. When I was standing at the deep sinks scrubbing, I had my back to him. The vegetable cooking was done in huge pots and when the vegetables were removed you were left with a heavy pot half-full of almost boiling water. He would lift the pots onto the floor and, using the aisle between the work surfaces as a well-greased bowling alley, send them barrelling down at me. I had to be continually alert as there was very little time to get out of the way between hearing the noise of the approaching pot and having it crash into me. I always managed to jump to the side before a pot and several gallons of scalding water crashed into the sink where I had been standing seconds before. The chef would laugh gleefully as I mopped up the spilled water and lifted the pot into the sink for a good scrubbing. One glorious day the chef carved a sizeable chunk of his thumb off while thickly slicing onion rings on the meat cutter. Taking the piece of thumb with him, he left to go to the hospital and we never saw him again.

The waiters were the elite of the restaurant staff and they knew it. After all, they were the image that a first-class restaurant portrayed and they had to keep the customers happy and absorb any complaints about the food. They were masters of keeping wonderfully calm, subservient and polite on the restaurant floor, but becoming foul-mouthed bullies at some perceived imperfection in the food the instant they stepped through the kitchen doors. Not even the crazy Italian chef was safe from their scorn if something was wrong with the food.

The clientele, who were mercifully ignorant of the goings-on in the kitchen, were a mixed bunch. Since we were considered a first class restaurant, well-off people dressed up to the nines and came to us in search of a decent a la carte menu and some drinkable French wine.

Being an airport restaurant, we were also subject to the whims and caprices of airlines' changing schedules. A flight would be cancelled and we would be notified that 180 passengers would be arriving for a meal in thirty minutes. It was total chaos, but it worked. Everybody got the same set menu. My job was to slice 90 grapefruit in half, lay the halves on trays, sprinkle liberally with brown sugar, artistically add a half maraschino cherry and pass the trays under a grill for a few seconds—the starters. The main course was always gammon steak with boiled potatoes and either boiled vegetables or salad, the latter also being my job. Dessert was a scoop of ice cream with a spoonful of canned fruit or a couple of crackers and cheese.

At the other end of the spectrum from the well-off crowd were the drunks with a few pounds in their pocket who came to us because we were somewhere they could drink after the pubs closed at 10 p.m. On one memorable occasion, the conversation went something like this:

Waiter: Good evening, sir. may I get you a drink to start with?

Man (who has had a sufficient amount to drink already): Aye, gi'us a pint o' heavy.

Waiter: I'm sorry sir, but we don't have any draft beer.

Man: Just gi'us twa bottles then.

Waiter: Certainly, sir. (offers the customer the menu).

Man (pushing the menu aside): Gi'us some fish.

Waiter (realizing that further detail would not be forthcoming): Would sir care for some *Pommes Frites* with that?

Man: Naw. Just gi'us some chips.

Waiter (struggling manfully to keep a straight face): Yes, sir. I'll be right back with your drink.

The waiter somehow managed to hold it together until he was safely through the doors into the kitchen where he collapsed in paroxysms of laughter.

My enjoyment of restaurant eating took a long time to recover from that summer but there were benefits. When the dessert trolley came in at the end of the evening, much of it could be eaten after the waiters had had their share. There were also good opportunities for theft. I developed a taste for many varieties of cheese that summer and even managed an occasional tiny piece of incredibly expensive, carefully-guarded smoked salmon. On one memorable occasion I left the airport with three very nice fresh trout stuffed into the belt of my trousers and the realization that there were other ways to catch fish than sitting in a small boat on a lake on Lismore with Jim. The other benefit was that I earned enough money for a thirty pound return red-eye flight from Glasgow to Barcelona and fifty pounds spending money.

I went to Spain with two friends, Ronnie and Jim, and we reckoned that the fifty pounds each—which was all the holiday money one was allowed to take out of the country at that time—would last us for a month. It almost did.

After a bumpy flight over the Pyrenees in a plane filled with raucous, heavy drinking, package holidaymakers, we landed in Barcelona before dawn on August 21. As the bleary-eyed tourists boarded their buses and taxis to their hotels and resorts, we hoisted our ungainly backpacks (mine had belonged to my sister Eelin and was of roughly the same vintage as the old Morris Ten Four), and trudged out to the highway to find a bus into town.

As the sun rose, the first bus appeared. It was packed with workers heading for their shifts in the ring of factories surrounding the city. The bus doors opened and we were faced with a wall of people. We stepped back to await the next bus but the workers beckoned us in. Through sign language they got us to pass up our backpacks, which we nervously watched disappear over the heads of the crowd. We were then physically hauled onto the bus and the doors closed.

This was 1969, Franco was still firmly in control and apart from a few places along the coast, tourism was not what it is now. Everybody on the bus wanted to talk to us and the fact that our languages were mutually unintelligible didn't seem to matter. Eventually, some way down the bus, a woman was found who spoke some English. Questions were shouted to her, she shouted the translations, we shouted replies, she shouted the translated answers.

As we wound our way through the industrial areas, the crowd on the bus thinned. Everyone who got off wanted to shake hands with us and no one left on the bus seemed to mind how long it took. We virtually had the bus to ourselves by the time we reached the Placa de Catalunya in the center of Barcelona. We tried to pay now that we could reach the driver but he waved us off, claiming that someone had already paid our fare. I was tired and stunned, but I had experienced my first example of the kindness of strangers that all travellers discover at odd moments, and the first tingling of a life-long love affair with the country, its history and its people.

Our holiday was probably fairly typical for three eighteen-year-old boys let loose in those days. We stayed in city-sized campsites at Palafrugell on the Costa Brava, spent our days on the beaches and our evenings chasing unattainable German girls in the discos to a soundtrack of Creedence Clearwater Revival's "Lodi", "Proud Mary" and "Bad Moon Rising", the Stones, "Honky Tonk Women", Crazy Elephant's "Gimme Gimme Good Lovin'", and Jane Birkin and Serge Gainsbourg's "Je t'aime…moi non plus", the last of which was an added bonus as it was banned in Britain. We caught an octopus, visited a weird cemetery where the bodies were entombed in the walls and went to a bullfight in Sant Feliu de Guixols. We spent far too much of our limited funds on Sangria and Cuba Libre and, with the notable exceptions of a couple of wonderful paellas in a tiny backstreet restaurant, we lived mostly on canned sardines and eggs fried in olive oil over a camping stove.

We arrived back in Barcelona with enough money for a shared breakfast omelette in an early morning workers' cafe but not enough for somewhere to sleep. We tried to find the beach and were stopped by a very short Guardia Civil with a very large gun. Fortunately he seemed to regard our attempts to find somewhere to sleep, or perhaps our terrified attempts to explain this to him, as humorous and directed us to a vacant lot where we settled down to a cold, uncomfortable night. We wandered around the town the next day and caught our midnight flight home.

I had to walk home from the airport and arrived on my doorstep as dawn broke. I hadn't slept in forty hours, eaten in twenty-four, shaved in four weeks or washed in far too long. I rang the doorbell with images of the Prodigal Son being welcomed with open arms, a big breakfast, a bath and fifteen hours sleep. What I did get was Jim opening the door, taking one look and saying, "My God, you look terrible." Eve took a kinder perspective and I ate, washed and slept.

Apart from my lack of success with the German girls in the discos, I was proud of what I had achieved and filled with a desire to see the world. I had left home a holidaymaker and returned a traveller.

Interlude

Travelling Without Leaving Home

Oh Martha look, the Taj Mahal
see how it glitters so
a masterpiece of ancient art
oh damn, its time to go

Oh Martha see, a Raphael
its filled with life and hope
the form, the lines remind me so
of that old ad for soap

Oh Martha hear, the symphony
the crystal, dulcet tones
its good to sit in here awhile
and rest the tourist's bones

Oh Martha now, how meaningful
affirmative not bitter
those zen boys really knew the way
to rake out kitty litter

Oh Martha well, at last we're home
to Kansas we're returning
with souvenirs and photographs
and not one ounce of learning.

Part 3

Such, such were the joys
(with apologies to William Blake and George Orwell)

saffron Buddha
contemplates eternity
above the flashing selfies

Sex, drugs and rock 'n' roll

As a member of the leading edge of the baby boomer generation going through my troubled formative teenage years in a decade that for better or worse supposedly defines my generation, this section should be, as the title suggests, about the wild free love and mind-expanding life in the sixties. Unfortunately honesty must intervene.

I admit that I spent far too many hours in the 1960s thinking about sex but, apart from a few fumbling and unsuccessful expeditions into this intriguing yet foreign land, the age of free love it was not. We knew about marijuana and LSD in a theoretical sense, but our drugs of choice and necessity were Players No. 6 cigarettes, pints of heavy and, if we could afford them, fifths of vodka and orange juice. As for rock & roll, we were more aware through weekly episodes of Top of the Pops, pirate radio stations broadcasting from Luxembourg or ships in the North Sea and, latterly, John Peel. On the other hand I spent a couple of years in the mid-sixties being into country and western music. Paisley was not Haight-Ashbury. While we knew about the goings-on in San Francisco and swinging London, for the most part Scotland remained stubbornly immune to the Summer of Love.

My six years of high school were not, as many people claim, the best years of my life. The moment I put my pen down at the end of my last exam in the spring of 1969, I stood up, walked out of Paisley Grammar School and never returned, not even for the end-of-year party and dance. While others hung out, reminisced and said goodbye, I took a deep breath and began scrubbing the grease off the kitchen walls in Glasgow airport.

That summer I felt truly free for the first time in my life. I was earning money, going to Spain on holiday and, despite some significant anxiety, heading off to university in the fall. I was only seventeen and still had many mistakes and stupidities ahead, but my troubled teenage years were over.

My less-than-stellar academic career had ended on a high note. In my fifth year, when we were all taking exams that would determine which university we would attend or if university was even in our future, my parents and I had a meeting with the school principal, Robert Corbett, to discuss options. I was nervous. I had been in Corbett's office far too many times listening to him tell me, and sometimes my parents as well, that I was on the brink of expulsion. I tended to blame Corbett for all my troubles at school, which was unfair but our relationship *had* sometimes descended to one-sided physical violence (in those days strapping a recalcitrant student on his outstretched hand with a leather belt was perfectly acceptable), and my view of him see-sawed between fear and hate.

Eve assumed university was a given and I had vague ideas of turning my passion for collecting fossils into something geological.

"What do you see your son doing?" Corbett asked Eve.

"Going to university," she answered.

"And you?" he asked looking at me.

"I want to do History or Geology," I answered.

My memory has Corbett laughing but he probably didn't. He did tell Eve a story though, "A few years ago we had a girl at the Grammar who was accepted into all four of Scotland's universities. She was an exceptional student, unlike John."

There was more about my poor marks in preliminary Higher Level exams—physics, chemistry, history, english and mathematics had all been just enough to allow me to sit the final exams. French, for which I had not seen the point of doing the slightest work, was a remarkable 19%.

Corbett went on to go over the various troubles I had been in and outlined the options for technical college. All of this must have been hard on Eve but I don't remember the details because I was sitting thinking, "Fuck you, Corbett," and other even less savoury things.

The upshot was that, in my anger, I applied myself and in fifth year passed four Highers: English, History, Maths and Science, (Physics and Chemistry were combined into Science since I was in the first year of a new curriculum and we hadn't got far enough through it to allow sitting separate exams), with good enough grades to be accepted into Glasgow and Aberdeen universities to do Geology. It wasn't enough for two reasons: first I had to show Corbett and second St Andrews was the best university in Scotland for Geology and their requirements were greater. I returned to the life I detested for another year and passed Physics and Chemistry, Advanced Maths and, to fill in time, O level Geography with good enough grades to be accepted into Edinburgh and St Andrews universities.

I dreamed of walking back into Corbett's office and waving the four acceptance letters under his nose while saying something suitably pithy. I didn't, and it was only years later that I wondered if the whole thing had been a setup on his part. Had he been smart enough to spot that, beneath all my childish rebellion there was something worth saving and challenging me would allow that rebellion to work in my favour?

So my high school years ended on a high note. They began on a similar one half-a-dozen years before. Can you answer these questions?

1) Make adjectives from these nouns: beauty, slope, glass, friend, doubt, expense, delight, sleep, danger, sport.

2) A motorist leaves home at 10.15am and drives at 32 miles per hour. He stops for lunch from noon to 1.45pm and then continues his journey at 30 miles per hour. How many miles has he travelled by 5pm?

3) Multiply 7,296 by 479 (Without a calculator).

4) What article of furniture is DWEBORRA an anagram of?

5) Pick the odd word out in each of the following lists.

    a)   alike, same, similar, somewhat.

    b)   pigeon, duck, goose, swan.

    c)   firm, rough, solid, hard.

d)   this, that, the, those.

e)   pretty, nice, charm, lovely.

f)   tumbler, cup, mug, jug.

g)   fishing, rowing, climbing, swimming.

h)   scarlet, blue, red, pink.

i)   sewing, cotton, needle, calico

6) Write an essay on "What life must be like as a cat."

Okay, but could you have done it in a strictly limited time frame when you were ten- or eleven-years-old?

The questions above are taken from the old eleven-plus exam, which was used in Britain in the 1950s and 60s to stream students academically in the last year of primary school. Your mark determined which secondary school you would go to, either a senior secondary that gave you five or six years of education and the chance to go to university or college, or a junior secondary that gave you a much more practical education until age sixteen with the expectation that you would then go into a trade. Once you were categorized, it was possible but very difficult to move from a junior to a senior secondary school, so the exam was important.

Eve realized that, although it was too late for her, a post-secondary school education was one way to avoid the trap that the collapse of the Raj had thrust her and Jim into. This was particularly true for girls and my sisters had, respectively, a science degree from Edinburgh University, an art college diploma and a teacher training certificate. The expectation was that I would do well in my eleven-plus as a first step on the way to university.

At eleven-years-old I had only the haziest idea of what university was and no idea what I wanted to do with my life, but I was okay with that. The difficulty was that I was a lazy student and didn't particularly care which senior secondary school I went to. There were three options in Paisley and which one you went to depended upon your mark in the eleven-plus, in ascending order, Camphill, John Neilson and Paisley Grammar. Eve was convinced that the last of these was the best, even though going to Paisley Grammar included the added cost of small fees and the purchase of a school uniform, which must have put a strain on the family finances.

Most of my friends were aiming for Camphill and regarded a desire to go to Paisley Grammar as snobbish. I would probably have coasted into Camphill had it not been for an event that strangely prefigured my experience with Corbett. After a pre-eleven-plus parent-teacher meeting, Eve came home annoyed that the teacher had said that I was not capable of getting a good enough mark to get into Paisley Grammar. Based on past performance that was an entirely reasonable supposition but it annoyed me too and, in a fit of juvenile bloody-mindedness, I worked hard and with one other person from my class made the grade. Am I really that easy to read and manipulate?

In any case, Eve was thrilled and I was scared. The only positive was that I had a crush on the girl who was accompanying me and, with the whole of high school ahead, maybe she would notice me—she didn't.

One of my most vivid memories of early learning was a Geography lesson. To illustrate whatever point she was making, the teacher drew a rough outline of Scotland on the blackboard. She had already told us that Britain was an island but I was totally confused by the zig-zag lines of her map. That wasn't what an island looked like. Islands were more-or-less circular or oval and had bays and beaches round the edges where pirates and castaways could land. I went home and looked at an atlas, only to discover that my teacher had been right. I learned that the sketches in *Treasure Island* and *Robinson Crusoe*, while useful to their stories, didn't constitute worthwhile geography textbooks.

The West Primary School, around the corner from Ferguslie Villa, was a combined primary and junior secondary and a very different proposition from what I was used to. The junior secondary half of the school was troubled. There were frequent fights in the playground and police cars were a common sight parked outside. Primary kids were fair game for bullying, which normally took the form of threats of a beating to extort school lunch money. It was good practice for honing my invisibility skills.

Games of conkers were replaced by marbles, sometimes for pennies, and knifey. The latter involved two boys standing about six feet apart with their legs together. Some arcane ritual that I no longer remember decided who began the game. The object was to firmly throw a folding penknife so that it stuck upright in the ground beside either of the opponent's feet. If the throw was successful, the other guy had to move the foot nearest the embedded knife and place it where the knife stuck. This opened a gap between his legs and the game was won by throwing your knife so that it stuck in the ground between his feet. The game was more subtle than it appears at first sight. It was easier to get the knife to stick upright with a short throw close to the opponent's feet, but that gave you less of an open target between the feet and hitting your opponent's foot lost you the game. On the other hand, successfully making your opponent spread his legs wide lowered his body and none of us had a desire to emasculate the other with a missed throw.

Unsurprisingly, knifey was against school rules but I recall playing it in plain sight on the grass verge beside Newton Street in front of the school, so the rules can't have been strongly enforced.

If you were a boy going into first year of secondary school at Paisley Grammar in 1963, the wearing of long pants was optional. When I look back on the photographs of my childhood, apart from when I was playing in the snow, I wore short pants. Therefore, I had short pants that would fit with the school uniform, so that's what Eve decided I should wear. What she didn't realize was that long pants were what big kids wore and short pants would mark me as a little kid and the last thing I wanted to do was stand out. I fought the decision, but to no avail and, at the beginning of September, I dressed in my brand new jacket, cap, shirt, shoes and old shorts, learned to tie a dark-blue crested tie, loaded my pencil case with erasers, pencils, pens, compass and ruler, and boarded the bus across town for my first day of secondary school.

~~~~~
~~~~~

Paisley Grammar School was universally known as the Grammar, although its full title, Paisley Grammar School and William B. Barbour Academy, was much grander. The pretensions of the Grammar didn't help its reputation for snobbishness. Founded by a royal charter in 1576, the Grammar charged fees, the students played rugby and cricket as opposed to football, which was what everyone wanted to play, and had a school song, the Oriflamme:

The torch of our yesterdays
Was kindled by a royal hand.
To bear the Oriflamme always,
And keep it splendid and ablaze,
Was his command.

The torch has ever burned with light
Inspiring, down the days of dust.
They held it sacred in his sight.
To pass it on, a beacon bright:
It was their trust.

The torch, long borne of storied fame
Our eager hands are grasping now.
That we shall tend its vital flame
In loyal service to his name
This be our vow.

Despite singing it on numerous occasions, I was never eager or inspired and made no vow.

The Grammar also had a Latin motto inscribed above the front door. It was "*Disce Puer Aut Abi.*" This translates as "Work boy or get out", which I didn't find particularly encouraging.

To be fair, the Grammar did, overall, provide a decent education. Of course, there were good teachers and bad. I had two favourites. Colin Campbell taught me history for two years. He made it come alive and was influential in giving me history as a source of the stories I now tell, so much so that I reconnected with him in 2004 and dedicated a book to him

(*The Flags of War*). I can still visualize the lesson he gave on the assassination of Archduke Franz Ferdinand in Sarajevo. I was so impressed that I went home and wrote the story down, complete with a map of the route the Archduke's car took and crosses where the assassins stood.

It helped that Mr. Campbell was closer to us in age than many of the teachers at the Grammar and so we could relate more easily. He also had a cool story about his brother who was in the RAF and told us how, during the Cuban Missile Crisis, Vulcan bombers loaded with atomic bombs had been distributed to civilian airports around the country and sat, fuelled and armed at the end of the runways with a pilot in the cockpit 24/7 for eleven days.

The story resonated because, like most teenagers in the sixties, I really thought the end of the world was round the corner. Our grandparents' generation had had a war, our parents' generation had had a war, pretty soon it was going to be our turn. I was hugely impressed and scared by Peter Watkins' movie *The War Game*, which in 1965 depicted in mock-documentary style the run-up to and consequence of a nuclear war in Britain. I even did a school project on the coming nuclear holocaust and went to talk to Civil Defence experts in the local government. I still have the faded and rather quaint brochures they gave me complete with instructions on how to build a "safe place" out of mattresses in the centre of your home.

I kept a diary during these years of living on the edge and make several references to the possible start of World War Three. For example, on Monday, May 15, 1967, the day I sat my last O level exam and recorded that today "everything goes back to monotony", I finish the entry with "I am of the opinion that if the war in Viet-Nam does not stop it will lead to Chinese intervention and an inevitable World War 3. It's pretty frightening but true I'm afraid. Cold sunny day." Two days later I sadly registered that Colin Campbell was leaving to become head history teacher at Greenock Academy.

My concern with the world and its end dovetailed perfectly with the second of my favourite teachers. I can't remember his name and we had him for only one year during which he taught Religious Instruction. My experiences learning First Corinthians and a burgeoning atheism didn't encourage high hopes but the teacher overcame those impediments. We were encouraged to research and discuss topics like the morality of having used nuclear weapons on Japan in 1945. The complexity of moral issues that I had always thought simple fascinated me and every scene I have written where a character wrestles with a problem that those around him see as straightforward owes a debt to that unfortunately nameless teacher.

The other side of the teacher coin were the teacher who got into a fist fight with a student outside the lunch room and the chemistry teacher who, for a strap, used a narrow, wickedly flexible strip of leather that left angry, painful weals on your wrist if you couldn't drag your shirt or jacket cuff far enough down your arm.

Oddly, within the culture of violence surrounding us, we admired both of these teachers. The first because he was one of those who had taken us to Austria and because we agreed that the student he hit had deserved whatever was coming to him. The second, his slightly sadistic streak notwithstanding, was a good teacher and, in any case, getting six of the strap from him gave one status in the strangely disturbing competition we boys had, to suffer as many of the strap as possible to prove our budding masculinity.

Other incidents stand out in isolation. There was the time I was tripped running along the school corridor and smashed my jaw into a door, loosening a front tooth and causing me to faint at morning assembly. One year a teacher was brought in from outside to give a lesson on Sex Education. Bizarrely it was only given to the girls and we boys were left hanging around outside fantasizing about the mysteries that were being revealed behind closed doors.

In one corner of the school library were two bookshelves containing titles that only fifth- and sixth- year students could sign out. In fourth year

I asked for a dispensation because those shelves contained treasures by some of my favourite authors: Hemingway, Orwell, Maupassant, etc. I was told no, so I got around it by stealing the books I wanted to read. It wasn't really stealing because I returned the books when I had read them but I doubt if the school would have looked at it that way had I been caught.

At the breaks during the day, we played a fast and vicious version of poker, three-card brag, for pennies. We played football with a tennis ball in the playground, often with more than twenty-a-side and long arguments about whether a shot was inside or outside the chalked goalposts on the gym wall. We hung out in the covered walkway between the school and the gym, which was the only place we were allowed any interaction with the girls who had a separate playground on the other side of the school.

We also hung out off the school property half a block down Mckerrell Street outside a tiny convenience store. The creepy guy who ran the store sold single cigarettes and it was here that all the serious business was carried out. Forbidden literature was exchanged. For a while, Lord Russell of Liverpool's two books on the Nazi and Japanese war crimes, *The Scourge of the Swastika* and *The Knights of Bushido*, held sway and we huddled round in groups reading and shuddering at the graphic descriptions of torture. It was not that we were young monsters preparing to perpetrate these horrors on others, it was more that our lives and experiences were so well-controlled and bland that we were naturally attracted to anything that gave us a glimpse of a darker world than the one we were supposed to believe in. Yet, even through my morbid fascination, I had a suspicion that listing atrocities was gratuitous and that there was more complexity to history than these books suggested.

Popular as Lord Russell's works were, they couldn't compete with sex. Well-thumbed, dog-eared copies of *Lady Chatterley's Lover* and *Fanny Hill* were breathlessly passed around. Tattered copies of *Parade* and *Girl Illustrated* and even the rigorously unsexual (although it always seemed to show bare-breasted women and not men on the cover), naturist magazine, *Health and Efficiency*, circulated. Compared to what any teen can access today on the internet this was all incredibly tame. Nothing was ever shown apart from bare breasts and bottoms but it was the only window most of us had into this foreign land of sex and the coquettish smiles on the model's faces seemed to offer so many more unknowns.

Once, I was spotted skipping class and heading down Mckerrell Street. A teacher followed me and I ran, dodging through tenement closes, alleys and back greens—if he didn't catch me he couldn't prove anything. I came back out onto Mckerrell Street, only to see that the teacher was still hovering about. I ducked into the convenience store and the creepy guy said I could hide in the back. Unwisely, I did. He came through and brought out two or three dirty magazines. These were ones I wasn't familiar with but were just as bland as all the others. As I thumbed through them, he tried to fondle me. I was wondering what to do, when the bell of the shop rang and he went through to serve a customer. Hurriedly, I stuffed two of the magazines under my shirt and brazenly walked out through the shop, ignoring the stare of the woman buying groceries. Of course there was nothing the creepy guy could do and the teacher was gone, so I got away scot free.

This was the first suggestion I had that sex was a much more complex part of human relationships than my simple, idealized, clean-cut imaginings promoted by *Health and Efficiency*. The next day I took one of the stolen magazines to pass round outside the shop and gained minor status for it. I still shamelessly went into the shop to buy my single cigarettes, but I was always careful that others were around. In time, I learned that my experience wasn't unique. None of us even remotely considered reporting the shopkeeper to the police. It was just the way things were, if you went through to the back of the shop the store owner would try to fondle you.

At the time I had no qualms and felt no guilt about stealing from the creepy guy, after all many of us tried to shoplift candy given an opportunity. I didn't even feel disgust at what he had tried to do, he had simply tried something that he could have got in trouble for and that gave me a certain power over him and a freedom from culpability in stealing from him. Today I feel very differently about him. He was probably just a sad and lonely man in a time when his sexual preferences could still draw him a hefty prison sentence. I wonder whatever happened to him.

For me, being a student at the Grammar was a world away from the image that the school represented and I never bought into the ethos that it tried to portray. It was a trial that had to be survived but, for all the ups and downs of the rocky journey, the Grammar served its purpose in getting me into university. University was an escape from school but it was also an escape from Paisley and its gangs.

Interlude

Otzi

The cold eats through your bones,
the blinding snowflakes freeze your beard,
and leather, straw and wool have lost their power to warm.
You stumble on on feet of lead
a roaring fire, a waiting wife
the only impetus
for that next agonizing step.
A feather bed of snow
beneath the wind,
you lay your quiver knife and axe aside
and rest.

Fifty centuries of calm blue ice
muffle with equal ease
an army's thunderous tread,
the whisper of a thought.
Asleep you lie
as Hannibal passed by
fooled by Rome's eternity
and Christ fished
in waters deeper than your sleep.
Your changeless dreams
a simple hut on legs beside a lake
a hearth
a meal of fish and grain
a family to pass your memory down.
Poor fool
even the lake has long since gone.

The ice withdraws
and leaves you naked
in our questing glare,
an ancient man so primitive
and yet so much like us.
We probe in awe
the arrow in your back,
the sacred marks upon your skin,

each tiny seed of gruel from your final meal,
and catalogue your trinkets tools and garb
as through those hollow eyes
you watch our petty quarrelling

I want to touch your face
feel the skin's dark leatheriness
let you know I am alive
and care.
Maybe then you will awake
and forgive us
for killing you.

Gangs and Sexual Wonders

Sir Christopher Lee, who played Dracula in a series of Hammer Horror films in the 1960s, never went to see his own films. In an interview he said that only once had he made an exception. On a rainy day when he was at a loose end he went in to see an afternoon showing of one of his early horror films. In the half-empty theatre, he sat behind a couple of teenage girls who squealed and clutched each other in delighted fear as Dracula attacked his victims on the screen. As the credits rolled and the lights had yet to go up, Lee leaned forward between the two girls and, in his wonderfully menacing deep voice, said, "Did you enjoy the film?"

I imagine the reaction Lee got from his live performance in the cinema outranked the ones his screen presence elicited, with one possible exception. In 1961, Lee was given his first top-billing in the Hammer movie *Terror of the Tongs*. In the days long before appropriation of voice Lee donned heavy oriental makeup and played Chung King, the leader of a gang in Hong Kong called the Red Dragon Tongs.

Nineteen-sixty-one was a particularly hot summer in Glasgow and a movie theatre in the east end offered free or cheap rates so people could take advantage of the air-conditioning. One afternoon, the members of two rival gangs, The Calton Team and The Spur from Barrowfield went into the packed cinema. Insults were exchanged, food was thrown and a fight broke out. The leader of The Calton Team, the charmingly and appropriately named Terror McCabe, stood and yelled out "Tongs Ya Bass".

Those with an interest in Scottish heritage claim that "Ya Bass" was derived from an ancient Gaelic battle cry "Aigha Bas" which has something to do with battle and dying. However the origin is almost certainly a more prosaic Glasgow rendition of "you bastard". In any case, the newly-named Calton Tongs became the paramount and most feared Glasgow gang in the 1960s and ruled an area of the city called Tongland. Terror McCabe's immortal battle cry became an unavoidable sign painted on walls far beyond Calton Tongs' territory and was taken up by almost all lesser gangs.

Between the park across the road from where I lived in Ferguslie Villa and where we moved to near the airport in 1963, there was a council housing estate called Ferguslie Park or colloquially, Feegie Park. It had been built after the war to house the burgeoning population and replace decrepit tenements and the houses lost in the bombing. It was a good idea except that no one thought to plan any amenities within the forest of low-cost housing.

It's possible that Feegie Park was never as bad as its reputation, but that still allowed it to be a place you thought twice about going to at night. Of course there were families who took good care of their houses, gardens and streets, but there were also streets where windows were boarded over with plywood, gardens were clogged with refuse and weeds as tall as small children, and pavements littered with refuse and broken glass. A friend of mine who had visited someone in Feegie Park told me in awed whispers that the council-supplied furniture was chained to the floor.

My life in Paisley skirted the edge of Feegie Park, totally unaware that one of my future favourite singer-songwriters, Gerry Rafferty, and his partner in Stealers Wheel, Joe Egan, were growing up there a few years ahead of me. What I was aware of was the local gang, The Disciples. They were the most feared and probably best-organized gang in Paisley. Membership was limited to 50 and once you had passed whatever cruelly imaginative entrance requirements there were, you could wear a blazer with the gang crest on the pocket. I avoided Feegie Park and The Disciples, but I saw their eccentrically spelled logo everywhere, "Mental

Disciples Rool Ya Bass." It struck me as odd that the graffiti artists had no trouble with spelling Disciples yet couldn't handle the much simpler, Rule. Although The Disciples 'rooled' Feegie Park, they did sometimes venture off turf.

There were a couple of boys in my year at the Grammar who were, or appeared to be, far in advance of the rest of us sexually repressed fifteen-year-olds and much more aware of the surrounding gang culture. In later high school years we had a boys' common room where we could meet at breaks, have our lunch and leave what we didn't need for any particular class. Monday mornings in the common room were often highly anticipated for the accounts these boys gleefully gave of their weekend exploits.

On one celebrated Monday morning, I arrived to find a boy called Tam regaling a couple of dozen of my peers with a story of the past weekend.

"I went doon tae Largs on the train fer the Sa'urday night dance at the Hydro. Got off wi' this bird. She wasnae brilliant but she came doon tae the beach wi' me. We're doin' good until she says it was her bad week. I was gonnae leave but she said she'd take it in her mooth."

This was back in the days before any fifteen-year-old could see anything on the internet, or anywhere else for that matter. Most of us were still virgins with only the sketchiest idea, if any, of a what a blowjob was, but the reverential silence that fell over us was positively biblical.

"Did she?" a hoarse voice whispered eventually.

"Aye," Tam said with a grin. "It was magic."

Tam's description of events was met with awed, sweaty silence and no one present in the common room that morning could focus on a word any teacher said that day.

Another famed Monday morning was after Tam and his mate Hugh had been to a local dance on the Saturday night. Both were drunk and had gotten into an argument. A fight broke out and, to prevent help being called, Tam had seized his opponent by the jacket collars and given him what was charmingly known as a 'Glasgow kiss.' This involved pulling your opponent forward while simultaneously driving your forehead into his face. If done properly, the adversary collapsed like a wet rag. In this case, Tam had done it with such force that the guy had shot backwards through a plate glass door. Sensibly Tam and Hugh had departed hurriedly.

Used to being reviled for going to such a posh school as the Grammar, we took some strange vicarious pride in Tam's achievements. Not only had he received a blowjob but he had now won a fight. However, the mood changed as the afternoon progressed and some seriously sketchy people began gathering at the school gates. Word filtered up that Tam's victim was one of the leaders of The Disciples and these were the gang members come to secure revenge. As the final bell of the day drew closer and the numbers on the streets outside grew, Tam and Hugh understandably became more nervous. At the end of the day they decided to stay in the common room in hopes that the gang would think they had missed them and disperse. The rest of us took a deep breath and ran the gauntlet.

One Disciple stopped me on the way out and said, "D'ye ken Tam?"

I shook my head figuring that was the safest course.

"Is he still inside?" This was a stupid question given my previous answer, but I wasn't about to point that out. I shrugged.

"If you see him," the Disciple went on, "tell 'im we're lookin' fer 'im." To emphasize his point, he opened his jacket and fondly stroked the head of a small axe that protruded from his pocket.

Asking me to tell Tam that he was being searched for was also a pretty stupid thing to say since it was obvious to everybody who theses guys were and why they were there, but I was impressed by the axe. Once more keeping silent, I merely nodded. With a deep sigh of relief that the axe wasn't meant for me, I headed home.

Tam and Hugh's ploy worked and, after some nervous hours, they managed to sneak out of the school. Both were off school for a couple of days and everything had blown over when they returned later in the week.

For the most part, my strategy of remaining invisible worked fairly well but there were a couple of occasions when, for one reason or another, it failed spectacularly.

I first went into a pub when I was 14. It was a school dance and three or four of us went to the pub along the road. It was a dive, long-since bulldozed, but the barman didn't care that none of us looked even close to the legal drinking age of 18. I was terrified that the police were going to burst in and arrest us all. We went up to the bar and, because I had already been introduced to the beverage by my Irish brother-in-law, I ordered a pint of Guinness.

An old regular standing beside me at the bar watched as I nervously sipped the drink. I had convinced myself that he was an undercover cop, when he leaned over, pointed to my Guinness and said, "Good stuff that, eh?"

I nodded and mumbled something.

"Aye," the old guy went on, "You drink that, son. That'll put lining on your shite."

We drank up and fled, but the next time was easier. Gradually I got to know the pubs where they didn't care how old you were. This was helped by me being tall for my age (by Scottish standards), but I wasn't fooling anyone. Sometimes, because I didn't have a girlfriend or a social life worth mentioning, I would go out and wander the streets on a Saturday night trying out different pubs. This was mainly done for the thrill of breaking the law because even in the days when a pound would buy you ten pints I never had enough money to get drunk.

There must have been an element of self-loathing in my sad, solitary Saturday night excursions. One night when I was fifteen, I went to a pub on Lady Lane off the High Street. Unlike many of the places from my childhood, it still exists, although now it's called Scruffy Murphy's, which it certainly wasn't in 1966. I don't remember what I had done with the rest of the evening, but I went in to spend my last pennies on a 'hauf and hauf', a whisky and a half pint. Oddly, I remember that the whisky was

VAT69, which I later discovered was Ernest Shackleton's tipple of choice in the Antarctic.

Having finished my drink and my money, I set off on the walk home. I turned into the High Street and stood for a moment looking up at the tenement where the girl who had moved with me to the Grammar from West School lived and on whom I had a strong, unrequited and probably unhealthy, crush. As I set off again, an old drunk stumbled up to me and asked for money. I said a curt "No" and walked on. A few steps farther on, two boys about my own age stopped me. "You botherin' auld Jimmy?" one of them asked.

I shook my head and kept going. As I did so, for some unfathomable reason, I turned and spat on the pavement. I heard footsteps coming up behind me. Why didn't I run? I have no idea. In any case, they caught up to me and I turned to face them. One pushed me in the chest so that I stumbled back into the doorway of a small jeweller's shop. I swung a poor, ineffectual punch and the next thing I knew I was down in the doorway getting what was called in those days, "a kicking." One kick jerked me back so that the back of my head broke the pane of glass at the bottom of the shop door. One of the boys tore my watch, which had an expandable strap, off my wrist and with a final kick they ran.

In tears, I got up, went around the corner into Townhead Terrace and hid in a corridor, or close as the access to the tenement flats was called. I checked to see if my head was bleeding. Luckily it wasn't. I was bruised but not seriously injured. What upset me most was that it was my grandfather Dyer's watch and I would have to hide the fact that I had lost it from my mother.

The memory of this rather pathetic little incident is still vivid more than half a century later. I can go on Google Maps and spot exactly where it happened. Apart from the name of the pub, the demolition of the tenement where I paused wistfully and the jewellers being replaced by Hollywood Hair Styles, little has changed and the other side of the street is still dominated by the red sandstone, Neo-Gothic, Thomas Coats

Memorial Baptist Church and the Ionic capitals of the Paisley Museum and Art Galleries.

More mysterious are my actions or lack of them. Why was I so short with the old drunk? Why did I spit, an unquestionably aggressive gesture? Why didn't I run when I heard them coming after me? I was a fast runner and would soon have been among people downtown and safe. Why didn't I defend myself with more than a weak attempt at a single punch? I don't have the answers. Certainly I was a shy kid (shy being what anxiety disorder was called in those days), and was used to a reclusive existence. I actually enjoyed my solitary pursuits of reading, stamp and fossil collecting, and model-making, but the peer pressure to be a part of a large group of friends, socialize a lot and have a girlfriend, were immense. I suppose that the pop psychology explanation would be that the peer pressure to conform and be a part of the group, added to my slightly drunken loneliness as I stood before the tenement where the unattainable object of my lust resided, created a self-loathing that caused me, subconsciously, to welcome punishment for what I perceived as my miserable life at that time. I don't entirely buy this explanation but have little else to offer. I did, however, learn from the experience.

In later years, my options for going home after a late shift working at the Glasgow Airport were the direct route—crossing the highway and hiking across fields—or the longer and more expensive route—catching a bus into town and then one back out to my home. If I was tired or if it was raining I took the bus.

One Saturday night a friend and I were waiting for a bus outside the airport after long split-shifts. Two big guys, "hard men" in the local parlance, approached. "Kin ye gie us a couple o' fags?" one asked.

We both had cigarettes but denied it. They left.

The bus was a long time coming and we both forgot about the incident and took out a cigarette to while away the time. In those days you could smoke on the upper floor of a double-decker bus, so we wouldn't waste them. As the bus pulled up, the two hard men reappeared. "Ye got fags, ye lyin' bastards."

We dropped our cigarettes and sat downstairs near the driver at the front of the bus. The hard men, muttering obscenities, went upstairs. As the bus neared downtown, we could hear curses and threats from upstairs. As we approached our stop we stood at the front door.

"They're gettin' af," came from upstairs. "Let's get them."

We knew only too well that "Let's get them," meant at best a kicking, at worst a stabbing with the sharpened tail of an aluminium comb, which was the weapon of choice among gang members at that time.

As feet pounded down the stairs, I screamed at the bus driver. "Open the fucking doors."

He did and, despite the bus still moving at a frightening speed, we jumped. Fortunately neither of us fell and we shot off down the High Street heading for the Cross, the centre of town where we know there would be police patrolling. I vividly remember looking down and seeing broken glass from thrown beer bottles skittering past my flying feet.

Our last hurdle to safety was crossing the busy Causeyside Street. We didn't even break stride and hurtled over against the lights with angry car horns sounding all around. We went and stood panting close to a couple of police. The hard men, deciding that we weren't worth it and, I hope impressed by our suicidal dash across a busy road, gave up. We waited quite a while and then made our respective ways home.

Paisley when I was growing up was a dangerous place, or at least some parts of it at some times were. For whatever reasons, I sometimes got myself into riskier situations than necessary, but it wasn't always with hard men on the streets. Sometimes I pushed limits just for the hell of it and sometimes that pushing led into places that I am not particularly proud of all these years later.

Interlude

City Boy?

I used to think myself a city boy,
a child of smoke-stained walls and traffic noise
and tenements of wailing kids and drunken dads.
I relished walking streets of unknown people
anonymous and grey.
I thrilled at older boys with
gang-badge-sharpened tail-combs
ready for a fight.
I knew the streets to run on feet spurred on
by flying diamond shards of bottle.
I knew the darkened bars where age was never asked
and scorned the threadbare nature of the local park
below the council flats with only its population of
strutting crows and begging ducks of lower class
where grass was only something
treacherous to hide the broken bottles.

But now my years of search have found
another me
far older and hid deep below.
A memory of ghostly, fertile fields where lived
Jemima Puddle Duck and friends.
Where, like as not when I awoke,
the kitchen table would be clothed
with corpses sad of still-warm rabbits
helping to explain my dreams
of early morning firing squads.
A land of gaelic mists
and ocean waves,
with undertows of memory,
which brought debris from other lands mysterious
that one day I would call my own.

Which pole of truth should I pursue
as blindly stumbling on my road I go?
Who knows?

Avoiding Prison

On November 9, 1847, a meeting of Paisley's concerned and influential citizens resolved to establish and maintain a Ragged and Industrial School along the the lines of those already existing in Aberdeen and Dundee. They undertook this because there were, "a considerable number of destitute, neglected children in this town, who, having been left by their parents…without any regular means of living nor any moral superintendence…are allowed to grow up in habits of vagrancy and crime." Apparently, this was an "increasing source of juvenile delinquency, which is the disgrace of our large towns." The worthy citizens of Paisley determined to "take immediate steps to remedy this great social evil by reclaiming these children, and providing the means of raising their condition and enabling them to lead an honest and useful life."

From the perspective of someone being chased down the High Street by gang members with broken bottles one hundred and twenty-two years later, this admirable attempt could at best be said to be only partially successful. However, the Ragged and Industrial School thrived, housing 18 boys and 17 girls who were taught, "reading, writing, and the common rules of arithmetic, geography and music." The boys were employed teasing hair and cotton and the girls learned knitting and sewing by making their own and the boys' clothing, and helped in the kitchens.

In the 1850s, a Miss Elizabeth Kibble made a bequest to establish a reformatory "for the purpose of reclaiming youthful offenders against the laws." The Kibble Reformatory for Boys opened on the last day of August

1859 on three acres on the edge of Paisley. Its first inmates were the boys from the the Ragged School who were deemed to require reforming.

By 1865, there were 53 boys at the Kibble learning tailoring, shoemaking and gardening. In an inspection of that year, the boys' standard of education, at least in reading, cyphering and dictation, was considered above average to very good, but all was not perfect and in September 1872 there was an escape attempt by many of the boys. All were recaptured and four imprisoned.

The daily routine was rigid, up at 5:30 a.m. and bed at 9 p.m., with the intermediate hours dedicated to school, work, play, worship and three meals. Apart from the escape attempt, the regimen seems to have worked and the Kibble Reformatory thrived and grew. It ran a nearby farm and taught an increasing number of trades. The football team won five gold medals, the boys gave public concerts, camping trips were arranged and almost 200 of the former pupils volunteered to fight in the First World War. Many of the boys seem to have gone from the school into gainful employment and a steady stream emigrated to the hope of a better life in Canada and Australia.

In 1933, Reformatories were abolished and the Kibble became an Approved School for "all classes of neglected and delinquent children" and those "falling into bad associations, or...exposed to moral danger, or... beyond control." The act that established the Approved Schools also allowed for court-mandated punishment such as being "privately whipped with not more than six strokes of a birch rod by a constable."

While all these changes were taking place, Paisley was expanding. Rows of sandstone tenement flats were built on the opposite side of the road from the front of the Kibble and the RAF base at Abbotsinch was built behind the school's farm.

One day during the winter of 1963/4 I got on the bus as usual for my trip across town to the Grammar. What made this day special was that I got on a different bus to go home. While I had been struggling with my twelve-year-old self image in short pants, my parents had moved out of Ferguslie Villa and into the large ground floor flat on the corner of

Greenock Road and McFarlane Street, immediately opposite the Kibble Approved School, or the Borstal as it was erroneously but commonly known.

For the next six years, every time I stepped out of the front door of home I faced the Kibble. The boys of the Kibble occasionally hung out the windows and shouted at passers-by and Eve told me to keep away from the place and not to talk to any of them, as if I could somehow become contaminated by these delinquents. She had little idea how perilously close I came to looking at the world from the other side of the street through one of the Borstal's windows.

$$\sim\sim\sim\sim\sim$$

I kept a diary for two-and-a-half years from January 1966 to the middle of 1968. It's often a painful read filled with teenage angst, naïveté and political ideas that make me cringe today. It's also not as truthful as I would like, but it does give some uncomfortable insights into my fourteen- to sixteen-year-old mind. My main preoccupations were with world events and the weather, both of which come across as fairly miserable. I can go through my diaries and compile a list of every disaster, tragedy and war worldwide over a thirty month period. The worse the calamity, the more words I devoted to it. I wrote a short book on the Six Day War and came to the conclusion that the Middle East was the Balkans of the latter half of the 20th century—a not entirely erroneous historical analogy.

I also have a valuable almost day-to-day climatological record of the weather in Paisley—mostly cold, rainy or snowy, and grey, although I record a heat wave in June of 1968. The major climate event that warrants a longer entry than usual was for Monday January, 15, 1968: "Hurricane force winds hit Paisley and most of southern Scotland last night, killing 18 people [later upped to 20] and sending thousands of chimneys and chimney heads crashing to the street or through house roofs. The strongest gust in Paisley was an all time record of 106 mph [171 kph] at about 3 a.m."

I woke up about 3 a.m. and looked out the window to see all sorts of debris tumbling along the street and slate roof tiles crashing to the ground all over. By the time I got up for school the winds had died down. I walked through a town that veterans of the Second World War said looked like a city after a bombing raid. The roads were covered with shattered roof tiles and rubble from collapsed sandstone chimney heads. Cars on the street were damaged and some totally crushed. Our tenement lost three chimneys and our garden fence and gate disappeared. Few people were out and about at 3 a.m. and most of the deaths were caused by heavy stone chimney heads crashing through roofs and killing people in their beds.

Despite a constant rather dark interest in disasters, there is a progression in style and the first inklings of a growing maturity. In my *Letts School-Boys Diary 1966* I record that I am 5 ft 7 in tall and weigh 9 stone (126 lbs). After 64 pages of information that Letts thought would be of interest or use to a fourteen-year-old boy (ranging from fishing hints and lists of French irregular verbs and logarithmic tables, to notable events in history and four pages of recommended books, none of which I have read, although I admit to being intrigued by '*How I Became a Librarian*'), I note the two major events of 1965 as Churchill's death and funeral and Ian Smith's Unilateral Declaration of Independence for Rhodesia.

My first entry on Saturday, January 1 is: "Radio Scotland opened early in the morning. Hope it lasts. United States envoy had talks with H. Wilson on Viet-Nam. Pope appealed for Peace (it won't do any good). I stayed home today, weather very wet." From this can be deduced an early dissatisfaction with BBC Radio (Radio Scotland was a pirate radio station broadcasting from an converted lightship in the North Sea), and an early interest in politics, skepticism about religion and concern about the weather. All of which turned out to be reasonably valid.

In 1966, among other things, I read Alistair Maclean, Nevil Shute, Jack London, John Wyndham and Homer. I watched *The Collector*, *Paths of Glory*, *Fail Safe*, *The Birds*, *Nevada Smith* and many TV plays and shows, and listened to a wide selection of pop songs from the Small Faces to Jim Reeves. My sister Eelin came home for a holiday, I went to Armagh in Ireland for a holiday, I cycled around collecting fossils in many dangerous old quarries, and asked a girl out twice, noting in my diary with totally unfounded optimism, "third time lucky"—it wasn't.

I am ashamed to say that I supported Ian Smith's white racist government in Rhodesia and argued the point when Eelin, who was teaching at a mission in South Africa, came home. In my defence, I had spent my first fourteen years in a social monoculture where everyone was white and Scottish. Around Glasgow, with the exception of the occasional Chinese or Indian restaurant, diversity was religious and you were defined by whether you supported Celtic Football Club (Catholic) or Rangers Football Club (Protestant). I knew other cultures existed but knew virtually nothing about any of them.

I was sick a lot and, although I don't specify in my diary, I played it up to get more days off school. I received detention and the strap so often that I don't even mention what for. The school principal, Ninian A. Jaimeson, or NAJ to most of us, retired and was missed, mostly because, my detention and strap notwithstanding, he was a lax disciplinarian. The new principal when we returned in the fall of 1966, Robert Y. Corbett or The Boss as he came to be known, was a different story. On the very first morning of his first day he stood and watched as we trooped in from morning break. We all watched him to try and judge what he would be like. I was slouching along with my hands in my pockets. "Wilson," The Boss shouted across the playground, "get your hands out of your pockets." In shock, I responded immediately. It was not the order that surprised me, I was well aware that hands in pockets were not allowed when in uniform, it was the fact that he knew my name. That was the start of the fraught relationship between us.

It seems an odd thing for an anxiety-ridden kid to do, but I shoplifted as a teen. Sometimes I took things that I wanted, a book or a vinyl long-playing record (the latter not an easy thing to shoplift), and once a small fossil from the local museum, but mostly it was for the breath-stopping thrill of stepping through the shop doorway without an alarm sounding or a hand descending on my shoulder. I was never caught and if I had been I suspect that the anxiety would have kicked in and I would have stopped immediately.

At the beginning of my 1967 diary, which was much bigger than the pocket *Letts*, I filled a page and a half with a 400 word description of myself. At some later time, hideously embarrassed by the whole thing, I scored it out but it is still legible.

After a paragraph emphasizing the privacy of the as yet empty pages and the hope that what I fill these pages with will be read by future generations (this is you), I describe myself. I give my name, age, height (5ft 8in), weight ("10 stone +, but I'm not fat"), eye and hair colour (both brown), and admit to being educated at the Grammar. I then go on a long ramble about my character.

I profess to being generous, trustworthy to my friends and state that I would "much rather kill a cruel human being than harm an innocent animal of any sort." I am interested in History and Geology and hope to become a Palaeontologist. "I drink moderately because I enjoy it, but smoke very occasionally to keep up appearances."

On the down side, I "cheat in exams where possible" although I don't remember doing this, and "where something I do not enjoy doing is concerned, I am lazy", a characteristic that I have never fully thrown off. "I am rather nervous though not seriously so, but become tongue-tied near the opposite sex, much to my disadvantage". I admit to stealing things "regardless of value" and because "it seems to be fairly common in the school" and go on to say that "I suppose I will grow out of it." "I enjoy the fear of stealing…[and] also have the modern trait of senseless vandalism but can still see things in perspective and stop before I go too far." I claim to have "controllable cleptomania."

In the diary that follows, I tend to make only veiled references to my worst illicit activities, presumably to prevent my diaries being used against me if I am caught. I do mention that I sneak up onto the school roof and dodge the prefects on duty to prevent such activity. I also record skipping classes (usually French), swimming lessons or sports days to play billiards at the local workingmen's club, or to go out collecting fossils.

On June 29, 1967, the second last day of school before summer, there was a minor riot. Eggs were thrown, windows painted over and a cistern in one of the toilets was ripped off the wall. Not to be left out, I spread a mixture of ink and paint on the toilet wall and got caught. Mum was called in the next day and The Boss "raved on as usual and tried to lay it on thick, however nothing came out, thank god, and after mum left he belted me (8 of it but 2 missed)." I wonder what could have "come out" but didn't. In any case, when school reconvened in the fall, it cost my parents ten pounds for the repainting job.

Most of this was stupid teenage stuff not that different from what many of my compatriots were doing. It was done for cheap thrills by the shy kid trying to give himself a sense that he was more than the unpopular invisible person he saw himself as, and the consequences were rarely more than detention or the strap. But there was one thing I did that could easily have landed me across the road in the Kibble Approved School.

~~~~~

While my dad was doing his apprenticeship on Clydeside in Glasgow, he saw several famous people. He heard Lloyd George speak at a venue where people handed out ripe tomatoes to throw. He also heard John Maclean, a famous Scottish socialist who died in 1923 in part due to his ill-treatment as a prisoner of conscience during the First World War. He also watched the famous runner Eric Liddell score tries for Scotland at Rugby Union. I learned about Lloyd George through my reading on the First World War. As my politics swerved to the left and away from supporting Ian Smith's Rhodesia, I began to appreciate John Maclean, Willie Gallacher and the other socialists of the Red Clyde in the years after the First World War. I went to St Andrews University several years before the opening scene of *Chariots of Fire* was filmed on the beach there, but
~~~~~

my enjoyment of the movie was added to by Jim's connection to Eric Liddell and by my interest in Rugby.

I never enjoyed playing rugby at school, in part because I was not overly athletic but was big for my age so was always hidden away in the second row of the scrum, which was not a fun place to be. What I did enjoy were the bus trips to Edinburgh to watch Scotland play against England, Wales, South Africa and the New Zealand All Blacks. Once on leaving a game at Murrayfield I became turned around and ended up on the opposite side of the stadium from the bus. By the time I eventually found the bus, it was full of unhappy people and so, to cover my embarrassment, I made up a story about meeting a cousin and losing track of time. Storytelling has its advantages.

The bus would drop us off in the evening back at the school and I would walk home from there. On Saturday, February 25, 1967, I went to Edinburgh to watch Scotland being beaten by Ireland, 5 points to 3. There was a Young Conservatives' dance at the school that I tried to crash but my diary claims there was some unspecified trouble, so I left.

After three subsequent days of stormy weather during which I noted that the Boston strangler, Albert de Salvo, had been recaptured after an escape, there was a rail crash in Birmingham and my record player no longer worked, I wrote on Wednesday, March 1 that "Someone has written an anonymous letter saying that I was in the school on Saturday evening and stole a tape recorder." I ranted on about how The Boss didn't believe me when I said it wasn't me and had threatened to involve the police.

Other boys on the bus with me were interviewed, Jim went to the police after The Boss refused to meet him, but learned little, and someone sent the news to the Paisley Daily Express: "Paisley C.I.D were today continuing their investigations into the theft of a tape-recorder from Paisley Grammar School." The theft takes first place in my diary entries except for the weekend where I approved of Sandie Shaw being selected to sing "Puppet on a String" at the Eurovision song contest, watched the movie *Arsenic and Old Lace*, and moaned about the continuing stormy weather leap to the fore.

On the Monday (March 6) I note that the "The tape recorder was returned and the culprit escaped despite the police watching the school. Aren't our police wonderful." Eve and Jim both went to see Corbett that day and he told them that a second anonymous note had been received the previous Thursday accusing other boys. Police investigations had discovered that a group of boys had been seen running out of the school and a police line up is to be organized. My only comment on this is, "it sounds like fun."

After this, with the exception of noting a week later that I almost got into a fight for accusing another boy of writing the note, the tape recorder disappears and I go back to international news and the weather. At some later date, I make two changes to my diary entries. On Friday, March 3, I add in the margin "Took T.R. back". The entry quoted above for Monday, March 6, has "the culprit" scored through and "I" written in its place.

So, what's the true story of this criminal master plan? Back in January and early February, there are pieces of entries that are heavily scored out and mostly illegible. However, there are references to getting a key and making a "fair replica" of it. Later illegible entries probably refer to trying out the key and wandering around the school. I remember the thrill of walking along the school corridors and going into classrooms at night. I suspect that the buzz came from a combination of doing something forbidden and a feeling of being in charge in a place where I was normally definitely not.

I don't know if the entire tape recorder escapade was carefully planned as a way to replace my failing record player, but there was some forethought—not much, though. How I ever imagined I could safely walk away from the school and through the streets of Paisley carrying a fairly large reel-to-reel tape recorder and not be noticed, let alone how I could explain its sudden appearance in my bedroom to my parents, are lost in the mists of time. I do remember hiding it under my bed, which suggests a stunning level of idiocy.

When the whole situation blew up, I considered dropping the tape recorder off a bridge to get rid of the evidence. That might have been the sensible thing to do, but I decided to up the stupidity level and, despite the police being involved and supposedly watching the school, I resolved to return it. I remember lugging the tape recorder through back alleys and tenement closes to approach the school from the back. Did I assume that police surveillance involved a constable standing at the front door of the school to welcome me? In any case, after watching the back of the school from a dark corner, I darted across the road, placed the tape recorder by the gym door and fled. There were no further consequences although I never again rebelled quite so dangerously or so foolishly.

The 1968 diary is spotty until June and virtually non-existent after that. Thankfully it does not begin with a painful bout of tortured self-awareness, although the themes remain the same. Despite a statement on January 1 that the coming year is "unlikely to be worse than 1967," it was at least as bad. In addition to the usual train crashes etc., the first half of the year included: the Pueblo crisis, the Tet offensive, the Rhodesian crisis, the assassinations of Martin Luther King and Robert Kennedy, the Paris student riots, and various attempts to revitalize the staggering British economy. All of these events are covered in some detail with more thoughtfulness than previously, and my politics are changing. I note with some glee when the communist and anarchist flags fly over the Paris stock exchange during the riots. I don't record getting into any serious trouble at school, which might be a sign of growing up, and the year wasn't about constant disaster and excitement. On February 29, I note, "If anything at all interesting happened today then I'm afraid I had absolutely nothing to do with it."

Culturally, I only record reading *In Cold Blood* and *The Ragged Trousered Philanthropist*; seeing, *The 3 Faces of Eve*, *Psycho* and *Dr. Zhivago*; and attended The Johnny Cash Show at the Odeon in Glasgow—"FANTASTIC" —and John Cairney's stunning solo performance in Tom Wright's *There was a Man* at the Metropole, but even these fragments of what I read and saw indicate a broadening of perspectives and interests.

I end 1968 with a 600 word entry that acts as a bookend to the 400 words at the beginning of 1967. Interestingly, I am writing this during the 100th anniversary of the Armistice and I end my 1968 entry by wondering, "What will posterity remember the 50th anniversary of the Armistice for?" I go on to list the major events of the year and what was notable for me. In the middle, I do wander into self-pity, "I wish I could write my thoughts coherently or even express my feelings to other people...I want to tell people how I feel while I'm young...When I'm older the harsh practicalities of life will have destroyed my ideals." Note to fifty-year-younger self: it didn't, just shifted them left, added a patina of skepticism and rounded the edges a bit.

I conclude my diary-keeping phase with the less-than-cheerful, "1968 was a year where many hopes were shattered and where even unborn hopes died and I see, unfortunately, no reason why 1969 should be different." I then add, not entirely hopefully, "However the year has ended, I shall end with Apollo 8, which gives me something to draw hope and comfort from. Mankind still has a desire to learn, to explore, to know, and 1969 will be another step on the way to this great goal that can never be achieved."

Incomplete, angst-ridden and self-serving though they are, my two-and-a-half years of teenage diary writing offer some insight. Beneath my artless fifteen-year-old words there is an odd, rational awareness of my behaviour. I know stealing and cheating are wrong and that I shouldn't drink or smoke, and yet I seem to distance myself from my actions. I benefit from these activities either materially or emotionally or to gain status, but I fully realize that some of my activities are morally wrong and distance myself from them by citing either peer pressure or a belief that it is simply a stage I am going through. It is almost as if I am observing my life and my actions from one step removed.

Reality rarely provides the structure for a good story and it is the pacing, the control of the speed with which a story moves along that allows a storyteller or author to craft something that will involve and manipulate the listener's or reader's emotional state. Pacing is vital to a good story and it is impossible to accomplish until an emotional distance has been achieved by the creator. In my diaries I hadn't yet learned how to pace stories but, even when I was closely emotionally involved in them, I did seem to have developed an ability to distance myself from the events I was describing and placing myself as a character in a story. Already I have a vital element in effective storytelling, but it would be many years before I put it to good use.

Interlude

Tides

The shingle-clattering tide
came sidling up
to lap around our door.
You were not here
and so in sorrow slow
it left.

The moon arose in solemn pomp
to pass the nighttime hours
in talk of lunacy.
You were not here
and so upon its long decaying arc
it left.

The continents no longer slide
upon the ocean plates
and glaciers retreat to mountain tops
cry milky tears
and wrap themselves
in foggy loneliness.

This morning my kettle made two cups of tea
to sit in accusatory silence
upon the desolation of my countertop.
You were not here
and so I drank them both.

I shall go down and sit
beside the crying waves
and see if the tide
bothers to return.

Part 4

From Dylan to Land Mines

soaring sunlit cedars
a small child trips
on exposed root

Me, Dad and Bob

Growing up, my Mum's default position on anything I thought or did that she disagreed with was, "Oh, you'll grow out of it." This was applied to my dislike of coffee, but variations were adapted to many other interests: my nascent atheism, what Eve regarded as an unhealthy interest in the Spanish Civil War, and an admiration for Bob Dylan. She was wrong on all those counts—I still dislike the smell of coffee, my atheism is much clearer now than the uncritical views I expressed to her, I have written two novels set during the Spanish Civil War, and I have stuck with Bob through many ups and downs and been rewarded by his Nobel Prize. I suspect that if I could have a conversation with her tomorrow, her perspective would not have changed despite me being old enough to collect a pension. So I wouldn't try and change her mind, I would happily and proudly tell her all about her grandchildren and their achievements. I would have a different conversation with my dad.

A couple of years ago I went on a trip up to the Yukon. Somewhere on the Dempster Highway, I fought off swarms of black flies, climbed a mountain and walked along a spectacular ridge. At the top where a breeze discouraged the insects, I sat and read "The Cremation of Sam McGee" out loud. That had not been my intention when I set off but, on an impulse, I had picked up a slim volume of Robert Service's best-known poems at a gas station outside Dawson City. On the walk I had been thinking about Jim and how much he had loved Service's poetry and would have enjoyed a visit to Dawson City, so it seemed appropriate to read aloud in his memory. I then began thinking about a talent he had that is virtually lost today.

Jim was a product of his time, his class and his circumstances, as are we all. He was not a literary man, although he loved a good story and enjoyed a thrilling novel. Apart from *Old Possum's Book of Practical Cats* he had little time for Eliot, Joyce, Pound and his other contemporary literary greats, but among my fondest childhood memories of growing up are listening to Jim recite poetry. He knew "The Shooting of Dan McGrew", "Gunga Din", "The Charge of the Light Brigade" and a host of other poems off by heart. He loved Tennyson, Longfellow, Robert Service and could quote Kipling endlessly. Partly this was because his schooling relied much more on rote learning than today, but it was also because those poets said something that resonated with him.

From the days of Homer reciting in the Agora until very recently, poetry has been an important part of western culture for a large portion of the populace, literate or not. Western culture is richer for: "Better to have loved and lost than never to have loved at all," "Man's inhumanity to man makes countless thousands mourn," "A thing of beauty is a joy forever," "Into each life some rain must fall," "He travels the fastest who travels alone," and "Be still my heart." All come from poems that were well-known in their day and Jim could quote from all of them. How many people today can quote extensively from contemporary poets?

I once sat on a Canada Council jury to determine the worthiness of financial support for various proposals to hold literary events in the following year. I represented children's literature and sat with a novelist and a poet. We all read all of the applications prior to meeting in Ottawa to finally apportion available funds. Obviously, we each found it easiest to assess in our own fields but I found some of the poetry proposals virtually indecipherable. It was as if the proposers were speaking a language of their own that required a specialized vocabulary and knowledge to understand. This was underscored by the poetry events aiming for, at most, a couple of dozen participants (one even proudly proclaimed that ten people had participated the year before), whereas the novel-writing and children's events were talking several hundred attendees (in one case over a thousand).

None of this is to suggest that poetry festivals and events should not benefit from financial support, but it does indicate that much modern poetry does not fill a role in nearly as many people's lives as it did a hundred years ago. The exception is Slam or performance poetry, which regularly draws decent crowds but, nevertheless, there's a gap in modern western culture that poetry isn't filling—but that doesn't mean that the gap is empty.

When my dad was two years old, Rudyard Kipling became the first poet to win the Nobel Prize for Literature. Were he still alive, my dad would have been one hundred and eleven when the first lyricist and musician won the Nobel Prize for Literature, but he would never have been a Bob Dylan fan. Dylan speaks to my generation just as surely as Kipling spoke to my father's, but they fulfil the same roles in our respective cultures. As poetry has become the esoteric preserve of an intellectual elite, the gap left has been filled by poet-songwriters like Bob Dylan, Leonard Cohen and Neil Young. They are our poets and they are creating our popular literature.

Dylan's *Blood on the Tracks* and Cohen's *Songs of Love and Hate*, resonate with me and my generation in the same way that Kipling's *Barrack-Room Ballads* and Service's *Songs of a Sourdough* resonated with my dad. He knew the quotes above, I know:

"In the dime stores and bus stations, people talk of situations, read books, repeat quotations, draw conclusion on the wall."

"There's a crack in everything, that's how the light gets in."

"The ghost of 'lectricity howls in the bones of her face."

"Suzanne takes you down to her place near the river, You can hear the boats go by, You can spend the night beside her, And you know that she's half crazy, But that's why you want to be there."

"Take me disappearing through the smoke rings of my mind, Down the foggy ruins of time, Far past the frozen leaves, The haunted frightened trees, Out to the windy beach, Far from the twisted reach of crazy sorrow."

What's the difference?

Poetry, from Homer to Dylan, has always been spoken or sung. Dylan didn't win the Nobel Prize for Literature for songs, he won it for poetry that is put to music, that is rich in extraordinary imagery, that says something that the average person can relate to even if the listener doesn't understand all the references. As T. S. Eliot said, "Genuine poetry can communicate before it is understood." Much of Dylan's poetry wouldn't resonate with my dad any more than much of Kipling's does with me, but I think he would appreciate Dylan's place in my culture.

I am not a musical person. Apart from "When the Saints go Marching in" on the piano and a brief foray into guitar lessons that went as far as a stumbling version of "The House of the Rising Sun", I have never touched a musical instrument with any intent. My attempts at singing are worse and often seem to involve Christmas carols.

On one of her visits home from Africa, Eelin taught me the words to "Silent Night" in the original German. I thought this was cool and, in a rare and ill-advised foray out of my carefully-cultured anonymity, I mentioned this to my music teacher when we were discussing carols during the last class before Christmas. Unforeseen, yet in retrospect horribly inevitably, she asked me to sing it. I tried to decline but she insisted and the class, sensing my embarrassment, took her side. Although the teacher encouraged and occasionally joined in, the acapella performance was excruciating. I had expected laughter at the end but was met by an even worse stunned silence. In the midst of wishing for nuclear war to suddenly break out a girl, Alex, turned, smiled at me and gently applauded. I survived, fell in love and promised myself that I would never sing out loud again. Only once have I broken that promise.

An office Christmas party back in the 1980s—a pleasant evening of food, drink and good company—was ending around midnight with everyone standing around the piano singing carols. As usual in these circumstances, I was miming the words. My boss at the time, who was a fine cellist, was standing beside me. At the end of the song he turned and said, "John, you weren't singing."

I replied, "I can't sing."

"Nonsense," he said. "Everyone can sing. Maybe not well, but everyone can sing."

By a stroke of luck, the next carol was one of my favourites, "Good King Wenceslas", so, with my inhibitions weakened by alcohol and renewed confidence in my vocal abilities, I joined in.

After the song was over, my boss turned to me and said, "John. I'm sorry. I was wrong."

I have never again sung "Good King Wenceslas", or any other carol, in front of other human beings, but it did give me my favourite Christmas Card. It shows two medieval soldiers standing on a castle battlement. One is looking out over a snowy landscape to the edge of a wood where a ragged figure is leering evilly back. Beside him is a miserable-looking man wearing a crown and tied to a tree. The second soldier on the battlements is staring at a tattered note, which reads, "Bring me Flesh, Wine and Pine Logs hither, or you'll never see Wenceslas again. Signed, Yonder Peasant."

Just because I can't participate, doesn't mean that I can't enjoy music. True, I do not have the experience or skills to appreciate a finely sung aria or a complex experimental symphony, but I enjoy a good tune. The problem with a good tune is that it is never enough. After a while it becomes boring or worse, it lodges itself annoyingly in your brain at 2 a.m. and won't go away. So, for me the words of a song are important. This doesn't stop the annoying 2 a.m. repetition, but it does mean that I can enjoy a song more for much longer than if it is simply a catchy tune. Of course, I started off with catchy tunes.

The only concert I went to before university was in 1968, and it was the Johnny Cash Show at the Odeon Theatre on Renfield Street in Glasgow—the very place my dad fled thinking an earthquake was approaching in 1935. I went on my own since no one else at school was in the least interested in Johnny Cash. The big musical event in Paisley that year was a concert by Amen Corner at the ice rink where almost 50 girls fainted at being so close to Andy Fairweather Low. While I had nothing against Amen Corner, it was "pop" music and I was already looking for something more. Not that my fading interest in Country and Western music provided that, but having played inside Folsom Prison was impressive. I had to wait until the 90s when Johnny Cash had a resurgence and even my teenage son thought that having seen "The Man in Black" way back when, was cool.

The Johnny Cash Show also offered me something broader than traditional C&W with Ma Maybelle and The Carter Family, The Statler Brothers and Carl Perkins performing "Blue Suede Shoes". And then came Omnibus.

One day in the fall of 1968, we were asked in music class to write down our favourite pop stars and classical composers. Pop stars were mostly split between the Beatles and Rolling Stones, although I put the Hollies, partly because I was discovering some Dylan through their covers. I think Beethoven easily won the classical composers, but I put down Frederick Delius. When the teacher went over the lists, she looked pointedly at me and said, "Some of you put down obscure names just to be different." I thought this was grossly unfair despite the fact that there was some truth in it. It was a safe way for me to be different but, more importantly, I had just watched Ken Russell's *Song of Summer*.

Omnibus was a BBC documentary series that aired late on Sunday nights. It showed films on art subjects by often controversial directors like Ken Russell. I had no background knowledge of what I was watching and had little idea of how historically accurate these films were, but I loved them. They introduced me to Edward Elgar, Richard Strauss, Claude Debussy, Dante Gabriel Rossetti, Antonio Gaudi, Henri Rousseau, and Isadora Duncan, and later, Tchaikovsky, Henri Gaudier-Brzeska and Mahler, but my favourite was Russell's portrayal of Delius in *Song of Summer*. Admittedly, none of this gave my knowledge of these artists any depth, but then my knowledge of Beethoven did not extend much past the opening notes of his Fifth Symphony. However, I had probably listened to more classical music in Omnibus' strange biographies on Sunday nights than most of the rest of the class had in their lives, but that didn't mean much. In fact, I know little more today about Rossetti, Debussy and Delius than I did at the end of their Omnibus episodes. What I did get was a sense that there was a broader world out there and just because I had never heard of someone didn't mean that they weren't worth hearing about. I did follow up on some of them in the post-Omnibus years, Gaudier-Brzeska, Strauss and Mahler spring to mind, but there was one Omnibus show that had a much more immediate effect.

In October 1968 Omnibus showed Tony Palmer's documentary *All My Loving*. It gave me a new perspective on the pop music on the radio by giving me background on some of the musicians. Palmer also attempted, sometimes pretentiously, to put pop music in a broader cultural context by interspersing the songs I was listening to with graphic images of self-immolating monks, death camps and violent rioting. He seemed to be suggesting that the bad world of the past that the young were protesting against was going to change. This was emphasized by pop icons talking about how there was a new feeling in the world and a new age was dawning. It was simplistic, cliched and wrong but it was a powerful experience for a culturally and politically innocent seventeen-year-old. It made me think more broadly, something I hope I never stop doing, and it introduced me to a band I'd never heard of before—Cream.

By coincidence, my nascent interest in Cream was reinforced less than three month later when Omnibus showed Palmer's *Farewell Cream*, which gave me performances from their last concert at the Royal Albert Hall and interviews with Eric Clapton, Ginger Baker and Jack Bruce. I was enthralled, but I had discovered Cream at the very moment when they were no more. I spent the summer of 1969 to a soundtrack of top 40 hits at Tennis Club dances, parties and Spanish discos but, when I went up to university at St Andrews in the fall, I was ready for something new.

University didn't mean an end to an interest in country-flavoured music. Two of my favourite albums in first year were Elton John's *Tumbleweed Connections* and Dylan's *Nashville Skyline*. I also listened to Kris Kristofferson but that was more because I briefly dated a fan rather than a deep appreciation of the man and his music. In my first couple of years at university, I saw Santana, Deep Purple (twice), Leonard Cohen, and lined up all night for tickets to Led Zeppelin. I toyed with the fringes of rock going to see Colosseum and The Dick Heckstall-Smith Band and even trying Soft Machine, but a flatmate's passion for Captain Beefheart was a step too far. By and large I stayed middle-of-the-road in what would today be called 'Prog Rock'. I listened, sober or otherwise, to my fair share of Pink Floyd, King Crimson, Jethro Tull, Mike Oldfield, Tangerine Dream, Yes, ELP, etc. and this gave me some credibility with my son when he got into Porcupine Tree, Wilco, Muse and so forth. But my most significant musical development at university was due to my flatmate's (he of Captain Beefheart fame) friends.

If you were a teen in Britain in the 60s, unless you lived in London, Liverpool, or some other music centre, you probably knew Dylan mostly through covers of his songs by The Byrds, Peter Paul and Mary, Manfred Man, The Hollies, etc. His albums sold well enough but his best single chart performance, which was what most self-involved teens looked at and where the radio plays came from, was a number four with "Like a Rolling Stone". It was common to hear people say something like, "Bob Dylan, he's a good songwriter but his songs are better performed by other people." Despite having bought Nashville Skyline, that was still pretty much how I felt when I met Colin. He was an aficionado who owned a copy of *The Great White Wonder*, an eclectic sampling of Dylan's work and the first major bootleg album. It was so precious that he refused to lend it to me, which was probably just as well since I doubt if I was ready for it then. However, he did lend me the three classics from 65 and 66: *Bringing it all Back Home, Highway 61 Revisited* and *Blonde on Blonde*. I transferred them to my, honestly acquired, reel-to-reel tape recorder and sat listening to "Desolation Row" over and over again. I was hooked.

In these days of streaming and the internet, it's hard to recapture the feeling of going into a record store to pick up a totally unheard new album by a favourite artist, or the excited anticipation of taking it home, placing it on the turntable and dropping the needle on the first groove. In January 1975, I went to the local record store on Church Street in St Andrews and bought a copy of *Blood on the Tracks*. From the first chords of "Tangled up in Blue" coming out of the tiny speaker of my mono record player, the Bob Dylan hook was driven deep.

Since then, Bob has occasionally worked hard to dislodge the hook, but he wouldn't be Bob Dylan without the gospel years or the weird Christmas album. I think my dad had an easier time with Kipling, but then perhaps the Raj encouraged a more straightforward view of the world than the 60s. In any case, we both have Nobel Prizes to boast about for our respective poets.

Interlude

An Insanity of Gardening

The bees have drained the flowers.
Nectar-drunk they realize that flying is impossible
and crawl beneath cold stones
to hug their furry abdomens
and fondly recollect a happy dance
on honey-laden hives.

Earthworms conquer flight.
On tiny wings of gossamer they carry vital mail
between nasturtium continents
while gazing down on beetles,
ironclad and rumbling
with blitzkrieg speed
to breach the lines of worried ants
and thrust toward
some distant, grassy Stalingrad.

Beside the herbs the butterflies
are bombing helpless lines of ladybugs
who push their prams of mattresses
towards their fiery homes.

From my imposing perch,
I sit and watch while uncontrolled
my hand with spastic jerks destroys
the little scrap of paper
with which you turned my garden mad
and said
farewell.

Student Life

Legend has it that when the Apostle Andrew was crucified in Patras, Greece in the first century of the Common Era. He requested a diagonal cross since he did not feel worthy of expiring on the same kind of cross as Christ. Sometime after, a monk called Regulus dreamed that it was to be his task to put Andrew's bones on a ship, sail it to the ends of the Earth and wherever it was wrecked, build a church to the saint. Taking a kneecap, arm-bone, three fingers and a tooth, Regulus duly sailed west to the ends of the Earth—Scotland—where he was shipwrecked amongst the surprised Celtic inhabitants of the Fife coast. A church was duly built and over the centuries the town of St Andrews grew up. The bits of Andrew enshrined in Fife became a site of pilgrimage until they were destroyed during the Reformation, leaving only a few relics in Warsaw, Amalfi, Patras (skull) and Edinburgh (shoulder blade) for the faithful to visit.

Whatever the truth surrounding the peripatetic saint's bones, St Andrews thrived and the church grew into an impressive cathedral. In 1410 the monks of the Augustinian priory associated with the cathedral —who had themselves done their fair share of travelling, being expelled from Paris by one of the several current popes and Oxford and Cambridge as a result of the Anglo-Scottish wars—created a learned society and three years later persuaded the Avignon Pope, Benedict XIII, to confirm their charter. Thus began the University of St Andrews, Scotland's oldest university and the third oldest in the English-speaking world (after Oxford and Cambridge).

After my unlikely success in being accepted by all four of the Geology-offering universities in Scotland, I had a choice to make. Academically, St Andrews had the best reputation, but almost all the people I knew were going to Glasgow. Going there made sense, not only for the social support I would have, but also because it was the closest to home and therefore the cheapest. The temptation was there and the thought of going across the country (albeit a small country), and starting out somewhere I knew nothing about amongst people I had never met was terrifying. But, just as I had forced myself to get into the Grammar when all my friends were going to Camphill, I forced myself to go to St Andrews—after all, the only way not to be scared was to stay at home in bed every day.

On a September morning, five hundred and fifty nine years after the university's founding, my parents deposited me, a tin trunk and a couple of suitcases in the annex of a student residence named for the original deliverer of St Andrew's bones. Regulus' adventures notwithstanding, I doubt if he felt as scared or as close to the ends of the Earth as I did after the two-hour drive from Paisley.

My parents took their nervous son out for lunch. In our absence, my roommate, Ian arrived from Newcastle and received a shock. The tin trunk I had deposited in the middle of our room had been my sister's and had her name, Helen Margaret Wilson, stencilled boldly on the top. He never told me whether he was relieved or disappointed when I walked into the room. I survived the introductory week and signed up to take year-long courses in Geology, Botany and Chemistry. The Chemistry was a struggle, the Botany was okay and the Geology was fun, in part because I soon discovered that a large portion of the early curriculum was based on *Principles of Physical Geology* by Arthur Holmes, the 1,200+ page tome that I had read avidly for fun the year before. It seemed that not having had a social life was finally paying off. Not that I intended to keep that pattern going. This was 1969 and, although St Andrews with its conservative background and mere 2,000 students was no Berkley, I was hoping to make up for lost time.

The group photograph of the two hundred or so residents of St Regulus Hall—Regs for short—shows a mixed bunch. Some look as if they have been through at least part of the sixties while others are still stuck in the 1950s. Most of us, like me, are somewhere in between—we look a little bit scruffy and have hair on the way to becoming long. Some, again like me, are in the process of growing beards. Fortunately Ian was at the same level as me and we got on well. The guys in the room next door were a step ahead and we soon recognized that the laughter and the smell of oranges (eaten in a pointless attempt to cover sweeter illegal smells), seeping under the door meant that they had scored some dope.

Back then, and to some degree today, tradition at the University of St Andrews was very important. Students had to purchase a knee-length red gown with a burgundy collar, unless in the Divinity faculty where the colour was black. First year undergraduates (*Bejants* and *Bejantines*) wore the gown high on both shoulders; second year students (*Semi-Bejants* and *Semi-Bejantines*) could wear it lower but still on both shoulders; third year students (*Tertians*) wore the gown off the right shoulder, unless in the Arts faculty when it was off the left shoulder; and fourth year students (*Magistrands*) wore the gown off both shoulders so that it hung from the elbows.

If you followed the previous paragraph then you probably feel, as many of us did, that this was a bit silly. However we felt, we all bought a gown to wear at formal residence dinners, debating society meetings, chapel on Sunday, and the traditional walk along the pier after chapel. They also made decent dressing gowns and a useful spare blanket for cold nights. I suspect that, despite our expressed cynicism, many of us took a certain superior pride in wearing the gown appropriately after we had survived the first two years.

One of the stranger traditions at St Andrews was Raisin Weekend in November. Each first year student was supposed to have a pair of academic parents, third of fourth year students whose job it was to help guide them through the beginnings of university life. In exchange they were rewarded on Raisin Weekend with a bag of raisins, a valuable food item in earlier centuries. In my day, the bag of raisins had been replaced by a bottle of wine and the weekend had become a typical student festival of bizarre costumes, dumb games and excessive drinking. A part of me thought it was silly and a part thought that it was way better than anything Paisley Grammar had offered. Apparently, Raisin Monday is now dedicated to a giant shaving foam fight. I can't claim to be sorry that I missed that.

My memories of the years in St Andrews are fragmentary—rather like conglomerate, a sedimentary rock made up of diverse pieces of other rocks cemented in a matrix of finer material. The pieces of rock are the clear images, rounded by memory and set within a vaguer matrix of too much beer and not enough work. Just as a geologist can categorize the different pebbles in a conglomerate in groups of related types, so my memory-images of university life fall into several pigeonholes: golf, girls, gainful employment, academic work and the rest.

I put golf first not because I play—in six years in the Cathedral of Golf I never swung a club once and my closest contact with the Old Course was falling asleep one night in Hell Bunker on the 14th hole—but because it is an inescapable piece of St Andrews culture. I must also admit to a quiet satisfaction in talking about my golfless time in St Andrews to the intense annoyance of practitioners of the sport. What particularly disturbs them is that I was in a bar close enough to hear the crowd roar when Jack Nicklaus famously drove the 18th green and won the 1970 British Open. When in a golfing conversation, I have often felt an affinity with James II of Scotland who banned the sport in 1457 because it was interfering with young men's practice of archery.

Shortly before my arrival at university, the elite Royal and Ancient Golf Club of St Andrews received a letter from Dean Martin requesting a tee-off time on the Old Course. As with all major celebrities of the day, the clubhouse laid on a sumptuous reception and gave a choice tee-off time. The only problem was that the Dean Martin who showed up was a plumber from New York. To the credit of the R&A they treated him to the reception anyway.

Throughout my university career, girls were much more important to me than golf and my main focus in first year was to find a girlfriend. My initial attempt was not a spectacular success. Every hall of residence had a formal ball each year, which required dressing formally, buying your date a corsage and struggling to get hold of one of the town's limited number of taxis to get her to the ball. I invited Judith, an attractive and very nice girl who, as it turned out, could drink me under the table. A photograph of the room party we were in confirms this.

Alcohol also played a part in a later, more successful, dating attempt. I discovered early in my drinking career that, although I could hold my alcohol well and generally gave the appearance of being more sober than I was—or at least than my friends were—my memory the next morning was often patchy. I got around this by jotting down anything that seemed important on a piece of paper.

One morning after a dance, I awoke to find a scrap of paper on my bedside table with a girl's name, Jane, the name of a female hall of residence, Hamilton, a room number and a time, 7 p.m. I assumed that I had made a date for that evening, but had no recollection of doing so. Nevertheless, I rationalized that if I showed up at the right place and time I could wing it. I spent the day congratulating myself on my foresight, had a bath, dressed in my best scruffy clothes, headed over to Hamilton and knocked on the correct door. What I hadn't accounted for was that Hamilton, like St Regulus, allotted shared rooms to first year students. The door opened and there were two smiling girls standing there and I had no idea which one was my date. I had a moment of total panic when fleeing seemed my best option but I took a breath, looked vaguely between the pair and said "Hello". Fortunately, Jane was well brought up and so stepped forward, smiled and introduced her room mate.

That inauspicious start was the beginning of my first longish relationship. We went out for almost ten months, which included the summer between first and second year since Jane lived a short train ride from Paisley. In retrospect the relationship was doomed by my immaturity and desire to lead, at least a vague replica, of the wild 60s student life.

The subsequent years were filled with a diverse collection of, probably not unusual, experiences: one-night stands; painful rejections; stealing girlfriends from flatmates and having girlfriends stolen by flatmates; a long, complex, tormented on-off relationship with a Divinity student much more worldly-wise than me who was dealing with her own issues; and meeting and falling in love with the girl who has been my partner through the rest of this saga. The last experience did not begin auspiciously.

The start of every university year was marked by a succession of dances, the point of which was to make new students feel welcome and introduce them to their new world. Those of us already comfortably ensconced in university life would prowl these occasions helping the new arrivals feel at home.

In my younger years I looked older than I was, partly because of the first signs of early onset male pattern baldness. At university this was exacerbated by having long hair and a full beard, and my apparent age became a running joke amongst my flatmates. One night four of the flat's occupants had returned home from one of the dances and were sitting around the kitchen table bemoaning our lack of success in meeting anyone of interest. The fifth came in with a new student he had invited for tea. I was the disgruntled, hairy guy sitting at the end of the table and, in keeping with the joke of the moment, someone asks the new arrival how old she thought I was. Misinterpreting the purpose of the question, she guessed 25. Since I had just turned 21, this elicited chuckles. Thinking this must be some sage of learning and, possibly one of the professors she would meet in the next week or two, she upped her estimate to 30. Now open laughter erupted and, in a panic, she blurted out 35. As my flatmates fell about, I glared at this upstart. However, this was the girl who had grown up round the corner from the house where I spent my first months of life and three years later we were married. The flatmate who introduced Jen to me was my best man.

In the 1960s, there was a grant system for the 12% of high school students who went on to university. This was means-tested and consisted of tuition fees paid by the local education authority and a maximum non-repayable grant for living expenses of 340 pounds. Since Eve and Jim were retired and had little in the way of savings, I received the maximum grant. This was a generous system, which, in these days when 50% of students go on to some form of post-secondary school education, has been replaced with repayable student loans. However, the grant was only enough to support a monk-like existence and required gainful employment during the holidays.

My worst summer job was in a laundry where they washed the large roller towels that filled the machines in restaurant and bar toilets in the days before air dryers. These rolls were heavy and had to be tied into bundles of two for delivery to their destination. My job, along with a couple of dozen women, was to stand at a metal table and do the tying. A skip full of laundered rolls would arrive at one end of the table. I would lift two out, tie them together and place the pair in another skip at the other end of the table. Apart from the mind-numbing boredom of doing this all day, there were dangers. The string was nylon. We each had a plastic ring with a blade on it which, with a deft flick of the wrist was used to cut the string. The unpleasant part was giving the string a hard tug to tighten it around the towels before tying the knot and cutting. By the end of the first day, the small finger on my right hand was inflamed and bleeding. "Don't worry," the woman at the next table said, "you'll soon develop callouses." She showed me her finger, which sported a thick layer of hard skin that could have deflected a bullet. It took me two weeks to find a job pumping gas.

Other summers I worked pumping gas and, after Eve and Jim moved out of Paisley to a small town, as a *scaffie* on the garbage trucks in St Andrews. This last job I kept for a year after I graduated, waiting for Jen to finish her degree before we married, and the money earned helped finance a three month backpacking adventure through France and Spain on our way to the boat down to southern Africa.

Academically, my university career had not been stellar. I enjoyed a year of Botany and failed second year Chemistry, taking Psychology instead. In retrospect, a History course or two would have been interesting, but paths were less flexibly presented in those days and academic advisors not yet invented. I wandered through four years of Geology to a second class honours degree.

Geology was mostly fun, especially the annual field trips—mapping within sight of Hadrian's Wall and strolling over granites on the coast near Barcelona. The Spanish trip was in the early 1970s and everyone was waiting for Franco to die so that the country could move on. At a reception to welcome us I met my first anarchist. I think we gravitated to each other as the two scruffiest people there. Despite our mutual lack of command of each other's language, he told me about the time the Guardia Civil had opened fire on a student demonstration on the street behind the building we were in and how, despite his anarchist conviction, after Franco's death he would support the socialists as a step towards his final goal of anarcho-syndicalism. He seemed to me a direct descendant of the Catalan anarchists of the Spanish revolution of 1936/7 and his political knowledge and awareness stood out in stark contrast to the rather vague leftish sensitivities expressed by my student colleagues.

On a Spanish political side-note, a subsequent visit to Spain gave me the first and, if memory serves, only appreciation of political graffiti in a foreign language. On December 20, 1973, Franco's Prime Minister Admiral Luis Carrero Blanco was in his way to mass at San Francisco de Borja church in Madrid. As he was driven in his Dodge Dart car along the narrow Calle Claudio Coello, 80 kg of stolen Goma 2 explosives were detonated by a three-man ETA commando unit. The explosion hurled the small car completely over a five-storey building where it landed in a courtyard, killing Carrero Blanco, his bodyguard and driver. Over a year later I read on a seedy toilet wall in San Sebastian, "*Arriba, arriba, Franco. Mas alto que Carrero Blanco*", which translates as "Up with, up with, Franco. Higher than Carrero Blanco."

After the final written and practical Geology exams, an external examiner was brought in to look over the papers and give an oral exam to make sure everything was above board. In 1974, my external examiner was a charming Welsh professor who chatted about this-and-that for quite some time. I suppose my confusion about when the exam was supposed to begin must have shown on my face, because he said, "Oh, I don't need to ask any questions. Your final exam results are consistent with your performance throughout." I nodded, relieved to hear that I hadn't screwed up majorly in the finals. "I do have one question, though," he went on.

I learned early in my Geology career that, since precise description is such a large part of field Geology, when asked in a practical exam to identify a rock sample that you had never seen before, you could scrape a passing mark by writing detailed descriptions of the sample. This had happened in the final exam. We had all been given a sample of a limestone and asked to identify it based on the fossils within. I had no idea. Yes, it was a fossiliferous limestone and I could spot pieces of coral, trilobites, brachiopod shells, etc. but specific identification was totally beyond me (The reason was that I had never seen this rock before. It had been visited by the rest of the class on a field trip I had missed through illness). Falling back on old habits, I described everything I saw and made a guess at the age of the rock, which I knew was somewhere within a 200 million year range. I completed the rest of the exam and right at the end a name for the rock I had never seen before suddenly popped into my mind. Figuring that it might be worth a point and probably couldn't do any harm, I scrawled it down—Wenlock Limestone.

"How did you identify the sample in the practical exam as Wenlock Limestone?" the examiner asked. "Your description was very good, but there was nothing in that would lead to a correct identification."

I mumbled something about it seeming right, assuming that wild, panicked moments of irrational inspiration were not what my degree was supposed to train me in. To this day I have no idea how I came up with that answer and can only assume that a photograph from a book had lodged itself in some deep recess of my memory. However, the experience has taught me to trust my instincts.

In a postscript to my Geology career at St Andrews, when Jen was finishing her degree, she needed one first year course to graduate. I persuaded her to take Geology, after all I had found the first year easy. It seems that not everyone has read Arthur Holmes' impressive *Principles of Physical Geology* or that they find the Earth Sciences fascinating, but with my help over several long nights before exams, Jen scored spectacular results. As she stood looking at her final mark on the Geology department bulletin board the head of the department, Professor Ken Walton, peered over her shoulder and said, "I see John did better the second time around." St Andrews' years were very different from the confused and tormented times in Paisley that had spat out the troubled eighteen-year-old in 1969. They gave me the space to experiment, make mistakes and polish life skills. They failed to turn me into a golf aficionado nor, other than the experiences I gathered and the reading I undertook, did they turn me into a writer. The process that began with Sue's stories in Skye had to wait until Africa to take another step.

Interlude

A Love Song

If I were not Alexander
I would be Diogenes.
Would you love a dog as much,
sitting in a clay tub
ignoring mad thoughts of conquest?

If I were Diogenes
I would not be Alexander,
and Darius would sleep easy in Persepolis
while you could stand between the sun and I
to cloud these cynic thoughts.

But I am me,
a featherless cock,
hopeful lantern clutched
to seek an honesty
bright enough to dull Athenian suns.
Do not laugh.
If I were not Diogenes
I would be me–
and still love you.

Mfecane

A catastrophe that killed between 1 and 2 million people and left huge areas desolate hit parts of southern Africa between 1815 and 1840. The causes are myriad, including: the introduction of water-hungry maize into the agricultural economy, drought, slavery, changes in styles of warfare, and the rise of the Zulu nation under its first king, Shaka. In *isiZulu* this period is known as *Mfecane*, the time of scattering and forced migration.

One of the clans affected by *Mfecane* was the Khumalo led by a chief called Mzilikazi. Mzilikazi was a favourite of Shaka but they had a falling out in the early 1820s and Mzilikazi and a few hundred followers were forced to flee. They headed inland where they set up their own nation and contributed to *Mfecane* by slaughtering their new neighbours. The depopulation of vast areas helped the Boers in 1836 as they fled north from the British at the Cape of Good Hope and they managed to force Mzilikazi and his people to flee north. After years of wandering, the Ndebele, as they were now known, settled in an area of southern Zimbabwe now called Matabeleland and proceeded to dominate their new neighbours.

Mzilikazi welcomed early European hunters and explorers to his new kingdom, including David Livingstone who called the chief the second most impressive leader that he met in

Africa. After Mzilikazi's death in 1868, one of his sons, Lobengula put down a rebellion and became king. Lobengula's misfortunes began when George Harrison stumbled on the main Witwatersrand gold reef on

Langlaagte farm in South Africa in 1886. In one of the great mistakes in mineral exploration history, Harrison sold his claim for ten pounds and left the country just before the world's biggest gold rush began. The rush created the usual selection of super-rich and led to the founding of Johannesburg, railway expansion into the interior, the Second Boer War and the creation of a new country.

One of the first on the gold rush scene was Cecil Rhodes. Rhodes was already heavily involved in diamonds at Kimberly, where he created De Beers Consolidated Mines, but thought that the news of gold was worth checking out. It was and, using one of his favourite words, he created the Consolidated Gold Fields of South Africa company. Not content with making millions in Kimberly and the Witwatersrand, Rhodes sent negotiators north to broker a deal for the mineral rights to Lobengula's land. In 1888, in exchange for a hundred pounds a month and a thousand Martini-Henry rifles, Lobengula signed the Rudd Concession which read in part: "I, Lobengula...do hereby grant and assign unto the said grantees, their heirs, representatives, and assigns, jointly and severally, the complete and exclusive charge over all metals and minerals situated and contained in my kingdoms, principalities, and dominions, together with full power to do all things that they may deem necessary to win and procure the same, and to hold, collect, and enjoy the profits and revenues, if any, derivable from the said metals and minerals." The negotiators neglected to put in an earlier promise that the incursions into Matabeleland would only comprise ten miners. Rhodes was thrilled. His reaction to the document was that the concession was "so gigantic it is like giving a man the whole of Australia."

Lobengula soon realized the scope of the document he had signed and ruefully commented that a chameleon comes up very very slowly behind its prey and, when close, shoots out its tongue and devours it. He likened England to the chameleon and himself to the fly.

He sent emissaries to London to contest the concession. They were well treated and met Queen Victoria, but the assurances they were given meant nothing. On October 29, 1889, despite some very murky behind-the-scenes moves, Rhodes' British South Africa Company was officially granted a royal charter by Queen Victoria. Soon armed police entered Lobengula's lands and despite two wars in the following five years the Ndebele king was defeated. Lobengula died of smallpox in early 1894 and miners and settlers flocked in and gratefully named their new land, Rhodesia, in honour of its creator.

Rhodesia fitted nicely into the patchwork of the British Empire—at least until empires became unfashionable. In 1965, Ian Smith's Rhodesian Front party unilaterally declared independence (UDI) from Britain. A white-dominated state—essentially a British colony without Britain—fought a bloody bush war and managed to hold out until the country gained independence as Zimbabwe in 1980. In 1975, just as the war for independence was heating up, I joined the Rhodesian Geological Survey.

Eelin and Frank had gone out to South Africa in the early sixties. They lived and worked at Kokstad in the heart of what had once been Shaka's Zulu empire, but because of their liberal, anti-racist views, by 1969 they were no longer welcome there, so they followed Mzilikazi's path north and accepted teaching positions at St James Mission and School for girls' near Nyamandhlovu only 50 miles from Lobengula's old capital of Bulawayo.

After I graduated with a degree in Geology in 1974, I worked for a year emptying dustbins and sweeping the streets of St Andrews while my wife-to-be finished her degree. During the year, I answered an advertisement for geologists and went down to The Strand in London for an interview at Rhodesia House, the former High Commission but since UDI with no official status. The interview went well and they seemed keen (in retrospect suspiciously so) to have me. Since, as a new immigrant, I would be given five years before I was liable for military call up (a clue to the keenness), they offered me the chance to undertake a PhD at the University College of Rhodesia in Salisbury (Harare).

I accepted, but not being in a particular rush, Jen and I spent a honeymoon backpacking through France and Spain and travelling by boat from Las Palmas down to Cape Town and by train up to Salisbury. I arrived in October to discover that, while I had been gallivanting around Europe, the law had been changed to allow new immigrants only two years before military call up. Fighting a war wasn't part of my plan, so that meant that the proposed PhD was now out of the question.

Since the field mapping season was over that year, I was seconded to a geophysical survey. This involved driving around the country, navigating to specific landmarks (sometimes a solitary tree or termite mound), and taking readings of the magnetic field as a way of determining what might be under our feet.

Much to Jim's disgust, since he had been running a driving school at the time, when I turned seventeen I had failed my driving test. It was not a big deal since there was no way I could afford a car anyway, but it did mean that I had to sit a driving test when I arrived in Rhodesia. During the geophysics field work, I learned to drive on a long wheel base, late model series 2 Land Rover, which I discovered on a couple of occasions lost its brakes after it had forded a river of any depth. This turned out to be very good training for many of the situations I was to find myself in as a geologist.

This was all fun and kept us away from the border areas where fighting was going on against the military wings of Robert Mugabe's Zimbabwe African National Union (ZANU) and Joshua Nkomo's Zimbabwe African People's Union (ZAPU). Only twice did we go close to the border. The first time was a weekend visit to Ruth, whom we had met on the train from Cape Town and whose parents owned a farm north of Salisbury (Harari). We saw no guerrilla fighters, but her brother was a member of the Selous Scouts, a shadowy anti-guerrilla force. He was a quiet, rather strange guy who had a habit of disappearing for long barefoot, early morning runs through the bush. He would return when the rest of us were having breakfast and sit reading a book, totally unconcerned while his sister extracted long thorns from his bleeding feet. I often wonder what happened to him after his war ended.

The other trip was a holiday to Victoria Falls with my sister and Eve and Jim, who had come to Rhodesia to visit. From our hotel we could see

Zambia across the sanctions-closed border and yet, every night, we could hear the trains crossing the bridge over the gorge below the falls. We also went on a short cruise up the Zambezi River, staying close to the Rhodesian bank while we were shadowed by a boatload of heavily armed soldiers in case anyone shot at us from the opposite bank.

Our hotel was a graceful old imperial-era building with much wrought iron and wide verandahs. As we sat in the evenings drinking whisky and watching the spray rise from the falls—"the smoke that thunders" Livingstone was told it was called—Jim and Eve reminisced about India

My real work began on March 29, 1976, when I loaded up my Land Rover and headed south. The object was to remap two 1:250,000 map sheets, approximately 1,000 sq. km. of territory, southeast of Bulawayo. The rocks had been last mapped by Frank Amm in the 1930s but ideas had changed in the interim and the gold mining activity on the area made it of considerable economic interest to Rhodesia's embattled government.

Since I had accepted the job a mere year before the military situation in Rhodesia had changed quite dramatically. Prior to 1975, Ian Smith's racist government had been battling guerrilla incursions across the relatively short and easily defended border with Zambia to the north. The country was an international pariah with strict sanctions in effect, but with the support of South Africa, Rhodesia was holding her own. That changed on June 25, 1975 when, following a ten-year struggle and the Carnation Revolution in Portugal, Mozambique became independent. The new FRELIMO government established a Marxist, one-party state and immediately threw their support behind Robert Mugabe's ZANU fighters. This opened more than a thousand kilometres of virtually indefensible border and signalled the approaching end of Smith's regime.

Oblivious to the broader political and military perspectives, I established camp near the centre of the northernmost map sheet at a farm outside the tiny village of Essexvale (now Esogodini). The farm consisted of four dwellings. The main one, where the farm owners Mr. and Mrs Beit lived, and three other houses where Mrs. Beit's elderly parents the van der Merwe's, a Portuguese refugee family, and a young policemen,

Allen, and his wife and baby lived. One of the things I learned in Rhodesia in the 1970s was getting on with people who held opinions that I fundamentally disagreed with. On my first evening at the farm the Beits kindly hosted a *braai* to introduce me to the neighbours. The occasion stretched my tolerance to extremes.

Braaivleis is the Afrikaans word for roasted meat and a *braai* is a barbecue that is often undertaken using a split 45 gallon drum half filled with coals glowing below a staggering assortment of sausages and game meats. The food at the Beit's was incredible and I had my first taste of kudu, wild pig and a host of exotic fruits. The difficulty was the humans.

The Portuguese family seemed very pleasant but spoke little English, which limited conversation. My doubts about the upcoming eight-month field season began when Allen asked, "Have you found Jesus?" There are two obvious ways to answer this question, "Yes," in which case you can smile beatifically at each other and talk about how wonderful your life has been since the discovery, or "I didn't know he was missing." In my case, the first answer very quickly becomes an obviously blatant lie and the second usually promotes a deeply embarrassing silence, which is sometimes okay, but not when you are trying to fit in and get on with your neighbours.

In a panic, I glanced at Allen's horrifyingly skinny wife who merely beamed at me encouragingly. "Not really," I mumbled, which is actually a worse answer than the other two as it is always taken as a request to be introduced to Jesus. Fortunately, I was rescued by Mr. Beit whom, I suspect, had spotted the theological swamp I was wading into. He introduced me to the offerings on the *braai* and told me that his father had come north with the pioneer column in 1890.

After Cecil Rhodes got his agreement from Lobengula, he decided to invade Matabeleland. He was told he would need 2,500 men and a million pounds. In an incident that could be from a Henry Rider Haggard novel, an adventurer called Frank Johnson offered to take the country in nine months with 250 men and for only 87,500 pounds. In exchange for participating, each volunteer would receive 3,000 acres of land and 15 mining claims. Johnson added 180 civilian colonists, and with almost 100 wagons, 250 cattle, and armed with Martini-Henry rifles, field guns and Maxim machine guns, the pioneer column headed north.

The first thing that happened to Mr. Beit senior once he settled was that his oxen were stolen. The authorities refused to do anything about it since the Ndebele were preparing for war and Lobengula's *Impis* (regiments) were all around. Mr. Beit set off on his own and tracked his cattle to an *Impi*. Boldly, he asked to speak with the *Induna* (commander). As they were talking a young warrior began waving his *assegai* (spear) and shouting that they should kill the white man. Mr. Beit tripped him as he ran past, grabbed his *assegai* and hurled it away. He then proceeded to beat the warrior at boxing, which the Ndebele knew nothing about. When the warrior was knocked out, the crowd laughed and cheered and Mr. Beit was given his cattle back.

The younger Mr. Beit once asked his father why he had taken such as risk. His father answered that he had no choice, the oxen were all he owned in the world so he had to get them back. Since I had shown an interest in this story, Mr. Beit took me to meet his wife's father, Mr. van der Merwe, who was 83 and whose father had fought against the British in the Boer War.

I spent the rest of the evening listening to Mr. van der Merwe's stories. As a child during the Boer War he had been in a British concentration camp, and as a young man he had bought illegal diamonds, fought for the British in the First World War and been gassed at Arras, and was the first person to drive a motor car across the virtually trackless wastes from Hwange to Bulawayo—a distance of nearly 400 kms that took him three days and nights in an eight cylinder Chevrolet Series D.

My favourite story was from when he worked in the diamond mines in South Africa. An African worker approached him. "Do you want to buy some diamonds, Boss? Very good stones."

"Let's see them," Mr. van der Merwe said.

The man produced a small sack filled with diamonds. Mr. van der Merwe knew something about diamonds and reckoned that the ones he was shown were good blue/white stones worth about 6,000 pounds, which is several hundred thousand pounds in today's money. "How much do you want for them?" he asked.

"Twenty pounds, Boss."

"I'll give you twelve."

"Okay, Boss."

Since a transaction like this could earn seven years in prison, Mr. van der Merwe suggested they meet down the road to do the deal. They met and the worker produced the hide bag and opened it to show that the diamonds were the same as before.

Mr. van der Merwe was nervous and watched the bag very carefully since he'd heard stories of people being stabbed and the attacker running off with the diamonds and the money. He held out his right hand. "You give me the diamonds. The money is in the top pocket of my coat." The worker handed over the bag, reached into the pocket and took out the twelve pounds. "Thanks, Boss," he said and left.

Mr. van der Merwe went back to his house to proudly show his partner his score. When he tipped the bag out onto the table, all that tumbled out were a collection of plain pebbles. Somehow, even though he was being watched closely the whole time, the man had switched bags. The pair laughed and went to a nearby bar to tell the story and drink beer.

Listening to Mr. van der Merwe, I realized that his stories and the way he told them were very like Jim's stories of India. Of course, Mr. van der Merwe held views on the relative intelligence and worth of the different races that were shocking and to which my father would never have ascribed, but they had come from the same time period in similar imperial worlds.

After Mr. van der Merwe had retired to his bungalow, I found out another similarity with Jim. My dad had once told me that it was the women in India who tended to hold the most overt and harsh racist views. This was not necessarily because they were more inherently racist, but rather because of the isolated, privileged world they inhabited. The men worked with the local population and, for the most part, while there was no doubt who was in charge, there was often a level of understanding and respect between the races.

I kept a field diary in 1976 and, on day 2 at the Beit's farm, I wrote, "They're nice enough people—very kind. He's fairly moderate by Rhodesian standards but she would make Hitler proud. Believes in space men in the past (cf. Erich von Daniken), and that the Roman Empire fell because it had become contaminated by African genes!! I've had to bite my tongue several times." I close that day's entry with a wish to spend some simpler time the next day, "Hope to start looking at rocks tomorrow."

A counterpoint to Mr, van der Merwe, although still a character that Kipling and Rider Haggard would have recognized, was Jackson Mpofu, the family retainer to my sister and her husband at the mission school in Nyamandhlovu. Jackson was of significant yet indeterminate age although he claimed to have been born when Lobengula was king, which would have put him into his eighties when I knew him. He had two wives and several cattle, which made him a relatively wealthy man amongst the local villagers.

Jen taught at the school while I was doing field work and, to fill some time in the three hours each evening when the generator supplied electricity, sewed me a three piece suit out of one of the few materials available—pink denim (remember this was the mid-seventies!). When I came back from field work for a few days, I put on the suit and paraded around. Much impressed by Jen's prowess, Jackson cornered me in the kitchen that evening.

"She is very good," Jackson said admiringly as he felt the lapels of my new clothing.

"Yes, she is," I agreed.

Jackson leaned closer conspiratorially. "How much did you pay for her?"

"Nothing, Jackson," I said.

"No. No." Jackson said with an expression that told me he could see through my coyness. He went on to tell me how many goats and cattle he had to pay in bride-price for each of his wives. His great wife had been more expensive because she had stronger legs and was better at working in the fields. Convinced that his man-to-man confession would elicit the truth from me, Jackson then repeated his question.

My answer was the same. "There is no bride-price in Britain."

Unable to comprehend such a foreign and obviously stupid concept, Jackson pressed. Eventually, I said seventy pence, which was the cost of registering a marriage licence.

Jackson grinned. Now he was getting somewhere. "Seventy pence and two cows?" he asked, thinking that this seemed a fair price. "No, Jackson. No cows, no goats, just seventy pence. All wives are that price in Britain." This last statement was a mistake because I could instantly see Jackson working out how many wives he could afford if only he could get his cows and goats to Britain. Why didn't he come with us when we went back to Britain, he suggested. To try and distract him, I said that Jen and I were probably not going back to Britain but to Canada and he wouldn't like it there because it was cold. Jackson huffed dismissively and said he didn't mind the cold. Now, the concept of cold a mere seventeen degrees south of the equator is not the same as the concept of cold in Canada. Eventually, I opened the door to the freezer above the refrigerator, pointed to the thick layer of ice built up there and said, "cold like that." I don't think he believed me, but the idea of accompanying us to the magical land of cheap wives was quietly dropped.

Christmas in Rhodesia was different. In mid-summer only the staunchest expatriate Anglophile even considered a midday meal of roast turkey, stuffing, dumplings and Christmas pudding. Everyone else settled for a light evening salad and fond reminiscences of childhood snowfalls. Santa Claus still showed up at parties to excite children but more likely than not was wearing safari shorts and a bush hat rather than a false beard and pillow-stuffed red suit, although this sartorial inexactitude never seems to bother the small beneficiaries of his largesse.

For the Christmas of 1976 it was decided to add to the rather surreal festivities by giving Jackson new teeth. As long as anyone could remember, Jackson had been toothless except for one irregular incisor hanging from his upper jaw. A set of false teeth would make an appropriate present and greatly add to his culinary choices. By the time I arrived for the holiday, Jackson had been measured by the dentist in Bulawayo and the faithful old fang ground down. On Christmas Eve he was taken to town and the long-awaited teeth collected.

The anticipation of Jackson's return threatened to overshadow the festivity which had prompted the gift. Many of his ancient cronies were camped out on the lawn behind the kitchen, having trekked several miles through the bush to be there. An expectant hush fell over them as the old Land Rover wheezed onto the mission and came to a stop. With the agonizingly slow pomp of a visiting dignitary, Jackson descended. His face sported a smile that any Miss World candidate would kill for.

Like a true superstar, Jackson kept his audience waiting while he came into the house to show the rest of us his rejuvenated jaws. When my turn came, I haltingly complimented him on his new appearance. With an accompaniment of lecherous grins, I was treated to a series of stories of how these teeth would make him a new man. Eventually, the teeth were extracted for closer examination. I nodded politely as they were put through their paces; biting, chewing and clacking in the empty air before me. Finally, they were offered for the ultimate test, a personal trial. I declined, explaining hurriedly that I still had teeth of my own which, while not as good as these, precluded the addition of any more. This satisfied the owner, who continued his regal progress.

Everyone was pleased with the success of the gift and separated to complete arrangements for the following day. I strolled through to the kitchen in the hope of seeing some local colour when the teeth were presented for peer approval on the back lawn. What I witnessed was still in my mind when I sat down to my turkey salad twenty-four hours later. Jackson was already there, squatting with a toothless smile before an admiring semi-circle of equally toothless cronies. His joy was unalloyed as his new teeth were passed around, examined from every angle, tapped against rocks to prove their strength and, for the decisive evaluation, tried out in sequence around the circle with no one showing a hint of my squeamish sensibilities.

Interlude

Tyrannosaurus Tooth

seventy
five
million
years
of sleep
waiting
for this day's sun
and my transient touch
your fearsome edge no longer
tears through flesh past bones
now turned to stone
puny I will never run in fear
from your remembered victories
slavering and bloody
instead I'll sit you on my desk
a harmless curio for idle chatter
never suspecting your wish
to tear out my throat
for disturbing
seventy
five
million
years
of sleep

Part 5

The Birth and Death of a Geologist

dusty prairie backroad
a funeral procession past
trapped fossil bones

Geology

In the fall of 1964 I was thirteen, terminally shy and beginning my second year at the Grammar. It was a year when *Goldfinger* played at the local cinemas, Jean Paul Sartre won and declined the Nobel Prize for Literature and Martin Luther King Jr. won the same prize for Peace, and the U.S. Surgeon General affirmed that smoking cigarettes caused cancer. The Rolling Stones were taking America by storm, not yet looking as if they had been freeze-dried. It was also the year that I discovered Geology.

It all began because my worst nightmare seemed about to come true. Our English teacher had given the class a project—we each had to stand in front of our twenty-five or so fellow students and talk for five minutes. For the socially comfortable kids it was a piece of cake. For me, a self-conscious introvert who habitually spent most of my energy on making myself invisible, the five minutes loomed like an eternity.

To say I was unhappy at the prospect of my upcoming speech would be a gross understatement. I was petrified. I lost sleep, lying wide-eyed and struggling to think of something I could talk about for such a vast length of time. I wrote speeches and read them out, only to discover with horror that they lasted thirty seconds and left four and a half minutes for the class to laugh at me. I considered running away to sea or feigning leprosy, but I sensed that nothing would work. They would catch me and stand me up to speak anyway.

The day loomed so large in my imagination that I could see nothing past it. Life was coming to an end and that seemed a shame so early with so much yet to experience. Then Tom, who lived in Bridge of Weir a small town about eight kilometres away from my end of Paisley and was also something of an outcast because of his geographic inability to participate in the after-school tribal rituals, told me about a place where there were seashells in the rock. I was convinced he was lying to me, trying to get me to believe an absurdity so that I could be ridiculed, but he seemed so genuine that I got directions to this mysterious place to check it out.

That Sunday I cycled out and found it. The quarry was not large but it was old, dating back to the fifteenth century when local monks had dug coal there. More recently, a neighbouring tannery had used it to dump waste and it was half full of thick, black, utterly disgusting sludge.

The smell hit me as soon as I dumped my bike at the crest of the ridge at the quarry entrance. It was rotten eggs, and so powerful that I gagged.

What I should have done at that point was get on my bike, pedal home and stumble through a presentation on my Scotties, Meg and Mac. I didn't for two reasons. First, the odour didn't scare me as it should have. It was familiar from the stink bombs that were occasionally let off in the school corridors and I didn't know it was dangerous. It was only many years later that I learned the smell belonged to hydrogen sulphide, a by-product of the chemicals used to break down the hair on animal hides, and discovered that hydrogen sulphide is comparable in toxicity to hydrogen cyanide—"even a low level of exposure to the gas induces headaches and nausea, as well as possible damage to the eye. At higher levels, death can rapidly set in and countless deaths attributable to the buildup of sulphide in sewage systems have been recorded."

The second reason that I didn't get back on my bike and race home was a small piece of ribbed rock that stuck out of a boulder beside my left foot. I set to with my father's claw hammer and, after a few minutes' work, held a fragment of what was obviously a sea shell in my hand.

That was it! I was sold. The smell vanished from my consciousness, and I spent the rest of the day scrambling around the edge of the muck, uncovering impossible wonders from the quarry walls. My prize was a complete bivalve looking rather like a fat, ribbed clam. (I still have it and for fellow amateur palaeontological geeks it is a very nice specimen of *Sanguinolites costellatus* from the Visean Stage of the Lower Carboniferous between 330.9 and 346.7 million years ago). It took me at least an hour of careful chipping to extract the fossil, which promptly dropped into the tannery waste. Of course, I wasn't going to let it escape, so I plunged my arm into the filth up to my elbow and, trying not to vomit at the smell or wonder what horrors might lurk in the thick slimy black ooze, felt around. I retrieved it and cycled home, happy and stinking. I purchased a small book, *FOSSILS. A Guide to Prehistoric Life, A Little Guide in Colour*. The 481 rather garish yet surprisingly accurate illustrations were no help in identifying my new finds, but they gave me a view of a vanished world that it was in my power to visit, and the introduction presented a decent overview of the geological eras and their remarkable inhabitants. I still have the tattered copy with the pictures of the ten items essential for the serious fossil collector carefully ticked off as they were acquired.

In the short term, I learned the value of good props in a presentation. My classmates were as fascinated as I had been and, after a few introductory sentences, they were so engrossed in the treasures I passed around that they completely forgot to humiliate me.

In the longer term, armed with a proper rock hammer and the much more detailed 1966 edition of the British Museum's *British Palaeozoic Fossils* (price Twelve Shillings and Sixpence), I ventured ever farther afield collecting and labelling a wide variety of interesting examples of long-dead creatures. I have continued this activity wherever I have lived and, on occasion, had to lie to movers about the contents of a growing number of suspiciously heavy boxes which now sit in my garage.

For my degree in Geology, I took the "soft rock" option. This meant that I studied sedimentary rocks—sandstone, shale, limestone, etc.—as opposed to the "hard rock" students who revelled in igneous rocks, which I considered boring, or metamorphic rocks, which I thought unnecessarily complicated. Of course, I loved the fossils I came across, but I was also fascinated by the sedimentary structures. I could gaze at a row of bumps and be awestruck by the fact that they had been caused by waves passing over a sandy shore millions of years before. It was very interesting but utterly useless as a preparation for my first day of field work in Rhodesia.

With my field assistant, Leonard, I drove from the Beit's farm down to the Ncema dam where the air photographs showed good exposures of the rocks I was to map. After an hour I was close to tears. I could see several different types of rock, but I had no idea what they were. All were varying shades of green and there wasn't a fossil for miles, or millions of years, in any direction. I knew I was standing on part of the Bulawayo Greenstone Belt and that the rocks had probably once been lavas, but they were around three billion years old and had been bent, squashed and cooked to such a degree that they looked nothing like the civilized lavas I had seen on university field trips. Then I spotted a pillow.

When molten lava is extruded under water there is much bubbling and hissing and the lava forms large bulbous structures that some early geologists thought resembled pillows. The ones I saw that morning confirmed that I was dealing with ancient lavas and told me that the the lavas had been extruded under water and showed me, even though the rocks had been tilted nearly vertically, what had been the top of the lava flow. I was reassured that I wouldn't have to return to the office and admit to being a bad geologist whom they had hired under false pretences—I could do this.

For the following eight months, I mapped, measured, sampled and learned. I classified the rocks I came across and tried to place them in a rational sequence. Despite the incredible age of the rocks and the torture that they had undergone, I even found some delicate, beautifully recognizable sedimentary structures in the fine ash flows from some primordial volcanic event. Today, when I read over the reports that I wrote at the time, I am amazed at the level of obscure knowledge that I acquired, but it wasn't all plain sailing.

Working as a field geologist in Africa had its moments: hairy spiders the size of my palm scorpions lurking underneath rocks that I wanted to look at, four-foot-long Mozambique spitting cobras rearing up as I rounded a boulder (they can spit venom into your eyes from ten feet away), and kudu large enough to crush a Land Rover appearing from nowhere beside a dirt road. Of course, not all the wildlife was deadly, much of it was beautiful and harmless. In the field I had a pet snake called Humphrey and a tortoise called Hieronymus. Humphrey died and Hieronymus escaped, although I was told later that tortoises are considered a delicacy, so he may not have simply run off. However, while I was struggling to understand the complexities of ancient green rocks, the faunal dangers came primarily from my own species.

As the security situation deteriorated, the Geological Survey introduced rules designed to protect its enthusiastic young geologists. We were told to report to the local police camp in the morning when we set out and in the afternoon when we returned. We were told not to drive at dusk because that's when most attacks occurred, and to avoid driving on dirt roads as much as possible because of the danger of land mines. The last injunction was impossible since almost every road in the map area was dirt, but I did look out very carefully for any disturbed ground.

The field work progressed well and by early July I had finished the Essexvale map sheet and was looking at the southern (Matopos) map sheet for a likely farm to set up my camp. I'd selected one about ten miles to the south and was planning to visit the farmer to see if I could set up there when he was killed and his wife seriously wounded in an attack. They had been in the farm store one evening when a couple of men in camouflage fatigues walked in and opened fire with AK47s. Suddenly there were heavily armed soldiers everywhere, manning road blocks and escorting protected convoys on the drive into Bulawayo. I decided to abandon plans to map the Matopos sheet and instead work the northern map sheet, which was closer to town. The survey protested that it would use more petrol at a time of severe rationing. I was firm, resisting the temptation to point out that a little extra petrol would be better than having one of their precious Land Rovers and a geologist riddled with bullet holes. They sent me the maps and air photographs for the northerly sheet.

The Beits were most helpful, giving me a room in the house to sleep in since my caravan was not included within the wire fencing designed to prevent grenades being lobbed into the house. Mr. Beit also offered me a weapon. The choice was between a small revolver and a Second World War vintage .303 rifle. There were a couple of aspects that had to be considered in making this decision. The survey said that the revolver was the best choice since it could be concealed and therefore the sight of it would not antagonize the local population. However, I went for the .303, rationalizing that if someone was going to shoot at me I would probably not see them and would have to count on them missing with the first shot. Then I would be hiding behind a rock or a tree and would much rather have a rifle to fire back with. Fortunately, no one ever shot at me, but the rifle did get me into trouble.

On September 13, I returned from a long traverse in the northern area to have Allen tell me that the police post in Essexvale had received a call from a farmer, Mr. Fisher, accusing me of poaching on his land. Allen gave me the farmer's number and I nervously called him.

"Hello Mr. Fisher," I began. "My name's John Wilson and I work for the Geological Survey. I believe that I was on your land today and that there has been some kind of misunderstanding."

My hopes for a civilized conversation to clear up the misunderstanding vanished the moment I heard his gruff voice. "What were you doing there?"

"I'm mapping the area…," I managed before he cut me off.

"It's been surveyed."

"Yes," I said, deciding not to explain the difference between surveying and geological mapping, "but that was back in the 1930s. It's being remapped because…"

"I know that. The man who surveyed it stayed with me. Why didn't you come to the farmhouse?"

By now I built up a fairly good collection of reasons why I didn't want to go to the farmhouse, but I stayed with the conciliatory approach. "I'm sorry I came onto your land. It's marked on my map as three farms and I couldn't see your house from where I parked."

"That's nonsense. It's always been one farm. I know because my father surveyed it. You had a gun and you shot something."

"I carry a gun but I didn't shoot anything and…"

"You shot something and then reversed away."

I felt the conversation spinning out of control. "I can prove I didn't fire the gun. I borrowed…"

"You shot something and drove up and down to hide your *spoor* (tracks). My boys heard the shot."

"Mr. Fisher, I'm staying on the Beit farm down by the Ncema dam. I borrowed the gun from Mr. Beit. He knows how much ammunition he gave me and I still have that amount of ammunition." Proudly, I thought that I had finally managed to say enough to clear the matter up. I was wrong.

"My boys heard a shot and you drove up and down to hide your spoor. I chased you."

I took a deep breath and, clenching the phone tighter, tried once more, "Mr. Fisher. I did not fire a shot and I can prove it. I did not drive up and down to hide my *spoor*. And if you chased me, I never saw you."

"Funny map you've got that shows my farm as three."

The sense that the ground was moving from under me created the feeling that I was somehow caught in a nightmarish loop. "It's not a very new map," I stumbled on weakly.

"It's always been one farm. Fine surveyor who doesn't know where he is."

I swallowed hard and attempted to break out of the loop. "Will you be in tomorrow morning?"

"Why?"

"I'd like to come round and sort this out." It suddenly struck me that there was something on Mr. Fisher's farm that I wanted to shoot.

"Don't bother. I know you're here."

"I'll be in the area for a while and I'd like to drop in."

"You don't need to. I know you're here."

I bared the nape of my neck once more. "I'm sorry for any inconvenience I may have caused. I didn't realize I was on your land."

"Fine surveyor doesn't know where he is."

Dreading the following day, I decided to finish the conversation. "Well, I am sorry, Mr. Fisher. I hope to see you tomorrow. Goodbye."

The next day I did go and see Mr. Fisher. He had calmed down and was just normally gruff. He invited me in and told me about meeting Amm in the 30s and how his father had surveyed the farm in 1897. The most difficult part of the meeting was that, without asking me, he ordered his servant to bring me a cup of coffee. I have always hated the taste of coffee but there was no way I was going to turn it down. Fortunately, it wasn't strong and I forced half a cup down.

The next day, not wishing there to be any more confusion, I visited the farm beside Mr. Fisher's. When I got out of the Land Rover I noticed that there was a dog tied up by the front porch. It was a Rhodesian Ridgeback and many of the local farmers owned one or two. I took a step towards the house and something about the way the dog was looking at me made me stop. I was standing wondering how long and strong the chain tying it to the porch was when the house door opened.

"What do you want?" The old farmer demanded.

"Sorry," I said, thinking that I would cede dominance immediately. "I was a bit nervous about your dog. I didn't want to come up to the door."

"Just as well. He'd have had your leg off."

The conversation didn't improve much after that and I began to realize that, despite all their fundamentalist Christianity and racism, I had been lucky to find the Beits. I explained who I was and what I was doing and he grunted at appropriate moments. He ended by warning me not to shoot anything. I left at least relieved that he hadn't invited me in for coffee.

Over the course of the season, the letters from the office increasingly contained notice that yet one more member of the survey was resigning and leaving the country. I had plans to leave early the following year after I had written my report of the field season, but I had a backup. The government had a habit of announcing on the morning news that the law regarding military service had changed as of midnight the night before. Both Jen, who was teaching at St. James, and I listened to the news every morning. If the announcement came that I was suddenly liable for military service, the plan was that I would get in the Land Rover, drive to St James to pick up Jen and head into Botswana. It wasn't a great plan but it was reinforced by the news of what happened to my survey colleague, Jim.

Jim's field area was in the east of the country, too close to the particularly unsettled border area with Mozambique. One evening he was driving his Land Rover back to camp late in the day. He came over a rise and saw a group of men beside the road kicking a soccer ball around. Jim was suspicious, why play soccer by the road and why were they moving so stiffly? However, there was little he could do as the road was too narrow to allow a three-point turn. Determining that the safest course was to pass the group as quickly as possible, Jim gunned the Land Rover's engine.

Gunning a Series II Land Rover's engine, especially if it has been subject to many years of use, doesn't do much, but partly because he was going downhill and partly because he was urging his vehicle on loudly Jim was travelling at a fair speed as he reached the men. To his horror, he saw that the reason they had been moving so stiffly was that they were carrying AK-47s beside their bodies. These they now raised and opened fire on the speeding vehicle.

Jim hunched forward over the wheel and began rocking back and forth to try and make his vehicle move faster. Glass shattered and bullets flew through the door and into the dashboard. A bullet or a piece of Land Rover tore a gouge in Jim's hand but then he was past, bouncing crazily along the road and sweating profusely.

After several kilometres, Jim relaxed enough to be able to loosen his hands from the steering wheel. Sighing with relief, he slowed and leaned back, and back, and back. The entire back of his seat had been shot away.

If Jim hadn't been leaning forward to encourage the old Land Rover to greater effort…

I survived the field season and the months of research and writing up back in Salisbury. I resigned and acquired a piece of paper that stated that the Rhodesian army didn't want me at the moment and that I could leave the country.

There was, however, another issue. I had been earning good money with the survey but it was a sum that I wouldn't be allowed to take out of the country and, even if I could, it was in a currency that was recognized nowhere else. The news was filled with items about people trying to circumvent the restrictions by smuggling valuables, from precious stones to race horses, out of the country. I was too much of a coward to attempt that, but there was an alternative.

The travel agent, Thomas Cook, had an office in Salisbury. It had no official existence and could book no travel outside the country, but it could pass orders down to be filled in the Johannesburg office. I was by no means certain where we were going or what we were going to do after we escaped, but there was a chance that we might go to Canada where Dorothy lived on the west coast. So I booked tickets on the boat back to the UK, open tickets for flights from the UK to Montreal and then the train across Canada.

Finally, we boarded the train in Bulawayo and headed for the border. Oddly, despite the effect they had had on my nerves, I had never set eyes on a guerrilla fighter until, with a sigh of relief as the train chugged into Botswana, I began to see young Africans in camouflage kit and carrying AK 47 rifles lounging beside the tracks and waving cheerfully as we passed. It was a strange war.

Interlude

Words of War

OUR wars are just.
WE are right.
GOD is on OUR side.
WE must win!

WE have reporting guidelines and press briefings.
THEY censor news and spout propaganda.

OUR bombs are environmentally sensitive.
THEIRS pollute indiscriminately.

OUR rockets are precise and humane.
THEIRS are random and poisonous.

OUR leaders are assured statesmen.
THEIRS are demented evil tyrants.

WE attack pre-emptively.
THEY launch sneak attacks without provocation.

OUR dead babies are innocent civilian casualties.
THEIRS are unavoidable collateral damage.

WE are professional, cautious, resolute, brave, desert rats.
THEY are brainwashed, cowardly, ruthless, fanatical, mad dogs.

WE take out, eliminate, neutralize, attrit.
THEY destroy and
kill
kill
kill.

OUR wars are just.
WE are right.
EUPHEMISM is on OUR side.
THEY must lose!

Dicing with Death

As an author I have had my share of paper cuts, stubbed my toe on desk legs and, a couple of times, come perilously close to falling off my chair. In the real world outside my imagination I have probably experienced an average number of risks: the odd minor vehicle accident and one time when a deer very nearly came through the windshield of my car at seventy kilometres per hour, but after I managed to escape war-torn Rhodesia without being ambushed, blown to pieces by a land mine or conscripted into the army, I assumed that my life would settle into a safe pattern. I was wrong.

While in Rhodesia, I saw Canada as close to the safest place to live, so I attempted to begin the process of emigrating there. Since there was no Canadian representative in the country, this involved working through the embassy in Italy. This slowed things down considerably, but progress was being made, until a group of Canadian racists intervened. Thinking, for some unfathomable reason, that the white refugees from an obviously doomed Smith regime situated within spitting distance of the equator would flock to the prairies of Alberta and the mountains of interior British Columbia, they put forward the idea that the Canadian government should set up a homeland for them. Predictably, there was outrage and Prime Minister Pierre Trudeau had to stand up and make a categorical statement that Canada would accept no racist white Rhodesians. A polite letter arrived from Rome shortly afterwards informing me that no further progress could be made on my application. In May of 1977, I headed back to Scotland and began the process again.

From Rhodesia, I took away a camera, a set of local crockery, a soapstone chess set, various knick-knacks and a minor compulsion to draw the curtains in any room I am in when it gets dark enough outside to warrant turning on a light inside. When I was staying with the Beits in 1976 and the security situation was rapidly deteriorating, it was drummed into me that with a light on in the living room someone would be able to hide in the dark outside and see in. Thus, while the fence around the house would probably prevent a grenade being thrown in it would not prevent someone shooting in. So, as dusk fell, I learned to stand behind the curtains and close them from the side before illuminating anything inside. Now, more than forty years later, I live in a small village on Vancouver Island. Arguably, major earthquakes notwithstanding, I am in one of the safest places on the planet, and yet if I am sitting reading in my living room of an evening and the curtains are open, I keep catching myself glancing nervously outside into the dark.

Back in Scotland, I worked on a multi-disciplinary study of Arthur's Seat in Edinburgh. Arthur's Seat, named for the legend that it was the site of King Arthur's Camelot, is the glacially-carved remnant of a 340 million year old volcano. While I studied the erosional processes at work on the hill, Jen and I talked about what we would do and where we would go next. Australia was a possibility until I discovered that they were restricting immigration to trades and geology didn't apply. Then a job was posted for the Geological Survey in Edinburgh. They were asking for a recent graduate, preferably with some survey experience. I fitted the bill perfectly. Unfortunately, things were not booming in Geology in the UK so I wasn't alone in my application. Almost 700 of my out-of-work colleagues applied, giving the Survey the choice of Phd graduates for an entry-level position. Fortunately, Geology was booming in Western Canada, so we scraped enough points together to become new Canadians.

At the end of November 1977, Jen and I, with $47.00 in our pocket, three nights paid for in the Windsor Hotel and a train ticket to the West Coast where my sister lived, arrived in Montreal in the midst of a bus strike. We survived huge icicles crashing down from roofs, gorged on one

Big Mac a day and splurged on an afternoon show of the first *Star Wars* movie. All our friends in the UK would have been jealous of the last item since—although *Star Wars* had been running in Canada since June, it was not scheduled to open in Britain for another month. Staggered launch times were common in the pre-internet days, but the lack of technology also meant that we couldn't contact our friends and gloat.

The train was a luxury until we reached Winnipeg. There we stopped for an hour or so and, since it was a glorious sunny day, we decided on a stroll. Of course, what you can't tell through the double glazed window of a sealed train compartment is what the temperature is. Totally unprepared for -25 Celsius, we lasted about ten minutes on the platform before my beard froze up and we scuttled back to our heated carriage feeling a certain annoyance at Australia's immigration policy.

That winter we stayed with Dorothy in Courtney on Vancouver Island. It was a difficult few months. Dorothy had four teenage kids and she and Alan had just separated. We helped where we could—Jen got a job at a local restaurant and I took Dorothy's sons out to ice-hockey practice at ungodly hours of the morning. The situation wasn't helped when, in February, Courtney suffered a record snowfall (54 cm in 24 hours). Things improved in the spring when we moved to Calgary and I began geological work on a third continent.

The main thing I miss from my fifteen years as a geologist is the field work. I don't miss field work in a war zone (although my most frightening moment in Rhodesia was walking round a rock and coming face to hood with an angry Mozambique spitting cobra), but I do miss the preparatory research, interacting with the rocks and the chance to go to some out-of-the-way place that I would never otherwise get a chance to visit. Yet, the times I have come closest to death have been on field work in "safe" Canada.

Every Canadian geologist has an armful of bear stories and takes great pride in embellishing them for overseas visitors. In my fieldwork days I had my share of frights walking around a corner in the trail and freezing as a hundred or so kilograms of Black Bear, *Ursus americanus*, lumbered away, huffing in annoyance at being disturbed, but my best bear story doesn't come from field work.

In the 80s, four of us had been hiking in Banff National Park. It was a pleasantly warm day and we were strolling down a beautiful, wide valley towards the highway, looking forward to a cold beer back in town. I was in front and as I came out of the trees into a football-field sized clearing I saw something move at the edge of the trees across the open space. I stopped and watched as the "something" stood up and, endlessly it seemed, kept standing up. This wasn't a shy black bear but *Ursus arctos horribilis*, a full-grown grizzly. Jen came up beside me. "Turn around and go back," I said, because now I could see the bear clearly and also the two cubs at its feet. You're not supposed to run away from a bear because that will get it excited, but it's very difficult not to run when your legs are screaming at you to do exactly that. One of our party listened to her limbs and disappeared through the trees. The rest of us walked briskly. After crossing the next big clearing I stopped and looked back. The bear appeared and had another look at me. She wasn't chasing us, simply shepherding us away from her family.

We caught up with our fourth member and decided on another way back to the vehicles. Crossing a small creek we met a fisherman returning with several good trout in his backpack. We told him our experience and he seemed unconcerned. Realistically he was right, we weren't in any danger but we did make sure to keep the fisherman with his pack full of fresh fish between ourselves and the bear.

Notwithstanding all the bear moments that I dramatically elaborated for the entertainment of visitors and my kids, my most dangerous moments didn't involve encounters with wildlife.

The first life-threatening occasion was probably the closest I have come and was early in my new life. A colleague and I were doing helicopter field work along the McLeod River in Alberta. This involved flying low along the river at the bottom of the deeply incised valley, with the pilot swinging the helicopter from side to side as we searched the eroded sides of the valley for the telltale black smudges of eroding coal seams. Suddenly the pilot swore and, leaving my stomach hovering in confusion above the water, the helicopter lurched viciously to the side and up. Once we had all calmed down, we flew back to where we had been about to fly under the road bridge that crossed the top of the valley and the pilot pointed out a thick steel hawser hanging from the bridge almost to the river. We had been heading straight for it and missed it by a matter of feet. Had the pilot not seen it in time, that would have been the end of my field work.

The hawser from the bridge was only frightening in retrospect. In the moment, there was neither the time nor awareness to feel fear and real fear requires both those elements. On another occasion during that same spell of field work I had too much time to realize what was happening.

I was driving a three-quarter-ton pickup truck along a dirt road south of Hinton to ground check some locations on the McLeod River. The road had been recently graded and gravel added to it. On a corner that I attempted to take too fast, the back end of the truck slid. Before I had a chance to regain control, the sideways moving wheel hit the ridge of earth pushed up by the grader and the truck flipped. It left the ground, turned over, landed on its roof, bouncing once more and landed back on its wheels, leaving its canopy upside down beside it with all the field equipment lying in it, perfectly arranged but inverted. I was shaken but again had had little chance to feel fear. What I had felt was that strange slowing down of time that occurs in a crisis when the brain frantically tries to absorb every fragment of stimulus in case it might be useful. The sudden influx of so much information makes time seem too slow as the brain struggles to process it all. My abiding image of that experience is hanging from the seat belt and the truck landed on its roof, looking with interest through the windshield and thinking, "So this is what the world looks like upside down."

In the early 1980s I was working for the Alberta Geological Survey, collecting and describing abandoned exploration drill cores from the area south of Lake Athabasca in the northeast corner of the province. It's a beautiful part of the country, dotted with Saharan-like sand dunes and crystal clear lakes. Unfortunately, the summer I was there was remarkably dry and large wildfires had raged across thousands of hectares of northern Saskatchewan and Alberta. I had already lost two irreplaceable drill cores to a fire that had left nothing but blackened piles of rock.

I had saved the most promising location for last. It was an old camp by a lake with beautiful sandy beaches. There was a well-constructed hut where my field assistant and I could sleep (it had been built by the drillers as a sauna by the beach), and piles of well-labelled, organized drill cores. There was even a table to lay the cores out on for description. We both thought this was fieldwork heaven and, after the float plane dropped us off, we spent a couple of days working in the shade of some stunted pines and falling into the refreshingly cold waters of the lake whenever it became too hot. The sky was unremittingly blue and the only wildlife we saw were the northern pike that swam over the sandy bottom of the lake to check out the beer bottles we placed there to cool.

It was idyllic and the work went well. On the afternoon of the third day, we radioed for the float plane to pick us up the following morning. At dusk we sat on the dock (yes, the exploration company had even supplied a dock for us), drank our last two cold beers and watched a lightning storm move along the northern horizon. There was no rain but several bolts of lightning grounded spectacularly in the bush across the lake.

We were just about to turn in when I noticed that, although the storm had moved off, there was still an odd glow in the sky. We sat back down. The glow got brighter, and redder. One of the lightning hits had started a fire. It was a long way off, but there was a wind, and it was blowing toward us.

So how far away was the fire, we wondered? I had read somewhere that the horizon at sea, if you are standing on the deck of a smallish ship, is about ten kilometres away. The land was flat to the north and we weren't on a ship but it seemed like a good enough ballpark figure. The fire was becoming clearer so maybe it was a good deal closer than ten kilometres, but I'm an optimist.

How fast was the fire moving? We had no idea. It was getting brighter and bigger but that might just be because dark was falling. There was a brisk breeze and the underbrush was tinder dry. I had read stories of fires moving faster than a man could run but those must be extreme circumstances, so on a pleasant evening such as this, probably no faster than walking speed.

How fast did I walk? I stood up very quickly on the edge of the rickety dock as I remembered calculating hiking times. A brisk walk covered four to five kilometres an hour. Even a slow walk would cover two to three kilometres per hour. The fire would be coming round our little lake by midnight.

Next question: how long could we stand up to our necks in a cold lake with pike nibbling our toes? Long enough, I hoped, because there was no point in wandering off into the darkness.

I sat back down and watched. For hours we watched the fire get closer and revised estimates of speed and arrival time. They were certainly all wildly inaccurate but there was no doubt that the flames were becoming more clearly defined, the smell of burning forest stronger and pieces of burned vegetation were now drifted over our heads. We watched, guessed and felt frighteningly helpless. There was no point in discussing options as there was only one. If the fire came around the lake, we would wait until the last possible minute, wade into the water and hope for the best. It was not much of a plan but it would save our lives, we hoped.

Around midnight, with the flames very close to our lake, which appeared much smaller now than when we had arrived, the wind dropped. Then it picked up again, but now against my left cheek, not full face. The fire began to move away to the east. We jumped up and danced on the end of the dock, and very nearly ended up in the lake anyway. Eventually, we tried to sleep, although without much success.

The float plane picked us up the next day and flew us to Fort Chipewyan where we watched the water bombers unsuccessfully attack our fire. At dusk, a larger plane picked us up to fly to Fort McMurray. We told the pilot the story of the fire and he offered to fly in close and take a look at it. From the air it was vast and the hot air currents tossed our plane about. There was no sign of our cozy cabin by the lake.

As part of my introduction to cultural life on the Alberta prairies, I took up hunting. Sometimes when I went out with a .22 calibre rifle or 20 gauge shotgun in search of grouse and rabbits, an activity that pleasantly resembled the pigeon shooting of my childhood. However, I also purchased an 8mm Mauser that had been manufactured in Spain in 1942 under licence from Nazi Germany. It was very similar to the .303 that had got me into so much trouble in Rhodesia. I took it deer hunting.

The hazards of deer hunting in Alberta don't stem from the hunted but from the other hunters. All game hunters were required to wear bright clothing, usually an orange jacket to make themselves visible and so less likely to be shot by accident by fellow hunters. I thought this a splendid idea but my confidence weakened after a couple of encounters with other hunters standing around pickup trucks in the middle of the day drinking cans of beer. I began to see a high level of visibility as less of a warning and more of a target and, since I had no wish to have survived wandering through the bush in war-torn Rhodesia only to be shot by an over-enthusiastic hunter in Canada, I was very careful.

As far as I am aware, I was never shot at in Alberta but meeting poor hunters did have one unpleasant consequence. A friend and I were driving along a track when we came upon a pair of hunters. They told us that they had wounded a deer and been tracking it but were fed up and were giving up. A basic hunting rule is that, if you wound an animal you do everything possible to find it and finish the job rather than letting it suffer. Unimpressed, we asked which way the wounded deer had been heading, locked the truck and set off. We soon found spots of blood and followed them to a clump of trees where an exhausted deer lay looking at us. I put it out of its misery and reached for my hunting knife to clean the carcass, only to realize that it was lying on the seat of the locked truck some two kms away. Now, gutting a deer is a messy business at the best of times. With a small Swiss Army knife, which was all I had, the experience beggars description.

Despite the occasional unpleasantness of deer hunting, the only injury I sustained was the solitary time I went moose hunting. My buddy

Campbell had friends who owned a farm in northern Alberta and we decided that we could stay a couple of nights with them and hunt some moose. It sounded like luxury compared to sleeping in a trailer where it was possible to awake in the morning with the entire length of one's sleeping bag solidly frozen to the wall beside the bunk. It also seemed to Jen like the ideal time to come and experience whatever attraction it was that pulled me away from home every fall. I tried to explain that hunting is mostly tedium and that moose enjoy hanging out in wet unpleasant places but Jen was adamant and so we set off.

The first day was as boring as expected and we were heading back through the twilight to the nice warm farm when Campbell stopped the truck and pointed off to the side. "What's that?" he asked.

It was within the allowable half hour of hunting time after sunset and it was cloudy and getting dark, so all I could make out was a shape that might have been a large rock. "I'll go and have a look," I said.

The only problem with my trusty old Mauser was that it didn't have a detachable clip for the bullets. Since, sensibly enough, it was illegal to carry a loaded weapon in a vehicle, the only rifle to hand was Campbell's which had a detachable clip. The other difference was that Campbell's gun had a scope, which mine didn't. I grabbed the rifle, loaded the clip, exited the truck and gradually worked my way closer to the mysterious object, which eventually resolved itself into a moose. I dropped to one knee, aimed and fired. The moose dropped. As I went closer and finished the job, Campbell worked the truck closer until the headlights illuminated the scene. He came over to me, congratulated me on the shot and suggested that I go and see Jen in the truck's cab as she was a bit upset. I went over and opened the truck door. The interior light went on, Jen looked over at me and let out an unearthly scream.

Never having used Campbell's rifle before, when I aimed at the moose, I put the scope too close to my eye. The rifle's kick pushed the scope back and gave me a nasty, crescent-shaped cut above my right eye. In the cold, I hadn't noticed that I had been cut but, being a head wound, it bled profusely. The blood streaming down my face was what elicited the scream from Jen. She told me afterwards that her first thought was that I had undertaken some obscure pagan ritual that involved bathing in the blood of your kill. I still have the scar from the moose's revenge and Jen never again asked to come hunting.

Interlude

Dying

I do not want to die
between two cold and antiseptic sheets
while nurses tend
the hum and beep of some machine
which tells them when the bed is free.
I do not want my body
to be washed and scrubbed and
made presentable
for relatives who'll say
"It's for the best he's gone."
or
"He had a good innings."

I want to go and sit beneath a tree
and feel the earth between my toes.
I want to breathe in gulps of air
unpurified,
and chew the stems
of unhygienic grass
while ants begin to plan
my journey home.
I want to die
with dirty fingernails.

Black Gold

None of the shocked survivors huddled in the only surviving building of the Granduc Copper Mine camp remembered hearing the avalanche approach, the buildings had simply exploded around them as tens of thousands of tons of snow crashed off the mountain above. It was the morning of February 18, 1965 and as the men awaited rescue they thought about their missing companions. One man, Eino Myllyla, was dug out alive 79 hours later but 28 men were dead in one of the worst avalanche disasters in Canadian history.

Many of the injured from the tragedy were ferried 35 kms south to the the town of Stewart at the head of the Portland Canal, a 114 km long fjord running inland from the Pacific Ocean and forming the boundary between southern Alaska and Canada. In 1965, Stewart was only sixty years old. It had grown up to service the gold exploration boom in the wake of the Klondike Stampede and boasted a population of 10,000 by 1910. At one time, as a consequence of the discovery of high-quality anthracite coal near Groundhog Mountain inland from the town, it was promoted as the Cardiff of the west and a major port facility and a railway across the mountains to the east were proposed. Plots of land in the coalfield were even sold. Unfortunately, because of its remoteness and the heavy winter snowfall, the Groundhog Coalfield was only accessible for a few weeks every summer. The grand schemes fell through, the promoters disappeared with whatever money they had pocketed and only a station and 24 kms of rail line were ever built. Almost overnight, Stewart became a ghost town. Despite a population low of only 17, the town survived and even had a minor boom when John Carpenter's movie *The Thing* was filmed on a nearby glacier in 1981. The population was some 1,400 when I was there doing field work but after the Granduc Mine closed in 1984 it slumped back to its present level of around 500.

Thirteen years after the tragedy, there was no trace left of the destroyed Granduc Mine camp when I flew over the site in the summer of 1978. Despite my near-death experience on the McLeod River, I was in Stewart to do several weeks helicopter work. It was a part of my first job in Canada, a summer position with the coal division of British Petroleum in Calgary who were taking another look at the Groundhog deposits. Despite being deafened in a helicopter for several hours each day, the work was spectacular, flying over 8,000 foot mountain ranges, glittering ice fields and walking ridges that surrounded basins so large that the parked helicopter below was virtually invisible.

Other than taking a cab the three kilometres into Hyder, Alaska, waving at the border guard as we passed, and getting "Hyderized" in the local American bar, there was not a lot to do in Stewart. Fortunately, we spent a couple of days with the local ranger who took us fishing.

While we were there, the salmon were spawning in ponds at the headwaters of the Naas River. Some of the ponds were so packed with fish that it was impossible to see the gravel on the bottom. With the approval of the ranger and the help of the helicopter pilot, who always carried fishing gear when flying, we took a number of these magnificent fish. The fish were frozen by the time we were ready to return to Calgary, so we loaded them and considerable quantities of ice into black plastic garbage bags and boarded the bright yellow Grumman Goose of Trans-Provincial Airlines for the flight down to Prince Rupert. The changeover to the next flight went well and the fish were still nicely frozen when we arrived in Vancouver. That was when things began to go wrong.

The airline who had promised to fly us over the Rocky Mountains to home and our waiting barbecues was on strike. We put ourselves on wait lists and sat around, nervously watching our bags of salmon. After three flights had left, we had moved from thirty-third to thirty-first on the waitlist. Obviously, we would be cooking and eating the salmon in the departure lounge before we got a seat. In desperation, we took a cab to the Greyhound bus depot and booked seats on the seventeen-hour overnight bus to Calgary.

All very well, except the salmon had been in the garbage bags for some time already and the ice was now cool water. We emptied the water out and rushed over the road to a nearby motel where we raided the ice machines. The understanding driver let us put the bags in the belly of the bus and we settled in.

It was summer, it was hot and I couldn't sleep. Partly because I don't sleep well on buses but mostly because, with every kilometer, I expected the smell of fish to waft up from below my feet.

What saved us the embarrassment of rotting fish was that Greyhound buses have to stop every couple of hours for the driver to take a rest. At the first stop we leaped out and tore around finding ice to replenish the bags.

People were curious—well, not all of them. Some just shook their heads in pity and others looked at us as if it was a particularly cruel fate that had placed us on their bus. As the story of the fish spread through the bus, we acquired helpers. By the time we stopped at Golden, people were leaping down the instant the doors opened and fanning out in all directions in search of fresh ice. I like to think it was human kindness but I suspect no one was keen on spending the last five hours on a bus with kilograms of rotting fish. In any case, we and the fish made it safely to Calgary and the the barbecue was awesome.

In the fall of 1978, the only oil I had ever seen had been in the crankcase of a Series Two Land Rover. Fortunately, the Alberta oil industry was booming to such a degree that a young geologist whose only experience had been in the oil-free rocks of Rhodesia could walk into a high-paid consulting job on the drilling rigs. I realized that experience wasn't a crucial factor when I went out with the owner of the company and had to find a gentle way to tell him that the large crystals (phenocrysts) in the lump of igneous rock he was holding were not actually fossil animals.

The geological work was fairly simple and involved little more than checking to make sure the samples coming out of the drill hole matched the rocks we were supposed to be drilling through, telling the drilling engineer when to core the rocks and sending reports back to head office on a wonderful new machine called a Fax. The only time I had a decision to make was one time when the rock chips didn't match what we were supposed to be drilling through. I sent a report stating that, and postulating that we had drilled through a previously unrecognized geological fault that had thrown the rock sequences out of order. Over the magical spinning drum of my Fax machine, I received a curt response saying essentially that I didn't know as much as the company geologists (which was broadly true), and instructing me to keep drilling. At considerable expense (not mine), the drill kept turning for a couple of days and the bit dug deeper and deeper into the unfamiliar rocks. Eventually the company stopped the drilling and called in a company to run an electrical log of the hole, the results of which I was told to rush back to Calgary. I did so and later heard that the company geologists had identified a previously unrecognized fault that had thrown the rock sequences out of order.

The oil rigs in Alberta in the 70s were tiny individual, sometimes very dysfunctional, worlds, often isolated hours away from the closest community. Rig workers made good money and often didn't care about the job since they knew they could head down the road and walk into another one. Alcohol was forbidden on many rigs but it was tough rule to enforce, especially when the salesman travelling around selling drill bits would show up with a gift of a bottle of good rye whiskey. On one rig I was on in the foothills of the rockies, the weather was cloudlessly sunny but the temperature didn't rise above -40 degrees day or night for that week. The main crisis was that bottles of liquor placed in the snow to cool would freeze.

My theoretical schedule was three weeks of work and one week off, although the three weeks often extended to four and the one back home was commonly reduced to a few days by a crisis of some sort. On one occasion, on my way back from the north, I was asked to stop at a shallow gas well west of Red Deer to pick up the drill core since there was no geologist on site. When I arrived they were still coring so, since I had been up all of the previous night, I went into the engineer's trailer and slept for a couple of hours. When I woke up, I went up to the drilling floor to see if the core was being pulled. As I watched the drill log slowly record the depth beneath me, the engineer looked out the window, swore very creatively and clattered down the stairs from the drill shack. I looked out the window to see flames shooting horizontally 20 feet out of the end of the trailer I had just woken up in. As I watched, thankful that I wasn't still asleep and that I had left my suitcase in my vehicle, the engineer jumped into the water truck, which had flames leaping around it, and drove it to safety.

Eventually, the flames died down and I went to see what had happened. The end of the trailer was a charred mess and the two four-foot-high propane cylinders, which had obviously been the source of the flames, lay on their sides. Apparently, the propane had been running low and, in the cold temperatures, the pressurized gas had gelled in the bottom of the tanks. A common way to solve this problem was to play a blowtorch on the base of a cylinder to thaw the propane. The rig's toolpusher had done this but had then gone into town to get new cylinders and forgotten to turn off the blow torch. Fortunately there was no explosion but the connecting hoses had melted and the escaping propane ignited. Happy that this rig hadn't been my responsibility, I collected the core and headed into town.

The year that I worked on the rigs, we went to the SPCA pound and picked up a dog to keep Jen company while I was out of town. We called him Scruff since his reported name was Tuffy and Scruff was close enough that he recognized it. Scruff was three years old when he joined our family and, as close as anyone could tell, a cross between a Cocker Spaniel and a Poodle. He had inherited the intelligence of both breeds and accompanied us on many driving holidays through the Western USA, but Scruff had a dark past.

After he had been with us for several years, we began to notice that he was having back problem when out for a walk in cold weather. Concerned we took him to the vet, suspecting arthritis and hoping it wasn't cancer. He took Scruff in for x-rays while we waited. After what seemed an unusually long time, the vet reappeared with a frown, said there was something odd with the x-rays and could he redo them. We said "yes" and immediately leapt to the cancer scenario. Eventually we were called through and the vet pointed to an x-ray of Scruff's spine. "What do you think that looks like?" he asked, pointing to a small white mark beside the vertebrae. I puzzled for a minute and then guessed wildly, "It looks like a .22 bullet." The vet nodded. "At some time in his life, your dog has been shot."

The bullet explained the stiffness. In cold weather the lead chilled and froze the nerve running along Scruff's spine causing his back legs to seize up. The bullet was impossible to remove without damaging the nerve, so all we could do was knit him a warm sweater for the winters. This solved the problem and Scruff happily went back to marking his territory around our neighbourhood until a couple of years later when he began to have seizures.

The seizures didn't last long. He would get excited by a squirrel or one of us coming home from work, suddenly keel over twitching and evacuating his bladder for some 30 seconds before staggering panting to his feet and getting on with life. This time the vet had a prompt answer, Scruff was having heart attacks. Apparently dogs have much stronger hearts than humans and can go on for years having heart attacks. The only thing that can be done is to avoid getting them excited.

We organized Scruff's life as calmly as possible and discovered that leaving the TV on when we went out calmed him and helped when we returned home. However, it was impossible to keep him calm all the time, especially on walks to his favourite spots. Scruff didn't seem to mind, but this was horribly embarrassing for whoever was with him. Standing and doing nothing while holding a leash on the other end of which is a small dog is obviously having a seizure, appears to the casual observer to be particularly heartless, and saying, "Oh, it's all right, he's only having a heart attack," doesn't help much.

Despite his health issues and the consequences of whatever had happened in his chequered past, Scruff was a beloved companion for several years and moved up to Edmonton with us where he was joined by Salaidh, a very cute somewhat neurotic stray poodle who turned up in our yard one day and whose owner we could never find.

In spite of us arriving in Canada with less than $50, the money I made on the oil rigs enabled us to put a deposit on a Calgary house within eighteen months of getting off the plane in Montreal. It was a lovely old building in Sunnyside and we were very happy there. The only problem was that, month-by-month, I was hating my job more. The conditions were often harsh, the work was unchallenging and, although I got on well enough, I had little in common with the other workers on the rigs, but the worst things were the phone calls. Every time I was home and had caught up on my sleep, I would jump whenever the phone rang and pick up the receiver with growing dread, knowing that the voice on the other end was likely to tell me to go at a few hours' notice to some god-forsaken place for the best part of a month. The stress was becoming unbearable, so I looked around for something else. The job I was offered was geological survey work, much more in keeping with my temperament and training. The only downside was that it was a three-hour drive to the north along highway 2. After a tortured weekend of indecision, I accepted and we contacted a realtor in Edmonton.

Interlude

Lunchtime Strip

The Friday lunchtime striptease crowd,
raucous denim,
steel-tipped boots,
trays of beer—
the dancer half-awake,
less exotic than the crowd,
gyrates to Aeorosmith
and offers up herself
to feed the half-remembered fantasies
of half-a-hundred
marriage beds.

Young Jim is new at this,
too shy to stare
he glances at the open nakedness
reflected in his glass,
and concentrates
on limp and tasteless fries
while buddies banter at the girl
inviting her to join with them
in more ways than one.

The dollars offered
she collects
in any way her nakedness allows;
even Jim,
with sweaty palms and mumbled thanks,
manages to place his note upon the stage
and is rewarded with a smile
of teasing promise
to bring the colour rushing to his cheeks.

A man alone,
middle-aged,
Japanese,
his race sets him apart
much less than does

his pin-striped suit and tie
and offered twenty dollar bill.
She takes it,
anoints the queen with baby oil,
and listens as he talks
and points
and waves small scissors
and a folded card.
She shakes her head
moves away
forgetting to return
the money she had loved.

The show is done
the girl in open dressing gown
collects discarded clothes
each casual careless glimpse
of partly hidden flesh
now more erotic
than that freely offered
with the lunch.
"What'd he want?"
Jim's buddy asks.
"My pubic hair,"
she says,
"for his collection.
That's what's in the card.
He's been here every day this week.
Tips are getting bigger though,
if he gets to fifty
he can have some,
but I do the cutting."

She moves away
Jim returns to work
imagining
not her jutting breasts,
her gleaming oily flesh,
but a lonely man
whose intimacy
is catalogued by colour
in rows of private hair.

Radiation

In 1927, a group of women working for the United States Radium Corporation (USRC) brought a lawsuit against their employers citing dangerous abuses of safety regulations. The case had been slow getting off the ground partly because of the difficulty of finding lawyers willing to take on such a powerful company, but eventually the women appeared in court in New Jersey in January 1928. By that time, two of the them were bedridden and none had the strength to raise their arms to take the oath. Others took their places and in the press coverage of the case became known as the Radium Girls. The Radium Girls became a media sensation, and after a decade of struggle were awarded $10,000 each, $600 dollars per year and coverage of legal costs and all medical costs while they lived. Unfortunately, many of them had not lived long enough to benefit.

Radium, in the form of radium chloride, was first extracted from uraninite (pitchblende) in 1898 by Marie and Pierre Curie. One of the properties of this strange new element was radioluminescence, giving it the property of glowing in the dark. The benefits of this were recognized almost immediately and led to a boom in the manufacture and sale of watches and clocks that could be read in the dark. This was achieved by painting the markers on the faces and the hands of the timepieces with radium-enriched paint. The work was performed by girls who were paid a penny and a half per painted dial and expected to complete 250 or so dials per day. The girls had to mix their own paint and apply it using small camel hair brushes. Since the brushes lost their fine point fairly rapidly the girls of USRC and other watch manufacturers were encouraged to repoint their brushes by licking them. Because of the novelty of luminescent paint, the girls also sometimes painted their nails, faces and even teeth. What the employers didn't say, even though they knew it, was that the radium in the paint was deadly.

As the company prospered and its chemists were given lead shields, masks and tongs to protect them from the radium, the 70 girls of the USRC began to get sick. They suffered from anemia, weakened bones and a hideous necrotic deformity known as Phossy Jaw. When they began to make the link between their work with radium and the illnesses and deaths, the company tried to discredit them by putting it about that the girls were in fact suffering from syphilis. It took their hard-won court case and the public outrage it fostered to bring the deadly secret to light. The Radium Girls' case established a worker's right to sue for damages from his or her employer because of dangerous abuse and led to radical changes in labour laws.

The radium used by the USRC came from mines in Colorado, but there were other sources around the world that supplied the radium and uranium that were increasingly being used in clock painting and in the treatment of cancer in the 1920s and 30s.

In a local dialect of the Democratic Republic of the Congo (the Belgian Congo prior to 1960), Shinkolobwe is a slang term for someone who is apparently easy-going but who hides a deep-seated anger. It's an appropriate name for the place where the world's richest deposit of uranium was discovered by an English geologist in 1915. A deposit of around 1% U_3O_8 is considered rich ore. The Shinkolobwe pitchblende ore assayed at around 65%. This made it, along with the much less rich deposits beneath Great Bear Lake in Canada's Northwest Territories, a major source of uranium in the days before nuclear bombs and power plants. However, it was an unstable market and, in a wonderful irony, the outbreak of the Second World War destroyed it and led to the closure of both the Congolese and Canadian mines. As a consequence, in 1942 when the Manhattan Project to research the feasibility of producing an atomic bomb was underway, it could only get up and running as fast as it did because there was an almost forgotten stash of more than 1,000 tons of Shinkolobwe ore stored in a warehouse on Staten Island.

After Hiroshima and Nagasaki, the demand for uranium remained high as the cold war escalated. Exploration for ore increased and in 1953 Eldorado Mining and Refining Ltd. began production at the Beaverlodge Mine north of Lake Athabasca in Saskatchewan. Other prospects got underway and the imaginatively-named Uranium City grew on the shores of the lake. Despite only being accessible by air or a winter ice road across the lake, Uranium City thrived and by 1982 boasted a population of close to 5,000. On June 30 of that year, Beaverlodge mine closed and, overnight, the population plummeted to a few hundred. I did field work out of Uranium City that summer.

A good rule for a geologist to live by is: never buy a house in a mining town. The death of Uranium City is a classic illustration of why. Overnight, the value of a house dropped to zero. All an owner could do was nail plywood over the windows and walk away. It was also prohibitively expensive to either fly out your furniture or wait until winter and truck it out over the frozen lake. I saw parking lots filled with expensive furniture, large colour TVs and stereo systems free for the taking, but who was there to take them? The few people who stayed probably upgraded quite nicely but I know of only one person who made a profit from the disaster.

Doing field work in the years following the death of Uranium City, I was occasionally treated to the surreal sight of a two -or three-storey house moving serenely across the landscape. There was nothing magical about it, the houses were on barges being towed down the Athabasca River. A house worth nothing in Uranium City was valuable in the booming oil town of Fort McMurray, it was simply a question of getting it the 200 or so kms over the lake and then up some 250 kms of the river. It wasn't easy, but the rewards were substantial.

The average low temperature for Uranium City in January is around -32 degrees Celsius and the average high for the same month is only ten degrees warmer than that. The seventy or so people who live there today tend to do so because they love the north, and if you go there it is easy to see why. The landscape around Lake Athabasca is spectacular. On the south shore are vast areas of pristine sand dunes. They formed after the ice from the last glaciation melted and if you stand amidst them on a hot summer day it is quite possible to imagine that you are somewhere in the Sahara or the Namib. North of the lake is a rugged landscape of lakes, stunted trees and unimaginably ancient rocks. It has always attracted people who either want to live on the fringes of society or who want to push themselves to the limit.

One morning I was sitting in a snub-nosed Beaver float plane (the eleventh one built some time in 1948), preparing for a day looking at rocks.

"See that guy over here," the pilot said. I looked up to see a tall African-American with a huge backpack. "He's a doctor from Philadelphia. Comes up here every year for a couple of weeks."

"Camping?"

The pilot laughed. "You could say that. He hires a float plane, gives the pilot map coordinates to some remote lake and gets dropped off. Two weeks later he shows up in town."

"With only a backpack?"

"Yeah. Carries everything. Apparently he has a small inflatable boat in there for crossing rivers."

"What would happen if something went wrong?"

"Most likely, he'd die," the pilot shrugged. "He doesn't have a radio and never says which route he's taking. If he didn't show up, we'd go looking, but the chances of finding him out there..." the pilot waved his arm to encompass the world north of Uranium City and left the conclusion hanging.

"Every year? Why does he do it?" I asked, examining the man with new interest as he checked his pack and tightened the straps around what I assumed was his portable boat.

"He's a Vietnam vet. I guess he misses having a challenge in his life. You see a few up here."

The man climbed into the neighbouring beaver as I wondered what he needed that was satisfied by his annual northern trips. He wasn't the first vet I had met, I'd had a couple of helicopter pilots who had learned to fly for the American Army in Vietnam and they occasionally scared the hell out of me.

Usually on helicopter-supported field work, I would sit beside the pilot and navigate. Sometimes we would be dropped off in the morning and spend the day walking down a creek to a pre-arranged pick up spot. We would fly up the creek until we found a suitable clearing to land in. The normal procedure was for the pilot to check for hazards by circling the clearing a couple of times before cautiously setting the chopper down. The first time I flew with a vet, I spotted a clearing, pointed it out and began to say, "That looks like a good place to...." Before I had finished speaking, we shot over to the clearing and without any preparation dropped with stomach-shuddering suddenness into its centre.

I clutched my map and stared at the pilot, thinking that either he had gone insane or that something dramatic had gone wrong with the helicopter and that we were lucky to be alive. He simply smiled, shrugged and said, "That's the way I fly."

The approach made sense if you were flying a *Huey* helicopter gunship into a rice paddy that was under fire. But we were in a *Bell 206 Jet Ranger* and the only hazards I was about to face were blackflies and mosquitoes, but I guess if you are trained in combat flying it is hard to break the habit.

On another occasion I learned the limits of helicopters. It was a glorious afternoon, not a breath of wind and too hot for the blackflies, and we had had a wonderful day working down a creek to the clearing where we were to be picked up. The helicopter arrived on time, circled a lot and landed quite heavily in the clearing. We loaded our kit and samples and climbed aboard.

"Beautiful day," I said cheerfully.

"A bit too still," the pilot said distractedly. I wondered what he meant until we tried to take off.

In our little enclosed clearing there was, literally, not a breath of wind and it was very hot. That meant that the air was less dense and the helicopter rotors had less to grip. The first time we tried to take off vertically. The helicopter worked valiantly but we got no more than ten feet off the ground. The pilot landed and explained the air problem.

We tried a couple more times with no better luck and the thought of crashing back to earth amid fragmenting, wildly spinning rotors began to form. I had been in enough helicopters to know that, when taking off, they invariably tilt forward to get some lateral motion. I assumed it was to get us going on our way, but it also served the purpose of gaining lift on hot days. Our problem was that the clearing was too small to do that without the rotors catching the trees. We would have to rise above the treetops and we couldn't.

Options were to offload our equipment and/or us, try to take off again and come back to get us later when it had cooled down, or for us to sit there until night fell. The pilot decided on a third option. Lifting a few feet off the ground he manoeuvred over the end of the longest axis of the clearing, which would give us the chance to tilt the rotors a fraction. I tried not to think about what would happen if we didn't clear the treetops but we did and flew happily home.

The work in Edmonton produced two bulletins, numerous reports and papers and presentations at a number of conferences. Oddly, my favourite contribution to my science was the smallest. In some of the rock samples I was working with I noticed an unusual mineral that I eventually identified as *crandallite* (*aluminous hydroxy phosphate*, if anyone cares). The crystals being somewhere in the vicinity of 0.01 millimetres across, it required an optical microscope to even see them and an electron microscope to study them. Given their lack of significance in the search for uranium deposits, I probably spent far too long studying the varieties of *crandallite* but they intrigued me. Eventually, they ended up in a five-page Note in the *Canadian Journal of Earth Sciences*, with the riveting title of: "Crandallite group minerals in the Helikian Athabasca Group in Alberta, Canada". It was hardly earthshaking research but I was gratified to receive requests for reprints of my Note from a small group of *crandallite* aficionados scattered from Poland to Australia.

What I should have taken from the *crandallite* experience was the realization that I was more interested in the obscure minutiae of Geology than the search for economically viable mineral resources. In time this became an important distinction as geological survey work became more short-term and project-oriented. Budgets for pure research were being cut and the difference had to be made up by doing applied research whose focus was determined by the companies who footed the bill. I was becoming disillusioned by my chosen field of endeavour, but took two different aspects of my life and work in the 1980s to trigger a major change.

I learned to write at the Geological Survey of Alberta. I had pottered with writing little stories during the long hours of field work in Rhodesia, but they were undertaken to combat boredom and never with the intention publication. I had written a research thesis at university and reports in Africa, but they too were not for a wider audience and hence had gone through only minor editing. In Alberta my reports, papers and talks were for public consumption and required a higher standard. Fortunately, the head of the group I worked in in Edmonton, Wylie Hamilton, was a good writer and editor and took the time to mentor me. Admittedly, Wylie taught me scientific writing, which tends to be in the passive voice and is overloaded with qualifiers, but it is precise and mostly concise. His greatest gift to me was an edition of the 85 page classic *Elements of Style* by William Strunk Jr and E. B. White (the latter of *Charlotte's Web* fame). Commonly known simply as *Strunk and White*, this book is masterful in its brevity, it is also one of the very few grammar books that is actually readable. In fact, in 2011, Time magazine named it one of the 100 "best and most influential" books in English since 1923. It is rarely far from me and I have absorbed its injunctions to "omit needless words" and "use the active voice."

Important though *Strunk and White* was, I might never have become a writer had I not uttered seven fateful words one evening on a walk home along the North Saskatchewan River. Jen and I were discussing holidays we might take in the near future when I turned, gave her a kiss and said, "Let me take you round the World."

Interlude

Lebanon: October 23, 1983

The crispness of the morning air
took me on a fishing trip
to some lost Adirondack lake,
or Rocky Mountain trail,
or Arizona desert dawn.
To simple homes
a million miles beyond
this sad and ancient land.

Returning to a distant hum,
a speeding truck beneath the sun-touched roofs,
a singing dot,
where no foot touched a brake,
growing to fill my world.
Barrier, compound, front door blurred
as eagerly the spinning wheels
made their obscene rendezvous.

What elder God smiles down
upon the righteous zeal
of this young martyr's fiery end?
What forces move his feet and animate his hands
to drive ten tons of death
before my sleepy eyes?

This is his land,
its morning sun should call him
from love amongst the cedars.
Life is brief enough beneath these weathered hills
for which crusaders yearned.
Why choose to end it all
in headlines dust and mourning?

I am the only one who saw his face
in those few final seconds
of a quarter thousand lives.
Was he filled with holy ecstasy
or warped by unimaginable rage?
I do not know.
I only know he looked at me
and smiled.

Part 6

The Birth of a Writer

fall park bench
two war vets share
one leg each

The Saturday Night World Tour

On Saturday, November 8, 1986, Jen and I and two large backpacks flew down to LA, checked into a motel near the airport and went for a drink in a bar chosen because Smokey Robinson singing "Tracks of My Tears" was playing out the door. We discussed whether what we were doing was insane or not. The next day we were flying to Tokyo with only a skeletal idea of what would happen after that. We had cut ourselves adrift from employment and home. Friends were living in our house in Edmonton and looking after it and our two dogs. Our only news would be through letters delivered to a series of *poste restante* addresses around the world. It was the beginning of 358 days of travelling during which we covered more than 60,000 miles (close to 100,000 kms), slept in 152 different beds in fifteen different countries on four continents. We were nervous.

One thing we decided as Smokey urged us not to be fooled by his false gaiety was that, wherever we were during our travels, we would try and do something memorable on each Saturday night. This would give us things to look forward to and/or remember fondly, and break up the daunting prospect of a year into manageable chunks. On each of the subsequent 50 Saturday nights we aimed at splurging on a nice meal, and some were spectacular: stuffed lobster on the beach at Colva in India; a floating restaurant on the River Kwai in Thailand; a wonderful meal in a tiny family restaurant in Kekira on Corfu; a student dinner on the Left Bank in Paris. On occasion, Saturday night celebrations involved simply cleaning up as best we could and having a drink in the bar of a hotel where we could never afford to stay, while we ate as many of the free bar snacks as possible. We sat with cans of beer and a bento box on the banks of the Ota River mere metres away from Ground Zero in Hiroshima. We drank whisky in the Duntulm Lodge Hotel that Eve and Jim had owned on Skye, and amidst the topiary animals outside the hotel where the movie, *The Killing Fields*, had been filmed. Sometimes we were on a plane or an overnight bus and so had little control over the evening but we always tried to do something memorable. Here is the Saturday Night Tour itinerary:

California
  Los Angeles
Japan
  Hiroshima
  Kyoto
Korea
  Seoul
Thailand
  Hua Hin
  Chiang Mai
  River Kwai
Nepal
  Kathmandu
  Birethanti
  Chitewan
  Namche Bazaar
  Bus, Kathmandu to Benares
India
  Khajuraho
  Simla
  Jodhpur
  Hyderabad
  Mysore
  Colva Beach
Egypt
  Cairo
  Luxor
Greece
  Heraklion
  Mykonos
  Sparta

  Kekira
Italy
  Naples
  Florence
  Venice
Austria
  Salzburg
France
  Paris
England
  London
  Manchester
Scotland
  Edinburgh
  Cullen
  Duntulm
  Glen Luce
England
  Preston
  Crich
  Patterdale
  Upminster
Zimbabwe
  Harare
  Great Zimbabwe
  Nyamandhlovu
  St. James Mission
  Plane, Harare to London
Belgium
  Ypres
Scotland
  Edinburgh (x2)
Spain
  Madrid
  Seville
Canada
  Edmonton

~~~~~

I have stood in awe before some of the pinnacles of my species' achievements: Saint Chapelle and Chartres; The Sistine Chapel and the Altamira Caves; Sukhothai and Kajuraho; Stonehenge and Karnak, but I
~~~~~

have always firmly believed that, to know who we are, if you stand at the zenith you must also stand at the nadir. I have hiked along the trenches of the Somme and Ypres, climbed Cemetery Ridge at Gettysburg and walked among the haunted ruins of Oradour-sur-Glanes, but one place has stood out in my catalogue of human horror.

There is a museum that, since it opened in 1955, has been visited by more than one million people every year, including: Che Guevara, Richard Nixon, Jean Paul Sartre, Mother Teresa, Leonard Bernstein, Mikhail Gorbachev, Elie Wiesel and the Dalai Lama. The exhibits are well-presented and there are informative signs in several languages but the signs aren't needed. People walk around the museum in silence, many in tears, staring in disbelief at: a watch stopped at 8:15, a lunch that will never be eaten, a child's school uniform retrieved from a tree, a set of concrete steps with a ghostly human figure imprinted upon them. The museum is situated in what was once a thriving community of narrow lanes, wooden shops and houses, and 3,500 people. At the moment the watch in the museum stopped on the morning of August 6, 1945, and in the fires that resulted, all those people died and their community vanished. They had been only 200 metres from the point directly below where the first atomic bomb used in war had exploded. It is as well that Japan has some of most beautiful and tranquil gardens in the world to offset the emotional impact of a visit to Hiroshima Peace Memorial Museum.

Hiroshima notwithstanding, Japan was probably the best place to get settled into travelling mode. Of course it was frighteningly expensive and confusing, but it was well-organized, safer than many places in 1986, and we had arranged to visit for a few days with Masako who had been a homestay student with Jen's family. Our Saturday nights in Hiroshima and Kyoto fulfilled our requirements established in LA. In a sense so did the next one in Seoul, but not in any way that we had intended.

The flight from Tokyo to Seoul was only a couple of hours, but the security checks at both ends were surprisingly numerous and thorough. Eventually we escaped, changed some money and discovered the airport bus that could drop us off at the Koreana Hotel, the closest stop to our guest house. There was a minor wrinkle when the bus driver, who spoke the same amount of English as we did Korean, refused to drop us at the Koreana. He managed to indicate that it was something to do with the police but attempts to explain or understand why, were futile. We persevered and various passengers joined in taking either our side or the bus driver's. Eventually the drop-off-at-the-hotel faction won and the driver shrugged and set off. We sat feeling good that we had taken charge, overcome the language barrier and got our way.

As the bus progressed towards downtown, we noticed that the streets were strangely quiet for a Saturday afternoon and speculated that Korean weekend habits might be different from the ones we were familiar with. There was also a mist forming and we worried that the changing weather would prevent us seeing the sights we had planned to cram into our 24-hour stopover. At last the bus, which was travelling at a fair speed along the deserted streets, braked sharply in front of the Koreana. The driver hustled us out, threw our backpacks onto the pavement and sped off. Using a map we had picked up at the airport we set off for our guest house.

It was an eerie experience having Seoul to ourselves apart from a few people hurrying by with surgical masks over their faces and I began to think of all the post-apocalyptic movies I had seen. At the first pedestrian underpass, what was left of our confidence in having handled the bus situation vanished. I turned to see Jen crying and was about to ask what was wrong when tears began running down my own cheeks. Then we began to cough. By the time we emerged onto the street, our eyes were streaming uncontrollably, we were coughing and choking and there was a strange metallic taste in our mouths. It had never happened in quiet St Andrews, but I had read and heard enough about student riots around the world to recognize that we had been tear gassed.

The air was clearer on the streets and we hurried to our accommodation. We turned the corner and stumbled into a line of police in full riot gear. They simply stood, shoulder-to-shoulder and stared at us

—at least I assumed they were staring at us, all I could see were pitifully tiny reflections of myself on the impassive, mirrored face plates of their helmets.

I could see our guest house a block behind the phalanx of police and tried to indicate that that was where we wanted to go. The only movement this created was that the tiny images of me waved their arms about futilely. Eventually an officer in regular uniform showed up. He didn't speak English so I went though my, that's-our-guest-house-all-we-want-is-to-get-there-and-collapse routine. He stared at us for long enough that I began to wonder if he was debating whether it would be simpler just to shoot us, but then said something and a gap opened in the line of police. We hurried through mouthing profuse thanks and signed into our refuge. The room was sparse but even the smell emanating from the nearby toilet was better than tear gas.

Having survived the aftermath of what we later learned had been the New Korea Democratic Party demonstration, we didn't do many tourist things in Seoul. That Saturday evening we wandered the streets looking for something that wasn't closed. There were still riot police everywhere but they were much more relaxed now and waved and smiled as we passed. At last we fell into a hotel for a drink. It turned out to be the Hotel Lotte, the most luxurious and expensive place in Seoul, which we didn't realize until our bill for a couple of drinks and a plate of antipasto arrived. On balance, after the day we had had, we figured it was worth it.

The plan had been to visit Burma but instability there meant that flights were being cancelled or changed so we decided to add a week onto Thailand instead. This was a good decision since it gave us more chance to get out of Bangkok's noise and bustle and visit some remoter places. The beaches at Hua Hin, the bridge over the River Kwai, Chaing Mai and Sukothai were all highlights but the most surreal experience was visiting the Khmer ruins of eastern Thailand. We went there because of another place we couldn't visit. Vietnam had invaded Cambodia in 1979 and intermittent fighting against the genocidal Khmer Rouge was still going on in western Cambodia along the Thai border when we visited in late

1986. Going to the ancient Khmer ruins at Angkor was not recommended but we could see outliers of the 11th century Khmer Empire at Phimai.

The temples in the Phimai Historic Park were spectacular but travelling to them off the beaten 1980s tourist track was its own adventure. Most of it, crowded buses with their own flexible timetable, cockroaches, noise, dirt, smells and sketchy people offering to carry your bags were common to travel in much of rural southeast Asia, but a few incidents stand out. In Lopburi we found what looked to be a decent restaurant. It was large, airy, clean and the waitresses were well-dressed and friendly. Things began to go strange when we tried to order food. Despite other tables in the restaurant being served a wide variety of mouth-watering dishes, we were told there was only rice, eggs and fruit. Certainly, people were going upstairs via a long staircase bearing baskets of fruit, but we felt like more substantial fare. We ordered beer. A soldier came over and, in the face of overwhelming evidence to the contrary, seemed to tell us that the food was wonderful. Giving up and finishing our beers, we left. On the way out it all became clear. Our waitress came up, grabbed Jen's arm and using graphic hand and finger gestures propositioned her. When Jen pointed out the obvious fact that she was with me, the waitress shrugged and continued her gestures as if to say, "That's okay with me." Innocent tourists that we were, we had stumbled into a brothel.

At the other end of the culinary experience scale, in Phimai after a long day visiting temples and without knowing what the letters meant, we wandered into the VFW Bar. Suddenly we were in a 1950s midwest American diner, complete with Elvis-playing jukebox, formica tables, red vinyl seats and chrome trim. The only customers were middle-aged men with greying buzz cuts, drinking Mekong whiskey beneath American flags and military memorabilia. VFW stood for Veterans of Foreign Wars and the customers were American servicemen who had stayed on after the US airbases that had sent off the B52s to bomb Cambodia in the 1970s had closed down. Going with the flow, we ordered a hamburger steak, southern fried chicken, corn, fries and ice cream for dessert. The only clue that we weren't in Kansas was Singha beer in place of Budweiser.

Thailand was followed by—Christmas in Kathmandu, New Year below Annapurna, avoiding *amoebic dysentery* on the Trisuli River, startling a large rhino in Royal Chitwan Game Park, and wondering how long we would be stuck in Lukla when the king commandeered the Twin Otter planes of Nepal Airlines to go on a picnic, followed by our six weeks recapturing the Raj in India.

In mid-March we headed to Egypt and up into Europe. After more than four months backpacking in Asia, we were fairly beat up. We had both lost a lot of weight and Jen had brought with her a rather unpleasant, persistent bug that took several weeks and a couple of courses of antibiotics to disappear. The wonders and history of Egypt, Greece, Italy and Paris lifted our spirits on occasion, but often we felt lethargic and exhausted. Strangely we missed the challenges, the difficulties, the impossibilities sometimes, of travelling in Asia, but we were tired. We needed some stability, we needed to get to the familiarity of the UK and scrounge some comfort off relatives.

In retrospect, we were lucky to travel in Europe in the days before the ease of international travel gave us a 12-month long tourist season. However, even in spring back then, there were places where we were overwhelmed by tourists. We learned tricks—in Florence we lined up outside the Galleria dell'Accademia a full hour before it opened so that we could buy tickets before the tour buses, run through the corridors and have ten minutes or so more-or-less alone with Michelangelo's David before he became a head and torso floating above the picture-snapping multitudes (and this was well before cell phones and selfies). Reading the diary that we kept, the highlights were often the unexpected ruins or the sites that required a stiff walk on a hot day. I count myself lucky to be a part of almost the last generation that had a chance to visit some of the cultural wonders of the world in relative peace.

Unquestionably, Asia had been crowded and this had presented its own difficulties, but there is something about a mindlessly chattering crowd pausing only to snap a picture before moving on to tick off the next item on the tour that I find unutterably depressing.

The second half of our year's travel was very different. We based ourselves in the familiarity of the UK, bought an old beat-up Volvo and travelled to visit friends and the sites we had taken for granted when we lived there. We took three weeks to visit the Zimbabwe we had known ten years before and, in search of sunshine and responding to the call of a country we loved, on an impulse took a cheap charter flight to Malaga and wandered around the south of Spain before returning to the beginnings of winter in Canada.

We returned to Edmonton on the verge of changing our lives completely. This was not entirely due to the mind-broadening experiences of a year on the road. In November 1987, Jen was four months pregnant with our first child and I was gestating a mid-life crisis.

I had taken a year's unpaid leave of absence from work for our travel and a replacement had been hired on a year's contract. At *poste restante* in New Delhi, we picked up a letter from the department head saying that there was a fifty percent chance that I would be laid off at the end of the fiscal year in March. The letter had been sitting waiting for us for some time so we decided to phone and find out what was going on. Given the time difference between New Delhi and Edmonton and the multitudinous joys of using the international phone system, it took us two days to make the phone call. In those two days, using our considerable powers of rationalization, we decided that me being laid off would not be too bad— in fact, it might be an opportunity.

Over whisky in the bar of the Imperial Hotel, I went over all my dissatisfactions with my job. Geological Survey work, at least in Alberta was not what it had been when I started. It seemed that future career paths had narrowed to two options: becoming a government bureaucrat in the Ministry of Mines and dealing with permits and paperwork; or undertaking short term contract work for exploration companies. Neither particularly appealed. We decided that if the worst happened we could make a go of many things: we could lead trips in Nepal; I had met a Dutchman whose accent was so thick that I could barely understand a word he said and yet he was making more money teaching English in

Japan than I was as a research geologist; and perhaps there was money to be made in writing about our experiences. It helped too that, the summer before we had begun our travels, Jen had graduated with a Masters degree in Social Work, making her eminently employable in many places.

When I eventually connected with my boss on a crackling phone line, I learned that my job was secure for at least another year—my replacement had been laid off. We were happy and went back to the Imperial to celebrate, but a seed had been sown. Or, perhaps the seed had always been there, buried deep in the mulch of my growing up, awaiting its moment. Certainly it sprouted in fertile ground.

Interlude

The Erskine Men

They must be gone by now,
the Erskine men of Christmas time
who came by childhood's door
to sell their home-made trinkets
from a wicker nest
too large to hold their dreams,
yet far too small for even half their memories.

They always came in pairs,
these travellers in time,
released from road-end buses
to walk in baggy coats that sagged
and let the chilling air blow through
just as it had along that icy Wipers trench.

Some hobbled on a leg of tin
or waved a sewn-up sleeve in flapping sad hello;
some stumbled blind
and caught a rough-shod foot upon
the ragged rims of shell holes long filled in;
some gasped for uncorrupted air
to fill the nearly useless lungs
that once could fill the Kop;
and some, on laughter-ridden streets
where we could only hear the cars,
abruptly huddled down
at noises much more ancient
remembering to always tilt
their helmets to the blast.

At school we made up stories of the ones who weren't let out,
a harmless child's grotesquerie of gaping wounds still fresh
and hollow eyes and lipless screams,
designed to scare
but in reality less horrible by far
than Erskine's hidden congeries of noble man's debris.

Some children, from the safety of their youthful vim,
would taunt these swaying distant men
with shrapnel sharp from lack of comprehension,
but older folk just watched
with silent looks I never understood
as their own sepia memories of missing loves and brothers
in poppy-red abandon staggered by.

They must be gone by now,
the Erskine men of Christmas time.
The long sad years of hopeless basket work at last undone.
I pray whatever black explosion
pushed them off our narrow ledge of sanity
was also strong enough to wipe away the hope
they never were to realize
before their world went mad.

Discovering War

I am extremely lucky in that my chosen career has offered me three things that I love doing: crafting stories into books; telling stories before a library or gym full of students; and researching the historical background to my books. The crafting has obvious sources in the tales of betrayal and torture in Skye and skinning crocodiles in India, jotting down short stories in idle moments of field work, and years of freelance writing, but the step from that to telling the stories before a live audience has a more tortured history.

Regardless of my surprise success in introducing fossils to my classmates, it was many years before I felt comfortable making even the simplest public announcements. Presenting my work both in university and Rhodesia was a nightmare of anxiety despite, early in my university career, having been shown in the most obvious way possible how it should be done.

In the early 1970s, the History department at St Andrews organized for the famous historian, A. J. P. Taylor, the author of the classic and controversial, *The Origins of the Second World War*, to come to town and deliver a public lecture. Unimaginatively, the lecture was given the same title as Taylor's famed book but nonetheless the venue had to be changed when far too many people showed up than could be accommodated by the advertised location. Like everyone else, I went along expecting a summary of the book and was surprised when Taylor put forward the then novel idea that the Second World War was in fact about oil and could not have been said to be a world war prior to December 1941 and the

Japanese attack on Pearl Harbor. Taylor spoke for an hour without notes, answered questions and then, leaning casually on the lectern after he had been thanked, said that we had been privileged to glimpse how an historian's mind worked. He had been planning to give the regular talk based on his book but, on the train up to St Andrews, he had been thinking about the new ideas that he had presented to us. He had given a fluid, coherent and entertaining talk off the top of his head. My thought was, "That's how to give a talk—know your subject so well and be so passionate about it that speaking about it comes naturally."

Of course, I didn't put this revelation into practice immediately, although I did learn how to prepare talks and how to dispense with notes by using projected slides as keys to the different sections. It was only when I began to tour as an author, that I managed Taylor's feat. In 1997, with a mere three books published, I was invited to give two writing workshops at the Calgary Young Author's Conference (CYWC). I used the invitation to organize a tour of Alberta schools after the conference, loaded copies of my books into the trunk of the car and drove across the Rockies (we were now living on Vancouver Island). I had given a few talks already but they had been low-key affairs—free visits to my kids' school and a presentation to 12 people at a conference in Vancouver—nothing that would prepare me for what happened at the Calgary event.

The CYWC was and is huge, attended by over 1,000 kids and a couple of hundred teachers and parent volunteers. The morning began with a Keynote address to all attendees, followed by a day of workshops. I was scheduled for two writing workshops to around 20 grade 4 to 8 students each time. The Keynote that year was given by Hazel Hutchins who had recently been a finalist for the Governor General's Literary Award for Children's Literature. Having finished my tea and demolished a couple of the free donuts, I wandered down to catch Hazel's 45-minute presentation.

The school gym was packed with over 1,200 people, so I stood to the side of the stage. A few minutes into her talk, it became obvious that Hazel wasn't feeling well. She excused herself and was helped off the stage. I was wondering what was going to happen when the event organizer, looking very stressed, came down off the stage and hurried by. I still don't know what made me do what I did, but I leaned forward as she passed and said, "Do you need someone to go up and fill in?" She mumbled something and hurried out of the gym. I was relieved. I had shown willing thereby gaining brownie points for future invites and yet had escaped the horrors of getting up on a stage before such a vast congregation with not a word prepared.

My relief was short-lived. The organizer returned and asked if I could talk for 20 minutes as she had someone who could do the following 20. Not trusting myself to speak, I nodded, grabbed a copy of each of my three books and followed her onto the stage. To my incredulity, the next 20 minutes were an utter joy. With no preparation and no props other than my books, I wandered around the stage telling stories about my novels. I got a few laughs, left to thunderous applause and that day sold all of the three hundred books I had brought for my two-week school tour.

Since then I have calmly given many keynotes, conference presentations and workshops, and have talked at hundreds of schools to tens of thousands of kids. Only once have I been as nervous as I was in Calgary.

I had just finished three of my four presentations in the library of a high school in a run-down area of Toronto. The day had gone well until the librarian came up to me and said, "This last group is a bit special."

I had been doing this long enough to know that "special" was code for difficult or troubled, but I wasn't prepared for the dozen or so guys who filed in and slumped onto the chairs. They were all much bigger than me, dressed in black and many sported gang tattoos. As they stared sullenly at me, the last arrival came up and put his arm around my shoulder. He was shorter than me but built as if he could go through a brick wall. He looked at me and said, "So you're the writer guy, eh?"

I nodded agreement, wondering where this conversation was going.

"Tough crowd," he said, inclining his head toward his intimidating companions.

"I'm beginning to see that," I offered.

"Don't sweat it, man," he said, squeezing my shoulder, "I got your back."

And he did. He sat in the middle of the front row with his arms folded and looked from side to side to check that everything was in order.

The presentation went well (war stories and lost explorers resorting to cannibalism and dying of scurvy catches the attention of most tough crowds), and my new friend threw a, "Nice work, man" at me as he swaggered out.

I assumed at the time that he was the leader and simply liked to show his dominance by keeping everyone in order. He probably was the leader, but afterwards I wondered if the librarian, who must have understood the dynamics of the group, had had a quiet word with him beforehand.

Doing taught me how to write my stories and Calgary cured me of any fear of telling my stories in public, but what of my third love, research, and why history?

History has always been the main focus of my reading and has developed into the main underpinning of my view of the world. This is not to suggest that I am an historian, although were I transported back to the late 1960s it is a road I might well have chosen, but it is my passion. It is also a wonderful weapon in the arsenal of a skeptic. It proves my distrust of simple answers. Anytime someone claims that the world is simple I can immediately think of dozens of examples when it was not, so why should the fact that they are living through this particular period indicate that anything is different? Whenever anyone claims that they are right, historical facts and anecdotes line up to tap me on the mental shoulder and whisper something along the lines of: "Yeah. Robespierre knew that he was right and that led to a very busy guillotine." History has the wonderful ability to disprove any easy generalization but that does not explain its attraction. True, a wonder at vanished worlds was cultivated by those long ago overheard conversations around the fire in Paisley, but my love of history goes deeper and focuses on some specific events and periods more than others.

Growing up in Scotland in the 1950s, I was surrounded by stories from the Second World War—spitfire pilots battling bombers over southern

England, commandoes raiding the French coast, spies and resistance fighters trying to evade the gestapo, and POWs outfoxing their jailers and digging their way out of Stalags. They were my heroes. I read books about Douglas Bader and Colditz, and watched movies about The Dam Busters and Violette Szabo. Inspired, I lay in bed at night imagining myself the hero of countless death-defying escapades. But there was another, older war that gradually began to place demands on my imagination.

I was born a mere thirty-four years after the opening bombardments of the Third Battle of Ypres, or Passchendaele as it is better known. The survivors of that battle and the others of the First World War were the age I am now when I was growing up and were a part of the landscape I inhabited, but they weren't everywhere. In those days in Scotland, people with disabilities were not encouraged to become part of society, there were no wheelchair ramps, Disabled Adult Transport buses or facilities to make life easier. Those with severe handicaps, physical or mental, tended to be shut away—if they were lucky, to be looked after by family—if less so, in facilities.

In 1916, the Princess Louise Scottish Hospital for Limbless Sailors and Soldiers was opened in Erskine, a thirty-minute cycle ride from where I grew up in Paisley. By 1920, 9,500 artificial limbs had been fitted, most of which had been manufactured in the hospital workshops. Throughout the 20th century, the facility, which became known simply as the Erskine Hospital, cared for disabled veterans from numerous small and large wars. It was not unique, there were many of these hospitals spread around Britain specialized in treating: Shell Shock, Battle Fatigue, or Post Traumatic Stress Disorder as it became known; gas victims; amputees; or those requiring extensive plastic surgery. Only twice in the year were the long-term patients of these facilities in evidence—prior to Armistice Day when they sold poppies from trays on the street and before Christmas when they came door-to-door selling the woven baskets and trinkets they had manufactured during the year. Immersed as I was in the later war, I paid little attention to them until I began cycling round the countryside collecting fossils.

On my cycling expeditions I would take sandwiches for lunch and often stop in small villages and towns to eat. In many cases the obvious place was the steps at the foot of the cross, obelisk or sculpture that constituted the local war memorial in the town square. Idly, I began reading the inscriptions. There was always a "Lest We Forget, 1914-1918" and a list of names of those who left the community and never returned. Sometimes there was a later list carved at the bottom or on the back of the memorial with the names of the dead from 1939-1945, the war that I knew about. I soon noticed that the early list was always longer, often by an order of magnitude, and that many surnames were repeated. For example, carved on the plaque beneath the stone cross in Bridge of Weir—the village where I first salvaged fossils from the tannery waste—are 70 names from 1914-1918 and only 35 from 1939-1945. Even stranger, amongst the 35, there is one surname, Robertson, repeated. The repetition is statistically meaningless and may not signify any familial connection. However, amongst the 70 names from the earlier war, there are four Barrs, three each of Houston and Jackson, and seven other names that appear twice: Andrews, Brown, Burns, Fulton, Higgins, MacDougall, and Millar. It strains credulity to breaking point to believe that none of the repeated names from 1914-1918 do not represent members of the same family.

Added to my personalizing of the stark lists of names, the thought struck me one day that these were not large communities. Today Bridge of Weir, one of the larger villages I stopped at, has a population of just over 4,000. Even assuming a similar population 100 years ago, 70 healthy men between the ages of 18 and 35 being violently ripped from the community would have been a huge social wrench (somewhere around 7% of the eligible males), everyone would have either lost a relative or known someone who had, and that is not even counting those who came back to the Erskine Hospital.

I began to see this earlier war as not so much a war of heroes, which was how the books I was reading about the Second World War were presenting that war, but more as a vast, unstoppable tragedy where heroism counted for naught. My opinions were cemented in place in 1964 by the 26 remarkable episodes of the BBC television documentary, *The Great War*. Historical reading and research over the years has led me to regard most wars in this light, but the First World War has retained its place in my consciousness and provided the framework for seven books of fiction and non-fiction.

Musing about war memorials, watching BBC documentaries and reading Robert Graves, Siegfried Sassoon, Wilfred Owen and Erich Maria Remarque was incognizant research, unfocused and done simply to feed my interests. Geology taught me to do disciplined research although in a narrow academic field. The two came together when I began writing historical fiction and non-fiction, but my first novelistic foray into the First World War was written for a bet that was made in 2001 over beer with one of my editors.

A couple of years ago I reread *All Quiet on the Western Front*. It's still a powerful book, but what struck me was that the most compelling images and scenes in the book are cliches. Of course they weren't cliches in 1929, in fact Remarque's masterpiece was instrumental, along with Owen's poetry, in creating the cliches of today. The explosion of First World War literature in the early 1930s has created a code we use when talking about that war. In the English-speaking world the Somme conjures images of young men hopelessly stumbling in lines into machine guns; Ypres and Passchendaele trigger a desolate landscape with soldiers being swallowed in mud; mention of Haig demands recall of the trope, "lions led by donkeys." Although the code is simplistic and the ideas it engenders are questioned by many serious historians, it is a useful shorthand for writers. But what if the writer's readership hasn't read the defining literature of the First World War or been taught the history of the war?

That was the core of the discussion with my editor—how to write a novel set in the trenches for twelve- to fourteen-year-olds who don't know the code. I wanted to write a novel about the experiences of a young boy in the trenches. I wanted the boy to be sixteen, only a year or two older than the reader and I wanted it to be historically accurate. I didn't want the boy's experiences to be peripheral to the core reality of trench warfare or to sanitize those experiences—to create an adventure story that, by omission, glorified war. Consequently, I couldn't see a way that I could accurately describe the boy's experiences without making the story too gruesome for any children's publisher to touch. My editor bet me that I could and promised to promote it to the publisher when I did.

I thought long and hard about the story I wanted to tell. I decided on a diary format, which would help my readers relate to a boy in a past they knew nothing about. I went to the Imperial War Museum (IWM) in London and read letters and diaries written by real teenage boys to give my fictional character an authentic backstory and voice. I researched people my character might have met and events that he could have witnessed or been involved in to create his world. I didn't hold back on the harshness of his experiences but based them on actual soldiers' experiences. I trusted that I could draw the publisher far enough into my character's life and fate that she would not object to a friend having his legs destroyed by a shell, a soldier bleeding to death in the trench bottom before help can get to him, or the only slightly paraphrased description of an eighteen-year-old Irish soldier being shot for cowardice. It worked and, a couple of days after I submitted the manuscript, the publisher phoned me to say that she had cried at the conclusion of the book. So, I lost the bet and the book was published in 2003 as *And in the Morning*.

The highlight of the whole process was the week in the reading room beneath the cupola of the IWM. Amongst other historical events, I have since researched books set during: the lost Franklin Expedition; the crusade against the Cather heretics; the Spanish Civil War; and the battles of Stalingrad, Shiloh, and the Teutoburg Forest. I have loved every obscure, geekish minute, and my main struggle has been leaving out the cool stuff that doesn't advance the story. For example, while researching a story set during the doomed Franklin Expedition I learned that, at the Battle of Trafalgar, John Franklin was a Midshipman aboard HMS *Bellerophon*. After *Bellerophon* broke through the enemy line of ships, she was engaged in battle at close range with the 74-gun Spanish ship of the line, *Bahama*. Many of the Midshipmen on *Bellerophon* were killed or wounded by sharpshooters in *Bahamas*'s rigging, but not Franklin. Eventually, the ships broke apart and, shortly afterwards, *Bahama's* commander, Dionisio Alcalá Galiano, the youngest Admiral in the Spanish navy, was decapitated by a cannon ball. All very well, but when you add in that Franklin was on his way to becoming one of the most important European explorers of Canada, and Galiano had made his name exploring the waters around Vancouver Island and Canada's west coast, there is an eerie synchronicity to their encounter. Two men, one an important explorer of Canada who was, rather abruptly, ending his career and another who was soon to begin his, each in complete ignorance of the other's existence, spent half an hour that day busily trying to kill each other. Much could be done with that in a novel, but it did not advance the story in my book and had to be omitted, although it did sneak into a short biography I wrote of John Franklin.

The holy grail, dreamt of by every researcher, is finding that previously unknown diary that turns perceived historical wisdom on its head or that misfiled lost play by Shakespeare. It happens rarely but I found my grail in Pringle Creek Public School in Whitby, Ontario. It was Remembrance Day 2013 and I had just finished my first presentation to the students and was searching for a rejuvenating cup of tea when the grade three teacher, Melissa Rabjohn, approached me. She said that she had enjoyed hearing me talk about the First World War because her grandfather's uncle had fought in it. She told me that he had kept a diary and that he had published it privately for the family in the 1970s, shortly before he had died—would I be interested in seeing it?

Of course I said "Yes", I am interested in seeing anything relating to the First World War, but I didn't have high hopes of anything notable. The diaries written by soldiers in that war, unless they were literary men like Sassoon, tend to be a dull read unless you are a researcher looking for specifics. Men in those days tended not to talk about their emotions, even in the privacy of a diary and, with the notable exceptions of those moments of terror when a battle broke out, dealt with the boring minutiae of digging trenches, going on leave, picking lice out of clothes, receiving parcels and letters from home, etc.

What Melissa hadn't yet told me was that her ancestor, Russell Hughes Rabjohn, had left school at fourteen and spent several years at the Ontario College of Art in Toronto. The diary she showed me was 140 large pages of the most remarkable line drawings covering the time between his enlistment in January, 1916 and his demobilization in March 1919. Even more remarkable, since Rabjohn was a trained artist, he was used by the officers to draw training posters, dugouts and the graves of comrades. Because of this, while he was at Vimy, Ypres and Mons, he could walk around with an artist's sketchbook under his arm without the danger of being shot as a spy. So, in addition to his work, he drew sketches of his own which he added to, reworked and tidied after the war.

Melissa asked if I thought the drawings might be publishable. I struggled out of my shock and said that yes I thought so and could she photocopy half a dozen pages—whatever were her favourites. A few days later, I showed the random pages to a publisher in Toronto and she immediately said that, if the rest of the diary was this good, she would sign a contract on the spot. I drew up a proposal, submitted it to five publishers and received fours offers to publish. This was nice, but it was just the beginning and the best was yet to come.

In addition to his sketches, Rabjohn also filled five volumes of a pocket diary and I spent two wonderful weeks in the Canadian War Museum (CWM) in Ottawa reading every word of his diary, timing it where possible to the incidents he sketched and getting to know him. On the day he arrived in France in April 1917, Rabjohn wrote at the top of the page in capitals, "ARRIVED IN FRANCE". This was a big deal for a kid from Toronto, but sometimes the getting to know him was not what he wrote but how he wrote it.

Rabjohn was scrupulous about keeping each day's entry within the space allowed by the diary page, even if this meant cramping his writing into near illegibility to do so. On only one occasion does he willfully fill two days with one day's events. It was when he arrived in Ypres in

October, 1917 in the midst of the battle of Passchendaele. A German shell landed amongst C Company of Rabjohn's Battalion and he was one of the first on the horrific scene. He says nothing about how he feels but he describes what he saw in uncharacteristic detail, the burning vehicles, bodies and the pieces of his friends lying around him. The reader has to imagine Rabjohn's horror in the unusual length and detail of his unemotional writing.

The CWM also holds a few of his original sketches and research material, so it is possible to see how Rabjohn changed the sketches when he tidied them up and used photographs to get the details right in images he created after the war. I could also tie his experiences to the Battalion diaries and his son and grandson were kind enough to show me family photos of Rabjohn as a boy and the sketchbook he was given for his tenth birthday in 1908. It was the favourite piece of research I have ever done and resulted in the book that I am perhaps proudest of although it contains fewest of my actual words, *A Soldier's Sketchbook: The Illustrated First World War Diary of R. H. Rabjohn.*

Interlude

Lines on a photograph from the Holocaust

In moments uncluttered by life
your face returns across
the grainy, empty years—
your one escape,
an impossible flight
through the tiny timeless lens
which holds us both together
and apart.

On your arm,
a neatly folded overcoat,
the one you took on family walks
while noisy children teased your cautious fear
of unexpected showers
and coldly whispering winds.

But seasons end.
An awkward soldier stands behind,
too young to hold the clumsy rifle still,
and offers you the Earth
to be an overcoat.

Do you still stare at him,
across the pit
into the ageing nights he stole?
Does he awake and start
to see once more your head
swim in the gunsight of memory?

We are both lost,
the soldier and I,
within the tidy folds
and pointless sad humanity
of useless overcoats.

Writing Stories

Stephen King recommended that, "If you want to be a writer, you must do two things above all others: read a lot and write a lot." Good advice and, on the surface at least, easy to follow. If you are reading and understanding this paragraph then you can become a writer. The only uncertainty is a definition of "a lot." It's a cliche that to master a field of endeavour you must put in 10,000 hours of practice. Like most cliches it's based on truth. In dozens of studies of successful musicians, sports personalities, chess masters and writers, that number seems to broadly hold true. Does that then mean that to become a writer you need to put in 10,000 hours of reading and 10,000 hours of writing?

I began my full-time writing career in 1989. At that point, at a rough estimate, I had been reading seriously for around three decades or 11,000 days. To reach 10,000 hours I needed only an average of less than an hour a day. Since I read around 40 to 50 books a year and many are long (6-800 page) history books or novels (I put in about 18 hours reading time to absorb Vassily Grossman's *Life and Fate*), I don't doubt that I clocked more than my required reading hours before I even considered a writing life and have easily more than doubled that in the years since.

Writing hours are tougher to calculate. As far as story writing is concerned, I didn't do much before 1989: a few lost, angst-ridden stories when I was a teen, pastiche copies of Lovecraft and Rider Haggard to kill time on field work in Rhodesia, and one longer tale while travelling in India. But those few dozen hours were not all.

I firmly believe that, even if you're not conscious of the processes, when you read you absorb how the author creates the story, and when you write, you practice that, regardless of what you write. Therefore any reading, from Goosebumps to Shakespeare, and any writing, from emails to autobiographies, counts as training. Certainly this was the case with the scientific writing I did for the geological survey, but then I had a good editor and *Strunk & White.* Add to this the essays I wrote at school and university, occasional periods of diary-keeping and letter writing, and miscellaneous work-related reports, etc., and I probably came close to the magic 10,000 hours by the time I began taking writing seriously. Of course in the 30 years since, the hours have mushroomed as I've written my 3,000,000 plus published words.

One early morning in July 1988, I was watching my infant daughter happily spread breakfast around when the phone rang, "Hello, Mr. Wilson, this is the editor from the Globe and Mail." My heart leaped. I had submitted a short piece on my visit to Hiroshima for the upcoming forty-third anniversary of the bombing and promptly forgotten about it in the turmoil of parenthood. "Thank you for submitting your piece on Hiroshima. We'd like to run it on August 5th."

"Thank you," I managed.

There was a pause and I wondered if I was supposed to say something else. The editor continued. "Our rates aren't high, I'm afraid, but we can offer one fifty."

"That's great," I said. "Thank you."

That was it, my first attempt at getting published. "The Globe and Mail's going to publish my article," I breathlessly told Jen who had taken over the feeding role.

"That's great," she said.

"They're paying one fifty," I added proudly.

"One fifty what?" my practical partner asked.

I had no idea. I didn't know whether it was one dollar and fifty cents or one hundred and fifty dollars in total, or if it was one dollar and fifty cents per word. I hoped it wasn't one dollar and fifty cents in total but I didn't particularly care. I was in the company of Orwell and Hemingway, a published freelance writer.

It turned out to be $150 and over the subsequent winter I rose at 5.00 a.m. and wrote until the family demanded attention. As a consequence, my work rate at the Geological Survey flagged at about 2 in the afternoon but no one seemed to notice.

In the six months after my first success, I sold two further pieces to the Globe and Mail and one to the in-flight magazine for Canadian Airlines. The latter market taught me one thing that every freelancer must learn if he or she hopes to survive—research your market thoroughly and write what the editor wants.

The Canadian Airlines piece was on the Japanese, super-fast Shinkansen trains. The editor liked the piece but required two changes. When I had travelled on the bullet trains, the system had been in the process of privatization. This was causing fear amongst employees and several had committed suicide. I mentioned this but had to cut it—you don't talk about death in an in-flight magazine.

The other issue was the "hook". I already knew that every article needed to begin with a strong image or anecdote to draw the reader in and I spent significant effort coming up with good ones. The Shinkansen piece began with the statement that it had been Mussolini's claim that fascism would make the Italian trains run on time but, for a number of reasons, this goal had never been achieved. However, the Shinkansen had achieved this lofty goal to the extent that passengers on the platform became noticeably restless if a train's arrival was even close to a minute behind schedule.

"That might offend Italians," the editor claimed. Swallowing the impulse to ask if ageing Italian fascists were a significant demographic on Canadian Airlines, I agreed. Fortunately, I discovered that the first passenger train journey in 1825 arrived 55 minutes late, which served my purposes well enough. All subsequent articles for in-flight magazines were suitably bland.

All three of these early articles were based on the year travelling and all used some of my photographs, which increased the rate, in the case of the glossy in-flight magazine to ten times what I had earned for my first attempt. On the basis of this meagre beginning and with the hope of some contract work , the illusion that I could return to geology if freelancing didn't work and, most importantly, with Jen's support, at the age of 38 I quit my well-paid research geology job for an uncertain future. As mid-life crises go, it was a good one.

By continuing my relationship with the Globe and Mail, broadening the in-flight magazine market and realizing that it's possible to sell articles as reprints to multiple non-overlapping markets, I began to build a base for my business. I began to promote my photography, having a few photo essays published and winning a couple of competitions. The photography highlight was an award from National Geographic Traveller for a shot of a full moon over the floodlit Jaisalmer castle in India during the desert festival. The effect was somewhat undermined when the editor in New York called to get the camera settings to put in the magazine and I had to admit that it had been taken from the roof of a guest house after we had filled a considerable wait for dinner with several beers. When the moon rose so spectacularly, I had woozily balanced the camera on the edge of the roof and clicked the shutter a couple of times, so had not the faintest idea about f-stops and shutter speeds—not the sort of story they wanted to print. However, I did receive a sum of money and a very attractive and useful photography book.

After a couple of years, I came to realize two things: it was getting past the point where I could easily return to geology and, if I was determined to struggle through a career as a writer, as long as I had a computer, printer and internet access, there was no need to suffer through any more prairie winters, I could starve just as easily where the climate was milder. Consequently, in the spring of 1991, we decided to sell our house and move out to Vancouver Island. As a freelance writer eager for different experiences, I decided we should sell the house ourselves.

For five weeks my family and I felt that we were living in a fish tank. We cleaned the house at least three times a week, tidied up compulsively and lived with the pervasive odour of cinnamon wafting from our oven— apparently it gives a country kitchen feel. At a conservative estimate, 500 people tramped over our carpets, poked into our closets and turned on our kitchen taps. I even began to feel murmurings of sympathy for Britain's decaying, poverty-stricken aristocracy, forced to open their mansions to hordes of peasants every summer.

We put up a sign, advertised in the papers, handed out feature sheets and hosted open houses every weekend, even the one where Edmonton's spring blizzard dumped 36 cm of snow on us. We ushered out the old guy who went on a racist rant at the Chinese family checking out our living room and then politely declined the Chinese family's offer of $20,000 below the asking price on condition that we threw in all the furniture. We carefully hid the "DO NOT TOUCH. RABIES CONTROL" trap after a family of skunks took up residence under our porch, and began to run out of friends that our kids could take refuge with. The only consistency was Anne, a neighbour along the street who showed up every weekend with a different relative or friend in tow because, "...you have such a lovely house." She usually came at a quiet time, so we chatted and exchanged skunk stories.

On the fifth weekend we were exhausted, suffering from the flu and had arranged for a realtor to come round at 5 p.m. on Sunday to take the listing if our final attempt failed. At 4:30 p.m., Anne arrived to show yet another friend how beautiful our house was. This time, the friend added a surreal touch by carrying a whippet wearing a powder-blue wool coat. Feeling sick, miserable and defeated, I mumbled something ungracious about Anne knowing the house better than I did and slumped down to await the realtor. After ten minutes or so, Anne, her friend and the whippet returned.

"I love your house," Anne said.

I grunted and peered out the window as the realtor's car pulled up.

"I'd like to put an offer on it."

I turned and looked at the strange trio and, through the fog of my clogged brain a bubble of a thought rose: "Thank Christ. The whippet liked it."

Bizarrely, it turned out that the realtor Anne had contacted was the one who was by now walking up our drive, so everything went smoothly from then on and we could load up the car and drive out to the west coast and look for somewhere new to live. One of the first things I did when the chaos of moving was done and my computer was plugged in was write up and sell an article on my real estate adventure.

Freelance writing is a harsh taskmaster. You are only as good as your next article and spend much too high a percentage of time on the business aspects of writing. This is fine and part of the deal, but what I hadn't anticipated were the moral issues.

Writing is a craft, like carpentry, you practice and progress from hammering nails into 2x4s to creating Louis Quinze desks and should be able to turn your hand to anything carpentry related. Similarly, a freelance writer should—in fact must—be able to write anything, from real estate brochures to opinion pieces in national publications. I learned this early and worked hard to broaden my market base as much as possible. I wrote travel and popular science articles, book reviews and opinion pieces, a column of profiles of local artists and a series of satires where I imagined having tea with Jonathan Swift. I wrote for local publications with a circulation of a few hundred and national and international publications with circulations in the hundreds of thousands, but I only had trouble with one.

In the late afternoon of December 8, 1989, twenty-five-year-old Marc Lepine entered the Ecole Polytechnique, an engineering school in Montreal. He knew the building well, having visited several times and applied for admission to its program, although he had been turned down for not having the pre-requisite courses. He believed that his failure was due to women moving into traditionally male-dominated fields such as engineering and blamed feminists for ruining his life. Just over two weeks before he had bought a semi-automatic rifle and hunting knife at a sports store.

For some time Lepine sat in the registrar's office and rummaged through a plastic bag. He spoke to no one, even when asked if he needed assistance. Eventually, he got up and wandered around the building, arriving at 5:10 p.m. at a mechanical engineering class on the second floor. He entered the classroom and separated the nine women and fifty or so men, ordering the men to leave the room. He then declared that he was fighting feminism and opened fire on the women killing six and wounding the others. He went to the cafeteria and other classrooms, killing eight more women and wounding ten women and four men before turning the gun on himself. The day after the massacre, the Globe and Mail published a brilliant and powerful article on the massacre and its meaning by freelance journalist Stevie Cameron.

A freelancer doesn't have to agree with the philosophy of every publication that he or she writes for and, early on in my career, I contributed to one that I certainly didn't agree with. It was a politically conservative magazine in Alberta and I justified my work by only writing apolitical book reviews and science articles on topics ranging from crop circles to the potential for coal-bed methane production. All was well until I noticed an editorial on the page opposite one of my articles. It was December, 1990 and I had just read a reprint of Stevie Cameron's piece from the year before. As the father of two daughters who I hoped would grow up to achieve whatever they wanted, even a year later the article brought tears to my eyes.

The editorial in the magazine I wrote for was not a violent piece, however, it was anti-feminist and presented a view of a male-dominated world where women were assigned the role of child rearer and housekeeper. Obvious nonsense but, in publishing it under their banner, was the magazine not building a platform encouraging a climate where the sick imaginings of a Marc Lepine could exist? And, in writing for that magazine was I not providing nails for that platform?

I thought hard about it because, that early in my career, I was earning a moderate yet significant part of my income from the magazine and I enjoyed researching and writing the science articles, but responsibility does not end with putting words on paper, it includes the use to which those words are put. There was a moral line somewhere in all of this. I was not certain exactly where that line lay, but I knew I had crossed it and I never wrote for that magazine again. Being a freelancer though, I did write a piece on my moral dilemma and my reasons for ending my relationship with the magazine, which to my surprise they published and which I later sold to other markets. There is material for writing in every experience.

The opposite end of making a living as a freelance writer is writing poetry. Over the years I have had some 30 poems published in small literary magazines and the average payment has been two copies of the magazine, even on the two occasions when I was the featured poet and filled three or four pages. Occasionally, I earned a few dollars when a poem won a competition but, despite the satisfaction it gave me, writing poetry was never a serious option. Neither did it seem at the time, was writing children's stories.

I had a couple of short stories published in Chickadee magazine so I thought I was on my way. I hurriedly wrote several picture book manuscripts, sent them out and began adding to my collection of rejection letters. I was on the verge of committing my life to freelancing when I was rescued by Anne Millyard of Annick Press. Not that she bought my book manuscript, but she sent me a rejection letter that I treasure almost as much as any of my acceptance letters. She praised my writing, apologized for not being able to publish the story and, most usefully, explained at some length exactly how it didn't fit into any of the very precise niches for picture books. Revitalized, I wrote a short story (some 7,000 words), about a boy, his sister and dog who travel back in time to the age of dinosaurs. I sent it out and it too was rejected, however, one publisher offered suggestions: the introduction was good but too long for what little came after. Taking this to heart, I chopped the last thousand words off the story and divided what remained into the imaginatively titled Chapters 1, 2, 3, 4 and 5. I then ignored everything I had learned about how to submit a manuscript to a publisher, picked one at random from one of my writing magazines and sent it off bravely stating that this was the beginning of a novel.

Eleven months later, when I had long forgotten about this impulsive submission, I received a letter apologizing for the long delay in replying, saying that they had enjoyed the first five chapters and could they see the rest of the novel? The short answer was "No", since there was no "rest of the novel". In a panic I called the number on the letter, got through to the publisher, thanked her for her response and, praying that the answer wouldn't be two weeks, asked when they needed to see the completed manuscript. Fortunately things tend to happen with glacial slowness in publishing and she said before the editorial board meeting in two months' time. I thanked her and explained that there was still some manuscript polishing I wanted to do, hung up, sat down, pushed everything else off my desk and wrote the novel in six weeks. Two years later, in 1995, *Weet* was published to sit in solitary splendour on a bookshelf that I dared to dream might one day be filled.

I now considered myself an author. I still had a vast amount to learn and kept up my freelancing for the rest of the 90s, but Weet was a major turning point. It taught me that I could write a publishable novel in six weeks and the bookshelf gradually filled. I've seen publishers come and go, worked with wonderful and dreadful editors and seen the the book landscape change almost out of recognition, but deep down inside, I'm still that little kid staring into the terrible dark dungeon in Duntulm castle or sitting unnoticed by the fire listening to tales of the vanished Raj. All I have ever tried to do through my writing and storytelling is recapture the sense of wonder that those stories gave me and hope that a little of that shines through to the reader.

Yes, but why write for kids?

The short answer is that writing for children is easy. A lot of people would disagree with that statement, and they'd be right. I've met many aspiring authors who think that writing a picture book will be easy—it's only 1,500 words and there are lots of pictures, how tough can it be? Very. Writing a picture book is like writing poetry, every word counts and must be agonized over. I suppose I should be more specific. For me, writing historical novels for pre-teens and teens is easy.

This book has been about how I became a storyteller with a passion for history and both of those characteristics were in place before I became an author. The storytelling gave me a sense of pacing and the history gave me a background for my tales and, often, a structure. What I learned very soon after I began presenting my books in schools was that kids bring much more imagination than adults to their reading.

Kids, by definition, live in a world that they don't have the life experience to understand. This gives them the innate ability to create explanations for what they don't understand, they create worlds that satisfy their need to understand the weird stuff that is going on around them. Many adults lose this ability as they grow into the illusion that everything makes sense and that the world they live in is ordered and rational. This gives them the ability to read through long sections of character description and development. Kids don't need that, give them a couple of good, strong sentences and their imagination will fill in the blanks and get on with the plot. Of course, especially in historical fiction, longer descriptions of time and place are important: the thirteenth century was not the same as the twentieth and 1914 was not the same as 2020.

So I write primarily for kids because I find it easy. This is true but I have also written fiction and non-fiction for adults (*North with Franklin: The Lost Journals of James Fitzjames*, *Ghost Mountains and Vanished Oceans: North America from Birth to Middle Age*, *The Third Act*), and crossover novels and non-fiction for high-level teens and adults (*Heretic, Quest, Rebirth, The Alchemist's Dream, A Soldier's Sketchbook: The Illustrated First World War Diary of R.H. Rabjohn*). I do this by imagining them as slightly older, bigger kids.

There is one final reason that I write primarily for kids.

When I go in and talk to a library or gym full of kids, I always think of the high school history teacher who had such a profound influence on me and I look around and wonder, is there a kid here who will be influenced to a similar degree by the stories I am about to tell?

Mostly I will never know, just as Colin Campbell never knew the influence he had on the quiet kid at the back of his classroom until I sent him a book dedicated to him. Sometimes I have clues—fan mail or a teacher emailing to say that little Jimmy in grade 8 who had never set foot in the library before my visit appeared shyly the following day and asked for a book—but there is one incident that stands out.

Because I write exciting stories set in wartime or the Arctic, I am sometimes invited to schools with "difficult" classes. Mostly the are not "difficult", they just need something that interests them.

Once, in the early two thousands, I was invited to a high -school to talk about the history behind my first two books set in wartime (*And in the Morning* and *Flames of the Tiger*). I had finished my presentation to a mix of grade 10 and 11 students and was sitting at a table in the library signing books when a student came in and walked towards me. He was six one or two and dressed in the style of the time, black hoodie (with the hood up of course), scuffed basketball shoes and black jeans with the crotch around his knees. He slouched up to the table , loomed over me and, with the social graces of a newt, thrust a couple of books at me and said, "This is what I read." The books were ultra-violent Japanese Manga comics.

"Cool," I said as neutrally as possible.

He went on, "But I read *Flames of the Tiger*. I didn't know a book could be that interesting. I'm going to try another one." Then he slouched off.

Feeling stunned and humbled, I called after him, "Thanks. Good talking to you."

He is the critical reader who has sat on my shoulder for every book I have written since then, and he's the guy I aim for in every presentation— all the others are easy. He's also the prime reason I write for kids.

Interlude

The Seven Deadly Sins

For writers as for normal folk
The seven sins are not a joke
But I am doomed before I start
For sin is such a part of art
On lust and wrath my stories thrive
And greedy dreams of wealth my drive
My sloth is passed off as reflection
But pride I need to salve rejection
I glut myself on words of gold
And envy stories better told

Lust
I love you more than I can say
And think about you night and day
My waking hours your image fills
And you my dreaming body thrills
You are my life, my hope, my breath
And I shall love you unto death
No other love will I allow
For none can match our holy vow
When once a year I bare my breast
And send my writer's grant request

Wrath
Oh slavering, mewling, gutless swine
Spewing wisdom thought divine
You dare reject yet cannot do
The priceless work I send to you
You do not know the field I plow
My thoughts go sailing past your brow
And yet you say, you witless peasant
"We cannot use your work at present."
I hope the devil too abhors
The hellish host of editors

Avarice
I want a place where I can write
Beside the ocean calm and bright
From three miles down my private drive
I'll watch the eagles soar and dive
And on my desk of solid gold
I'll write great works already sold
But ere I reach these vulgar heights
There's just one thing to put to rights
The payment for my poems has been
Two copies of the magazine

Sloth
In Wordsworth's quiet reflective dream
I sit and watch the tidal stream
Without the busy keyboard's clack
Of time I fear I have lost track
I tell myself that this is work
We poet's need this nature's perk
To clear the mind of life's mundane
And trivial little daily strain
But if you wish the truth be told
I'm half asleep and too damn cold

Pride
When I write my next great work
No longer in the shade I'll lurk
Awards will shower upon my head
With Mr. Booker I'll to bed
My bank account will swell and grow
And I shall host a late night show
A household name I will become
As I shall strike the critics dumb
But 'fore the spark of fame doth glint
I'll have to get my work in print

Gluttony
Give me a line, a phrase, a word
It matters not that it's absurd
I'll take them all and then some more
And stuff myself from Oxford's store
On oxymorons I will feast
With verbs and nouns I'll be a beast
I'll read and read and read and read

Until my eyes begin to bleed
And when I'm full and nothing's new
I'll say it all in one Haiku

Envy
My dog lies sleeping in my room
Untroubled by my scribblers' gloom
She doesn't care she cannot talk
Her words are only food and walk
Her brain seeks not philosophy
But dreams of bones and strolls with me
Right now her role is hard to top
My pen for fleas I'd gladly swap
And I could sleep upon a whim
And she could write this bloody poem

So when the judgement day draws nigh
And it is time to say goodbye
I shall not hope I'm bound for heaven
Remembering just the deadly seven
And comfort I shall draw in part
If I am quick and very smart
The competition's fierce I know
I'll shine my prose before I go
And luck might land me at the bell
A column in The Daily Hell.

Epilogue

spring rain drips
in the hearts of
winter mountains

What is Truth?

So you have just finished a slice of my life, which I hope has been enjoyably told, but always in the back of my mind has been Pontius Pilate's question to Christ, "What is truth?" It was a rhetorical question, but that hasn't prevented attempts to answer it for 2,000 years. So, since I am primarily a novelist, a writer of fiction, a teller of beautiful lies, you are perfectly entitled to ask that final question—is it all true?

In the Prologue, I described an evening in 1961. The events described all happened, all the elements of the story are true—the description and location of the room are as accurate as memory allows: I did have four sisters, one of whom died before I was born; my father did have a limp and did, or at least claimed to have done (other people's fiction is not my responsibility), all the things I described him doing in India; and I was a silent listener to many tales of a lost world. However, is it a faithful recapturing of a scene from my life, accurately describing the nine-year-old me sitting in a corner of a room beside the A726 out to Greenock in the presence of relatives, a soda syphon and tales of India? Have I really spent six decades trying to return to the Indian Raj that my parents missed so much over their whisky and soda?

Yes and no. Despite the accuracy of specific details, I wasn't to live in that room in that house for another year or two, and I have no idea if that exact configuration of relatives ever gathered there or elsewhere or whether I ever had that specific conversation with Jim. The tales of India *were* overheard and the nostalgia of their telling was undoubtedly a formative influence on my upbringing and my lifelong passion for the past, but I have given myself much more self-awareness of the process than I had at nine or ten. Only much later did I examine where my fascination with history came from. At the time I was mostly bored and trying to stay warm, although I do still love the sound of ice chiming in a crystal glass.

To give another example, the poem "Last Call" *is* about saying goodbye to Jim for the last time in Melbourne airport. When I began writing poetry, I recognized almost immediately that that event in January 1985 was a subject for poetry, both in terms of personal resolution and as a compelling experience that might resonate with others. I tried numerous times to write that poem but always ended up with something mawkish and simplistic—something that, however powerful the memory was to me, would mean nothing to the reader. It was only after dozens of attempts had blurred the image of that morning and the distance of time had smoothed the painful emotional corners, could I create something that, I hope, captures for the reader a tiny fraction of what I felt.

All well and good, but the events in reality were not as I describe them in the poem. To begin with, the event was so emotionally dramatic for me precisely because I knew at the beginning that Jim was dying of bone cancer. Had I presented the information to the reader up front, it would not have created the same impact—Jim was not the reader's father. So, I put the cancer information at the end and built toward it for the sake of impact. In addition, the announcements, the conversation, the details of the setting are made up. In one sense, what I did as I struggled to write that poem was take the most emotional thing that has happened in my life and lie about it.

There's an old proverb that one shouldn't let truth get in the way of a good story (no, Mark Twain didn't say it first), and all writers live and die by that axiom, but it does raise the question of whether manipulating truth, especially a very powerful personal truth, for the entertainment or even edification of others is a normal thing to do? Probably not, which is one reason why a skill in writing does not necessarily make a storyteller. The complete, literal truth of an incident told as it happened would be mind-numbingly boring and would take longer to tell than the incident took to happen. Fortunately, telling that kind of truth is impossible.

Imagine a simple scene from real life: a man walks into an office in a high rise building, pulls out a gun, shoots the person sitting behind the desk and leaves. It could be portrayed as the opening of a mystery thriller or the climax of a non-fiction book. Either way, the instant the assailant walks out the door, the truth, the total truth, of that moment is forever lost. Some of it can be recaptured: the pattern on the office carpet, what the desk was like and what was on it, the view out the window, the type of gun and a host of other details. What can never be recaptured is what has left no trace: what were the clouds like, was there a plane flying overhead, was anything said, what went through each person's mind, was there a spider busily weaving a web in the corner?

The totality of the truth of even such a brief dramatic event is impossible to recover. We can recover a legal truth, a moral truth, an emotional truth or, in the case of a writer, a narrative truth, but even in those fragmentary truths, reality must be massaged to convince a jury, or to resolve moral dilemmas or emotional trauma in participants who weren't present. The difference with the narrative truth is that only a writer consciously choreographs the elements of the event and changes events in the service of manipulating an unknown reader's emotions so that the reader ends up feeling whatever the writer wishes: fear, disgust, joy, etc. or, as in the case of Last Call, a tiny fraction of the emotional impact experienced by the participant—telling a deeper truth through beautiful lies. Or is that just rationalization?

I am no closer to answering Pilate's question than anyone else. Nor can I explain convincingly why I have spent decades of my life using nostalgia for a lost world and a passion for history to create narratives that make people I have never met happy, sad, angry, scared, or whatever I want. I fully acknowledge that it is a rather strange thing to do with one's life.

I make no claims as to the importance or significance of this tale. It is merely the imperfectly told story of my life within what I see as its historical context in hopes that there are dust motes of truth or a hint of honesty buried deep within. In all my novels over the years, I have shamelessly used family, friends and strangers in the service of a good story, occasionally in ways that would shock them. Perhaps now it's my turn.

A Sample and a Selection

If you enjoyed **Lands of Lost Content**, you might enjoy others of John's titles. Here's a sample of his novel of a search for the Northwest Passage

—

North with Franklin: The Lost Journals of James Fitzjames

"...a richly re-imagined fable which goes far beyond anything the historical record alone might suggest."

The Arctic Book Review

Here's how the tale begins—

Prologue

On April 25, 1848, three men huddled in a wind-blown tent in one of the coldest, most remote, places on earth. They were composing a message. One had just trekked four miles to get the paper; another dictated; the third laboriously thawed the ink and wrote the words. Outside, as an incessant wind blew mournfully between piles of clothing and supplies, 102 British officers, sailors and marines made final preparations for a desperate escape. Many were sick. Not one would live to see his home again.

The officer who wrote the note was James Fitzjames, perhaps the most promising young Naval officer of his generation. In addition to the bleak missive of 1848, Fitzjames kept a journal in which he wrote entertainingly and at length. Unfortunately, only the first few thousand words of this remarkable document survive.

North with Franklin has been a labour of love. From the moment I read the existing fragment of Fitzjames' journal, I knew I would have to tell the rest of his story. I felt a close kinship to the man. He had an almost modern sense of wonder at the world about him and I would have liked little more than to meet him over a glass of port and discuss his world and mine. So I read his letters and the letters of his friends. I read the books he would have read and marveled at the inventions that changed his world. I researched his culture and immersed myself in his life and times. I read the stories the Inuit told Charles Francis Hall and others of their encounters with Franklin's men alive and dead. James Fitzjames became my friend.

The writing of this journal, more than a century and a half after the real author dipped his quill pen into ink, has been more than recreation, it has been a rediscovery, the uncovering of a voice long silent and a glimpse into the mind of a man who lived and died in a world very different from our own.

Bringing Fitzjames back to life has been my primary purpose but, implicit in this task was an attempt to explain the mysterious fate of Franklin and his men. To this end I have used what little direct evidence we have of the expedition's fate, the more rational speculation put forward over the years, the published Inuit testimony and my imagination. These diverse threads I have attempted to weave into a coherent tapestry and I live in hope that one day someone will stumble upon the brittle, stained pages of Fitzjames' actual journal, wrapped in sailcloth and cached beneath a lonely pile of stones on some bleak Arctic shore. Then I will know how close my ghosts have come to the real ones.

Summer, 1845
Her Majesty's Ship Erebus, off the coast of Greenland.

Sunday, July 13, 1845, 11 p.m.—My Dearest Elizabeth. We are begun. All the endless preparation is done. The supplies are loaded and we have said a last farewell to civilization, or what passes for it in this barren land. We weighed anchor on the tide last night, beneath the most beautiful clear sky you could imagine. The sea was as flat as a glass and peppered with a most remarkable assortment of icebergs which shone on the horizon like a twelfth cake with each occasional gleam of the midnight sun. This really is the most extraordinary of lands we have entered.

Around eight the wind picked up and has moved us quite briskly northwards all day. There was some discussion before we sailed as to whether we should head straight across Baffin's Bay to Lancaster Sound or sail north and around the top of the ice. A Dane from Lievely who had married an Esquimaux came over to visit us at Disco and indicated that this was the one of the mildest seasons and earliest summers ever known in these lands. We are presented with a very open year for ice, but the pack—as a solid mass of sea ice is called—can still be a formidable obstacle in the centre of the bay.

It was decided that we should sail north along the coast in the direction of Cape York and yet be prepared to take advantage of any favourable winds or intelligence from the whalers we shall meet. It is generally agreed that we shall be in time if we reach Lancaster Sound by the first of August or thereabouts. Everyone is very sanguine about our prospects and I wrote to William that I would shake hands with him on February 22nd next.

Yet, I cannot stop myself from wishing for some small hindrance to keep us in this land for a winter—we have ample supplies for three years and our scientific work would benefit greatly from the extra time. I do not think one can get to know this place without experiencing it when the sun is both never down and eternally set. So if I am not back with you as my promise to William, do not fret for I shall be enjoying myself in complete security and comfort.

My dear sister—for thus I think of you just as I think of William as my brother—and wife of him I love best; I leave you knowing you as a woman and no longer a mere description in one of William's letters. I feel the parting from you full as much as from William—and of course the children. I am often to be found taking much pleasure in the remembrance of my little friends. My time on land between the Clio's return and this leaving was so brief, and busy, that I scarce had time to do one quarter of the things I had promised myself. My memories are too much filled with details of supplies and crew lists and the like. However, foremost in my mind is the short time I had to become acquainted with Elisabeth and Robert. Their visit to the Erebus at Greenhithe breathed a fresh draught of life into the dull life of a sailor at dock with their eternal questions concerning every knot and billhook they espied. In particular, Elisabeth's opinion that the rigging made the ship look as if it were held in the web of a spider and her scream of fright when she stumbled over a coil of rope which she mistook for a snake shall make me eternally look upon the tools of my trade with fresh eyes.

Perhaps you will think I am foolish to care for little children—but so it is. I was as much pleased with little Elisabeth's expressions of regard— exaggerated though they were—as I should have been with the more studied and carefully phrased, but perhaps less genuine expressions, of grown up people.

I hope to celebrate Elisabeth's birthday (this one or the next) in Behring's Strait or close by it. Little Robert, the son and heir, will be three or four by then and I promise I shall find time to devote to my Godfatherly duties.

After all your anxiety that I should keep a journal for your especial perusal and here I am already rambling on and wearing out the porcupine quill. I have never been one to waste the hours lying abed more than necessary and can always find some dark corner of the night in which to put down my thoughts. Indeed, I have managed to keep up my official journal which I will submit to the Admiralty upon our return, but it is dry piece of work talking in the same official voice of all our doings from the weather to a man being flogged. Not fit reading for a fair lady, to be sure, so I shall use it only to refresh my overfilled memory. These writings will be mere notes to please you, of such things as may strike me, either in the form of a letter, or in any other form that might at the time suit my fancy. So I do not feel obliged to fill a page every day. To keep my thoughts fresh I shall not read over what I have written, so you must excuse all inaccuracies.

And so having made a beginning and my excuses I will to bed. I wind up this and call it a letter just for the sake of adding that I am as ever your affectionate friend and almost brother, James Fitzjames.

July 14—A fine day and we make steady progress. The air hereabouts has the clarity of desert air, but with a cold sharpness I have not experienced before. It is most refreshing to both nose and eye, imparting a hard-clarity to the views which I have never perceived through the soft, moisture-laden air of England.

The coast of Greenland is in sight—a rugged place of black rock cut by white furrows and ravines of snow and some of the most magnificent glaciers the equal of any in Switzerland. The whole is canopied with a mass of clouds and mist. In bold relief, at the foot of this black mass, the most fantastically formed and perfectly white bergs shine out. Grand scenery, but desolate beyond expression.

Our time at Disco was longer than we had hoped, the off-loading of the transport being a more arduous undertaking than expected—but we used the time to advantage. We commenced by beating up to the Whalefish Islands, which are in the bay formed at the south end of Disco and the mainland. There we planned to clear the transport. By some mistake, Reid, our Ice-Master, fancied we were off-course, and led us away up to the end of the bay, thirty miles to the mouth of Waigat Channel. It is a not an auspicious beginning for our expert on the ice conditions of this land, but no harm was done. In fact, the wind favoured us right around the bay which was full of the most glorious icebergs packed close along the shore. But for the loss of a morning, it would have been the most delightful sail. I went on board the Terror that evening, and found Crozier aware of the mistake. He fancied we had given up the idea of going to the Whalefish Islands. It was around midnight that we finally ran into a bay. Of course, the sun was up all this time, it being almost as bright at midnight as at noon.

We were met by five of the local Esquimaux, in the smallest possible canoes, all in a row. The two going ahead kept near the ship and piloted her into a safe place among the rocks, where we moored in a channel just four times the ship's breadth, and perfectly landlocked. Feeling brave the following day, I resolved to try one of the Esquimaux craft. They are very small and necessitate the removal of trousers to enter them. I paddled about happily for some time but at last over I went and remained there, upside down in a most undignified position until rescued.

One of the party gave a quite remarkable display of skill in repeatedly severing a weighted string hung over the stern from a distance of several boat lengths with nothing more than a type of small throwing dart which they use to bring down birds in flight.

The Esquimaux have the most unusual aspect, being short and stocky, like folk used to a life of hard labour. They have very flat and wide faces. Some resemble a type of face I came across in China to such a degree that it made me wonder on the origins of these odd people. Many came aboard and traded for whatever they could. They were particularly taken with any metal which they could fashion into spear points. In exchange they offered many items made of sealskin. Our crew almost universally smoke clay pipes and many obtained tobacco pouches from the natives who, although they do not much use tobacco themselves, make the pouches for trade with passing vessels. It seems the European influence on these lands extends to establishing new trade customs.

Crozier went quite overboard and kitted himself out with a complete set of native clothing. It consists of a shapeless jacket and pair of leggings, cunningly sewn from the complete skins of several local deer and still bearing the distinct aroma of the wilds. He also procured a pair of skin boots, or mukluks as they are called. I cannot imagine what he will do with this outfit or how strange he will look in the Strand dressed—and smelling—like an Esquimaux. When I joked him about it, he replied with a serious explanation on the principles by which air is trapped in layers beneath the clothing and, warmed by the body beneath, serves to protect the wearer from the extremes of the local climate. He even went so far as to explain to me that the Esquimaux have been living in these lands, in all probability, since before Caesar conquered Britain and, for all their savage appearance, must have learned something of adapting to its vagaries. He really can be quite humourless at times. None-the-less, I could not deny the natives a superior skill to mine in the handling of their small craft.

I used this time to take magnetic readings with an early version of the 'Fox,' which we find quite cumbersome and awkward to use. Still, we must make what we can of it as there is no scientific supplier in these parts. I was frequently very wet and cold at this work; but plunging into cold water, when I got on board, made me quite warm. I could not help thinking of the Frenchman who, after a long account of the misery of the rain and fogs of England, rued—'Pour quitter ce triste sol je m'embarque à Liverpool.'

The land of Disco was bold, black, and topped with snow. The seas were covered with bits of ice, which rushed through the channel as they broke away from the icebergs with a noise like thunder. Every man was allowed on shore and they ran about for a sort of holiday, getting eider duck's eggs, &c; we collected some very curious mosses and plants, also shells. Le Vesconte and I spent a day on a small island surveying. It was very satisfactory to me that he took to surveying, as I said he would. Sir John was much pleased with him.

I also spent a day on land with Fairholme measuring angles of the magnetic lines of force of our dear old Earth. It is important work, but tedious in the extreme as it involves sitting for long hours in a little square wooden house recording minute variations in the movements of a tiny, suspended needle. To add to our woes, we were continually bitten by very large mosquitoes and I fancy we each lost some pounds of flesh. I have saved you one of the beasts.

Both the Erebus and the Terror are very heavily laden, the Terror less so since she left some supplies in Disco. We have taken on the extra tons of coal. The Erebus is, without doubt, the sturdiest ship I have ever been on. She is not overly large, being 370 tons to the Terror's 340. Both ships are 'Bomb' vessels, built solidly at first to carry the mortar cannons that were used to bombard Napoleon's coastal fortifications.

Oddly the Terror is the very same vessel I rescued south of Lisbon when I was a lowly fifteen-year-old first class on the old Pyramus in 1828. We found her 70 miles south of the detestable hole we were blockading. She lay on a bed of sand surrounded by rocks with the surf beating over her tremendously—her crew living in tents and six other merchantmen wrecked nearby. She was refloated and towed back to England, very leaky and with the pumps working continuously. I thought then she would see no more service in His Majesty's Navy yet here she is on this new adventure.

Both ships were much strengthened for the ice they encountered while with James Ross in the Antarctic, and they have been further strengthened with oak beams and iron hull sheathing for this endeavour.

We draw some seventeen feet fully laden which a few feel might handicap the work we have ahead of us. Thomas Blanky, the Ice-Master on Terror, was with John Ross from 1829 to 33 and saw as much as any man of the kind of waters we must navigate. He has expressed the opinion privately—but what can remain private in the confines of a ship at sea—that the waters are shoaly and treacherous and that we would have done well to bring a small yacht with us to take out if the going got tight. I think he worries overly for our aim is to sail through the open spaces near Banks Land and, when possible keep well clear of narrow passages which may well be ice-clogged traps.

Both ships are very full with three years' provisions and coals for the engine. The engine on Erebus takes up space most inconveniently. It is an entire locomotive (which but a few months ago was running on the Greenwich line) with only the wheels removed and set by crane in our aft hold. It weighs 15 tons and its bulk makes passage below deck quite a trial at times. Many of the crew are not to be convinced of its import, especially as it can only push us along at a poor three or four knots. Still, I am certain we shall have reason to be thankful for such foresight when we have need of a push through the ice and the wind is uncertain or contrary.

Some men of vision, Sir John Ross among them, even talk of a day when flotillas of ships powered by steam boiler alone will conclude all recourse to sail. It is a stirring idea especially given Ross's unfortunate experiences when he had to dismantle and dump the unworkable engines from his Victory at Felix Harbour in 1829. Yet perhaps he is right for certainly the steamer Rattler was of great assistance to us on our way to the Orkneys. Perhaps the day will come when we see the great navies and merchant fleets of the world steaming around the globe without a care for the movements of wind and tide! For all that they may change our world, the engines are, as Irving on the Terror says of their trials, prone to make the most dreadful puffings and screamings and will undoubtedly astound the Esquimaux not a little.

Meanwhile, our deck is covered with coal piled chest high and casks of food and liquor, and there is but a narrow pathway fore and aft which must look to the untrained eye as if it winds around like fallen knitting wool, yet which in fact defines the most convenient routes that the crew must take as they go about their sometimes complex tasks.

We sit very low and the two ships handle rather like logs in the water. You will please picture to yourself our having a smooth passage between the icebergs for we had enough rolling and pitching on our way across the Atlantic to last us all the voyage. The old Terror pitched so much she appeared as if tossed around by some playful undersea serpent—but no doubt we appear to do likewise from her decks. We can only hope that we do not meet with an unseasonable gale before we make Lancaster Sound and the opening of the passage.

I have no fear but that we shall complete the passage before we have time enough for scientific work and adventure, and if we do not, what wrong can befall us? Since Parry revived our English claim to these northern lands in 1818, all the expeditions, even those that met with misfortune, have lost but a handful of men, and most of those through accident or some pre-existing medical condition. Surgeon Stanley had to invalid one man back to the Whalefish Islands and Peddie did the same for two in addition to both the Terror's Armourer and Sailmaker who Crozier classified as "perfectly useless either at their trade or anything else." So we are now 129 hardy souls in two of the sturdiest ships ever to set sail. We have the best of supplies and the keenest hearts that could ever be wanted. How can we not succeed?

But here I am rambling on about hearts of oak when all you want to hear is gossip of my shipmates and stirring tales of adventure. All I can pass on in this regard is that our Purser, Osmer, beat me soundly at chess this evening. I pray the voyage is long enough so that I may improve to such sufficient degree that I might take a game or two from him before we reach home.

July 16—I was beginning to write last night, but the ship was tumbling about to such an extent that I went to bed but had to turn out again immediately and get the top-sails reefed, as it blew very hard in squalls. The ship pitched about as much as I ever witnessed. Reid is a most extraordinary rustic and prognosticates endlessly on all manner of topics, nautical and otherwise. After the experience at Disco I am disinclined to give much weight to his sayings, but they are undoubtedly quaint and sometimes amusing. Today he was saying that he does not like to see the wind "seeking a corner to blow into," and followed this with a rough comment on the impracticality of kilt wearing in windy climates.

The weather moderated this morning, and all day we have had little wind and tolerably smooth sea. This allowed us to get the proper 'crow's-nest' up. The construction is a hooped canvas cylinder attached at the main-top-gallant-masthead (if you know where that is). According to Reid, who will have the peculiar privilege of being perched up there to search out channels through the ice, this particular crow's nest is a very expensive one.

Blanky on the Terror proclaims this to be a very open season, much like the one he experienced when he sailed these waters in 1829 with old

Captain John Ross. Of course the weather cannot be taken as a good luck omen since Ross and his crew spent four years trapped in the ice and were given up for dead before they were rescued. But you need have no fears for us. I am told by Osmer that we could easily make supplies last a farther one or even two years taking no account of what fresh meat we might obtain with musket and ball.

Osmer is a delightful fellow. He was with Beechey in the Blossom when they went to Behring's Strait to look out for Franklin. At the time Sir John was surveying the north coast of America in 1821, and was within 150 miles of Beechey. Osmer was also at Petro Paulowski in Kamschatka, where I hope to go, and served since on the lakes of Canada. It is said that if the Purser is plump then the crew eat well. If there is any truth in this saying then we will surely benefit for Osmer is almost as broad as he is tall and his skin exudes a most ruddy glow. I was at first inclined to think him a stupid old man, because he has chins, takes snuff, and has an extraordinary nose; but he is as merry-hearted as any young man, full of quaint dry sayings, always good humoured, always laughing, never a bore, takes his 'pinch after dinner,' plays a 'rubber,' and beats me at chess—and, he is a gentleman.

By the time you have read a quarter of this poor document you will have a fit picture of all my messmates. We have the following whom I have or shall from time to time give you descriptions:—First Lieutenant, Gore; Second, Le Vesconte; Third, Fairholme; Purser, Osmer; Surgeon, Stanley; Assistant-Surgeon, Goodsir; Ice-Master (so called), Reid; Mates, Sargent, Des Voeux, Couch; Second Master, Collins; Commander, of himself you know better; and over us all, Sir John Franklin, the hero of so many past adventures in the lonely and unexplored regions of the world. But for now I must to bed. Good night sister.

Continue **North with Franklin: The Lost Journals of James Fitzjames** by picking up your copy at any Amazon site.

Other Titles

Norman Bethune: A Brief Biography

As a young man, Norman Bethune served as a stretcher-bearer in the First World War. The experience left him with the dedication and passion to lead crusades to find a cure for tuberculosis, to introduce universal health care in Canada, and to introduce mobile blood transfusion units to save wounded soldier's lives on the battlefield. He served with the Republican armies during the Spanish Civil War and in China where he died of blood poisoning in 1939. Because of his left wing politics, Bethune was ignored for decades in his home country. His childhood home in Gravenhurst, Ontario sees large numbers of visitors each year, although a majority are tourists from China where he is revered as a hero for his work with Mao's army in its fight against the Japanese. Regardless of politics, Bethune deserves to be more highly regarded everywhere for his lifelong struggle against injustice and suffering wherever he encountered it.

"I couldn't put the Bethune story down...It is an inspirational tale as well as a historically important one."

-Times-Colonist

"...John Wilson makes the private man come alive...[a] gripping story of a larger-than-life Canadian hero."

-Quill & Quire

John Franklin: A Brief Biography

Sir John Franklin was many things in his life: an officer in the great naval battles of Copenhagen and Trafalgar; governor of Van Diemen's Land; an explorer from Australia to the Arctic, but it is for his mysterious death and the deaths of all 128 of his crew that he is remembered today. The mystery of the disappearance of the Franklin Expedition to the Northwest Passage has captivated thousands in the 174 years since his men buried Franklin in an unknown grave in the frozen land that kept calling him back. For most of that time only a handful of graves, scattered bones, fragments of debris and Inuit stories have fuelled the speculation as to what killed them all. Now, the wrecks of both of Franklin's ships have been found, preserved in the frigid waters off King William Island, and may contain answers that have been sought for generations. This is the story of the man whose name will forever be associated with the greatest tragedy in Arctic exploration history.

"This book, admirable in its succinctness…is the best life of Franklin yet produced…there could be no better introduction to the life and journeys of Franklin than Wilson's…wonderfully engaging book."

-Russell Potter, Arctic Book Review

An *"…excellent overview, the reader is left with an appreciation of the enormous task early exploration of the Arctic represented…a first rate story and a very useful addition to our understanding and appreciation of an important and unique segment of Canadian history. Highly Recommended."*

-CM Magazine

Heretic: The Heretic's Secret book 1

In the style of Bernard Cornwell, The Heretic's Secret Trilogy is a rollicking historical adventure set during the bloody 13th century wars against the Cathar Heretics of Languedoc. When the armoured knights of Pope Innocent III swept south in 1209, most thought they would be gone by summer's end but, led by the fanatical Arnaud Aumery and the ambitious Simon de Montfort, they stayed for three fiery decades. In that time they slaughtered thousands of Cathars, burned countless towns and castles, destroyed a thriving country that rivalled France in power and culture, and created the foundations for the shape of western Europe we recognize today. John and Peter enjoy arguing about their differing views of the world. Peter sees the Church and an unquestioning acceptance of God's word as the way to salvation. John sees developing an understanding of the wonder of the world around him as a way of becoming closer to God. As the chaos of war erupts around them, the friendly differences of childhood demand that they take sides. Troubled by mysterious visions, Peter seeks refuge in the Church and becomes an assistant to the militant Aumery. Repelled by the horror he sees around him, John finds himself drawing closer to the persecuted Cathar heretics. As the brutal holy war expands and the flames of the Inquisition spread, Peter and John find themselves on opposite sides of a dangerous search for a secret that may have the power to change the world. **Quest** and **Rebirth** follow John and Peter's thrilling adventures to their heart-rending conclusion.

"…a brave book, an unsettling book, and one that is very much needed at this time."

-The Globe and Mail

"…an astonishingly nuanced and masterfully told story…"

-Quill & Quire

The Alchemist's Dream

"In this engrossing historical adventure, John Wilson paints a vivid picture of a bygone era involving Henry Hudson's fateful search for the elusive Northwest Passage, an alchemist, mysterious passengers, and enigmatic maps. The Alchemist's Dream fascinates from start to finish." (from the Governor General's Award jury). In the fall of 1669, the Nonsuch returns to London with a load of fur from Hudson Bay. It brings something else, too—the lost journal from Henry Hudson's tragic search for a passage to Cathay in 1611. In the hands of a greedy sailor, the journal is merely an object to sell. But for Robert Bylot—a once-great maritime explorer—the book is a painful reminder of a past he'd rather forget. As Bylot relives his memories of a plague-ridden city, of the mysterious alchemist John Dee, and of mutiny in the frozen wastes of Hudson Bay, an age-old mystery is both revealed and solved. Set against the thrilling backdrop of the quest for the Northwest Passage, The Alchemist's Dream is a riveting tale of exploration, ambition, and betrayal. Also available in an expanded edition that includes extracts from Hudson's journal, **The Final Alchemy**.

"In this engrossing historical adventure, John Wilson paints a vivid picture of a bygone era involving Henry Hudson's fateful search for the elusive Northwest Passage, an alchemist, mysterious passengers, and enigmatic maps. The Alchemist's Dream fascinates from start to finish."
-Governor General's Award jury citation

The Third Act *(soon to be a major live-action movie)*

The Third Act deals with the intercultural struggles faced by Chinese students studying in North America in the present day and by an American playwright, Neil Peterson, caught up in the Nanjing Massacre of 1937. The contemporary story focuses on three Chinese friends (Tone, Pike and Theresa) who grapple in their own ways with the pressure to succeed in an unfamiliar culture. The historical tale concerns Peterson's effort to find his literary voice and save the woman he loves amidst the chaos and horror of the fall of Nanjing in the Second Sino-Japanese War. The two stories are tied together by a play that Peterson attempted to write after his return to America. The students in the present day get caught up in putting on a performance of the missing third act of Peterson's play, and in doing so they are forced to confront their cultural and personal pasts and futures.

"I recommend The Third Act to students who enjoy both historical fiction and mystery novels. The novel has a strong, well-developed female character in Theresa...Highly Recommended."
-CM Magazine

The Ruined City: book 1 of The Golden Mask *(The inspiration for the upcoming animated feature, Heroes of the Golden Mask)*

Howard is a lonely, geeky tenth-grader dealing with a father who's had some kind of breakdown, a flaky, overprotective mother and frightening waking dreams. Then he meets Cate, a strange girl who convinces him that he is an Adept, which means he can communicate through dreams with other dimensions and, under certain circumstances, travel between them. Howard discovers that our world is only one of several dimensions swirling in time and space, and that one of the others, peopled by unimaginably powerful monsters, is approaching Earth for the first time in millennia. The last time the dimensions coincided, our world was saved by the breaking of a powerful golden mask in the Bronze Age Chinese city of Sanxingdui. Together, Howard and Cate travel through time and space, meeting other Adepts and avoiding lurking monsters, in a quest to find the three fragments of the golden mask and prevent it from falling into the wrong hands.

"A tale of adventure and monsters, The Ruined City, with more than a nod to H.P. Lovecraft, should appeal to readers who enjoy a mystery and slimy monsters from another dimension. Highly Recommended."

-CM Magazine

"An ambitious story...Fascinating."

-Kirkus Reviews

A Soldier's Sketchbook: The Illustrated First World War Diary of R. H. Rabjohn

A unique First World War diary, illustrated with more than a hundred stunning pencil and ink sketches, for children learning history and also for adults interested in a new perspective on the war and authentic wartime artefacts.

"The extracts from the diary describe intimate wartime experiences of death and destruction in gruesomely dispassionate terms...it's a story of unmitigated horror, highlighting more than any textbook the futility of war...This unique compilation of firsthand impressions of the Great War will be a valuable resource for adults and teens with an interest in this turning point in world history."

-Kirkus Starred Review

"The excellent and succinct text . . . provides context for Rabjohn's short diary entries, many of which merely scratch the surface of the suffering he experienced during his time at war."

-Starred Review, Quill & Quire

Ghost Mountains and Vanished Oceans: North America from Birth to Middle Age *(new edition complete with the original maps and appendices included)*

This book is more than the story of how a continent formed over 4 billion years. Told in readable, entertaining prose and filled with personal and geological anecdotes, Ghost Mountains and Vanished Oceans tells the story of our world and, in doing so, it tells our story. As the author puts it, "We are not just passengers on a dead piece of cosmic debris whirling through space; we are an integral part of an exceptional, dynamic system that produced both our earth and us."

"...a fascinating read for anyone interested in the planet on which we live and how it came to be as it is..."

-Geoscience Canada

...this book is a true, well-crafted page-turner...if you've ever wondered how the continents and the particular slab of rock you live on came about, you will love this book...Highly Recommended."

-Amazon Reviewer

Shot at Dawn

Allan McBride has fought in some of the First World War's bloodiest battles. He has seen his comrades, and his best friend, killed. But tonight he waits in a shed outside Amiens, accused of desertion, to discover if dawn will bring a last-minute reprieve—or execution by firing squad.

"...the powerful writing and strong characters will grip readers from beginning to end."

Quill & Quire

Graves of Ice

Thrilled at being a part of such a great adventure, George Chambers volunteers to join Sir John Franklin's expedition in search of the elusive Northwest Passage. But as the ice traps both *Erebus* and *Terror* in a desolate, frozen landscape, the explorers' search for the fabled passage deteriorates to a grim struggle to avoid death by starvation, freezing or scurvy. Eventually, only George remains alive searching vainly for a rescuing sail on the horizon.

"...a compelling story...a haunting story that keeps the reader riveted."

CM Magazine

Lost Cause *(The SEVEN Series)*

Steve travels to Spain and uncovers his late grandfather's involvement in the Spanish Civil War. Followed by a sequel, **Broken Arrow** and a prequel, **The Missing Skull**

"I had to force myself to take a break for food and sleep. I just wanted to keep reading."

ALSA's Top Ten review program

The **Caught in Conflict Collection** is an imprint of fast-paced, historically accurate, morally-complex quick reads for Adults and Teens. They can be read in any order.

And in the Morning: Somme 1916

"And in the Morning joins other outstanding novels about the First World War—an invaluable resource for libraries and classrooms."

-Jeffrey Canton, Quill & Quire

Flames of the Tiger: Berlin 1945

"Equal parts philosophical debate and historical fiction, this book... presents a compelling and thoughtful story of war that should appeal to a wide range of readers."

-Quill & Quire

Four Steps to Death: Stalingrad 1942

"This absorbing, well-crafted tale...is a haunting description of the tragedy and irony of war...In this vivid narrative, the awful cacophony of war comes to life...the skilled author succeeds without moralistic preaching in highlighting the harsh reality, the utter misery, and the heartbreak of war in this intricate but fascinating book."

VOYA

Lost in Spain: The Spanish Civil War 1936

"Wilson offers a unique perspective on this fascinating era...even minor characters are brought to life."

-Library Journal

Flags of War: Shiloh 1862

"...action-filled, tightly written prose. Realistic battle scenes illustrate the senselessness of war...the story offers a fresh take on the conflict - the idea of Canada as refuge for fugitive slaves and the irony of how it was nearly drawn into the war on the side of the South."

- Albany Public Library, NY

Battle Scars: Libby Prison 1865

"Readable and exciting."

-Booklist

Germania: The Roman Empire 9 A.D.

"This riveting, haunting tale will leave readers clamouring for more."

-Best Books

Where Soldiers Lie: India 1857

"This is an absolutely terrific book…Never lagging with a credible hero and an exotic setting…The pacing is flawless."

-Geoffrey Bilson Award for Historical Fiction Jury Citation

"The tension and action of the battle and the intense danger of the escape from the massacre will keep readers turning these pages."

-Quill & Quire

Find out more about these and other titles by John Wilson at www.johnwilson.com

All of John's 50 books are available through Amazon.

9 798223 060895